Lecture Notes in Artificial Intelligence 4118

Edited by J. G. Carbonell and J. Siekmann

Subseries of Lecture Notes in Computer Science

Zoran Despotovic   Sam Joseph
Claudio Sartori (Eds.)

Agents and Peer-to-Peer Computing

4th International Workshop, AP2PC 2005
Utrecht, The Netherlands, July 25, 2005
Revised Papers

 Springer

Series Editors

Jaime G. Carbonell, Carnegie Mellon University, Pittsburgh, PA, USA
Jörg Siekmann, University of Saarland, Saarbrücken, Germany

Volume Editors

Zoran Despotovic
EPFL Lausanne
School of Computer and Communication Sciences
1015 Lausanne, Switzerland
E-mail: zoran.despotovic@epfl.ch

Sam Joseph
University of Hawaii
Dept. of Information and Computer Science
1680 East-West Road, POST 309, Honolulu, HI 96822, USA
E-mail: srjoseph@hawaii.edu

Claudio Sartori
University of Bologna
Department of Electronics
Computer Science and Systems
Viale Risorgimento, 2, 40136 Bologna, Italy
E-mail: claudio.sartori@unibo.it

Library of Congress Control Number: 2006938336

CR Subject Classification (1998): I.2.11, I.2, C.2.4, C.2, H.4, H.3, K.4.4

LNCS Sublibrary: SL 7 – Artificial Intelligence

ISSN   0302-9743
ISBN-10   3-540-49025-6 Springer Berlin Heidelberg New York
ISBN-13   978-3-540-49025-8 Springer Berlin Heidelberg New York

Springer is a part of Springer Science+Business Media

springer.com

© Springer-Verlag Berlin Heidelberg 2006
Printed in Germany

Typesetting: Camera-ready by author, data conversion by Scientific Publishing Services, Chennai, India
Printed on acid-free paper   SPIN: 11925941   06/3142   5 4 3 2 1 0

Preface

Peer-to-peer (P2P) computing has attracted enormous media attention, initially spurred by the popularity of file sharing systems such as Napster, Gnutella, and Morpheus. More recently, systems like BitTorrent and eDonkey have continued to sustain that attention. New techniques such as distributed hash-tables (DHTs), semantic routing, and Plaxton Meshes are being combined with traditional concepts such as Hypercubes, Trust Metrics and caching techniques to pool together the untapped computing power at the "edges" of the Internet. These new techniques and possibilities have generated a lot of interest in many industrial organizations, and has resulted in the creation of a P2P working group on standardization in this area (http://www.irtf.org/charter?gtype=rg&group=p2prg).

In P2P computing, peers and services forego central coordination and dynamically organize themselves to support knowledge sharing and collaboration, in both cooperative and non-cooperative environments. The success of P2P systems strongly depends on a number of factors. First, the ability to ensure equitable distribution of content and services. Economic and business models which rely on incentive mechanisms to supply contributions to the system are being developed, along with methods for controlling the "free riding" issue. Second, the ability to enforce provision of trusted services. Reputation based P2P trust management models are becoming a focus of the research community as a viable solution. The trust models must balance both constraints imposed by the environment (e.g., scalability) and the unique properties of trust as a social and psychological phenomenon. Recently, we are also witnessing a move of the P2P paradigm to embrace mobile computing in an attempt to achieve even higher ubiquitousness. The possibility of services related to physical location and the relation with agents in physical proximity could introduce new opportunities and also new technical challenges.

Although researchers working on distributed computing, multi-agent systems, databases and networks have been using similar concepts for a long time, it is only fairly recently that papers motivated by the current P2P paradigm have started appearing in high-quality conferences and workshops. Research in agent systems in particular appears to be most relevant because, since their inception, multi-agent systems have always been thought of as collections of peers.

The multi-agent paradigm can thus be superimposed on the P2P architecture, where agents embody the description of the task environments, the decision-support capabilities, the collective behavior, and the interaction protocols of each peer. The emphasis in this context on decentralization, user autonomy, dynamic growth and other advantages of P2P also leads to significant potential problems. Most prominent among these problems are coordination—the ability of an agent to make decisions on its own actions in the context of activities of other agents—and scalability—the value of the P2P systems lies in how well they scale along several dimensions, including complexity, heterogeneity of peers, robustness, traffic redistribution, and so forth. It is important to scale up coordination strategies along multiple dimensions to enhance their tractability and viability, and thereby to widen potential application domains. These two problems are common to many large-scale applications. Without coordination, agents may be wasting their efforts, squandering resources and failing to achieve their objectives in situations requiring collective effort.

This workshop brought together researchers working on agent systems and P2P computing with the intention of strengthening this connection. Researchers from other related areas such as distributed systems, networks and database systems were also welcome (and, in our opinion, have a lot to contribute). We seek high-quality and original contributions on the general theme of "Agents and P2P Computing." The following is a non-exhaustive list of topics of special interest:

- Intelligent agent techniques for P2P computing
- P2P computing techniques for multi-agent systems
- The Semantic Web and semantic coordination mechanisms for P2P systems
- Scalability, coordination, robustness and adaptability in P2P systems
- Self-organization and emergent behavior in P2P systems
- E-commerce and P2P computing
- Participation and contract incentive mechanisms in P2P systems
- Computational models of trust and reputation
- Community of interest building and regulation, and behavioral norms
- Intellectual property rights and legal issues in P2P systems
- P2P architectures
- Scalable data structures for P2P systems
- Services in P2P systems (service definition languages, service discovery, filtering and composition etc.)
- Knowledge discovery and P2P data mining agents
- P2P-oriented information systems
- Information ecosystems and P2P systems
- Security considerations in P2P networks
- Ad-hoc networks and pervasive computing based on P2P architectures and wireless communication devices
- Grid computing solutions based on agents and P2P paradigms
- Legal issues in P2P networks

The workshop series emphasizes discussions about methodologies, models, algorithms and technologies, strengthening the connection between agents and P2P computing. These objectives are accomplished by bringing together researchers and contributions from these two disciplines but also from more traditional areas such as distributed systems, networks, and databases.

This volume is the post-proceedings of AP2PC 2005, the Fourth International Workshop on Agents and P2P Computing,[1] held in Utrecht, Netherlands on

---

[1] http://p2p.ingce.unibo.it/

July 25, 2005 in the context of the Fourth International Joint Conference on
Autonomous Agents and Multi-Agent Systems (AAMAS 2005).

This volume brings together papers presented at AP2PC 2005, fully revised
to incorporate reviewers' comments and discussions at the workshop. The volume
is organized according to the following sessions held at the workshop:

- P2P Networks and Search Performance
- Emergent Communities and Social Behaviors
- Semantic Integration
- Mobile P2P systems
- Adaptive Systems
- Agent-Based Resource Discovery
- Trust and Reputation

We would like to thank the invited speaker Hector Anthony Rowstron, Senior Researcher from Microsoft Research in Cambridge UK, for his talk entitled
"Removing the Overlay from an Underlay!"

We would also like to thank Omer Rana, from the Department of Computer
Science at Cardiff University, UK, for chairing the panel with the theme "To
Trust or Not to Trust." We express our deepest appreciation to the workshop participants (more than 40) for their lively discussions, in particular for the invited
panelists: Simon Miles, Maria Gini, Martin Purvis and Cristiano Castelfranchi.
Many thanks also to Raj Dasgupta and Karen Fullam for chairing sessions in
the workshop.

After distributing the call for papers for the workshop, we received 27 papers.
All submissions were reviewed for scope and quality, and 13 were accepted as full
papers. We would like to thank the authors for their submissions and the members of the Program Committee for reviewing the papers under time pressure
and for their support of the workshop. Finally, we would like to acknowledge the
Steering Committee for its guidance and encouragement.

This workshop followed the successful third edition, which was held in conjunction with AAMAS in New York City in 2004. In recognition of the inter-
disciplinary nature of P2P computing, a sister event called the International
Workshop on Databases, Information Systems, and P2P Computing[2] was held
in Trondheim, Norway in August 2005 in conjunction with the International
Conference on Very Large Data Bases (VLDB).

September 2005   Zoran Despotovic
                                                           Sam Joseph
                                                         Claudio Sartori

---

[2] http://dbisp2p.ingce.unibo.it/

Organization

Executive Committee

Organizers

Program Co-chairs   Zoran Despotovic
School of Computer and Communications Sciences,
Ecole Polytechnique Fédérale de Lausanne (EPFL)
CH-1015 Lausanne, Switzerland
E-mail: zoran.despotovic@epfl.ch

Sam Joseph
Dept. of Information and Computer Science,
University of Hawaii
1680 East-West Road, POST 309, Honolulu, HI 96822,
USA
E-mail: srjoseph@hawaii.edu

Claudio Sartori
Dept. of Electronics, Computer Science and Systems,
University of Bologna
Viale Risorgimento, 2 - 40136 Bologna, Italy
E-mail: claudio.sartori@unibo.it

Panel Chair   Omer Rana
School of Computer Science, Cardiff University
Queen's Buildings, Newport Road,
Cardiff CF24 3AA, UK

Steering Committee

Karl Aberer, EPFL, Lausanne, Switzerland

Sonia Bergamaschi, Dept. of Science Engineering,
University of Modena and Reggio-Emilia, Italy

Manolis Koubarakis, Dept. of Electronic and Computer Engineering,
Technical University of Crete, Greece

Paul Marrow, Intelligent Systems Laboratory,
BTexact Technologies, UK

Gianluca Moro, Dept. of Electronics, Computer Science and Systems, Univ. of Bologna, Cesena, Italy

Aris M. Ouksel, Dept. of Information and Decision Sciences, University of Illinois at Chicago, USA

Claudio Sartori, IEIIT-BO-CNR, University of Bologna, Italy

Munindar P. Singh, Dept. of Computer Science, North Carolina State University, USA

Program Committee

Martin Purvis, University of Otago, New Zealand
Omer F. Rana, Cardiff University, UK
Douglas S. Reeves, North Carolina State University, USA
Thomas Risse, Fraunhofer IPSI, Darmstadt, Germany
Pierangela Samarati, University of Milan, Italy
Heng Tao SHEN, ITEE, UQ, Australia
Christophe Silbertin-Blanc, University of Toulouse, France
Maarten van Steen, Vrije Universiteit, Netherlands
Katia Sycara, Robotics Institute, Carnegie Mellon University, USA
Peter Triantafillou, Technical University of Crete, Greece
Anand Tripathi, University of Minnesota, USA
Vijay K. Vaishnavi, Georgia State University, USA
Francisco Valverde-Albacete, Universidad Carlos III de Madrid, Spain
Maurizio Vincini, University of Modena and Reggio-Emilia, Italy
Fang Wang, BTexact Technologies, UK
Gerhard Weiss, Technische Universität, München, Germany
Bin Yu, North Carolina State University, USA
Franco Zambonelli, University of Modena and Reggio-Emilia, Italy

Preceding Editions of AP2PC

Here are the references to the preceding editions of AP2PC, including the volumes of revised and invited papers:

- AP2PC 2002 was held in Bologna, Italy, July 15, 2002. The Web site can be found at http://p2p.ingce.unibo.it/2002/ The proceedings were published by Springer as LNCS volume no. 2530 and are available online at: http://www.springerlink.com/content/978-3-540-40538-2/
- AP2PC 2003 was held in Melbourne, Australia, July 14, 2003. The Web site can be found at http://p2p.ingce.unibo.it/2003/ The proceedings were published by Springer as LNCS volume no. 2872 and are available online at: http://www.springerlink.com/content/978-3-540-24053-2/
- AP2PC 2004 was held in New York City, USA, July 19, 2004. The Web site can be found at http://p2p.ingce.unibo.it/2004/ The proceedings were published by Springer as LNCS volume no. 3601 and are available online at: http://www.springerlink.com/content/978-3-540-29755-0/

Table of Contents

Trust and Reputation

P2P Infrastructure

Semantic Infrastructure

Community and Mobile Applications

Optimizing an Incentives' Mechanism for Truthful Feedback in Virtual Communities*

Thanasis G. Papaioannou and George D. Stamoulis

Department of Informatics, Athens University of Economics and Business (AUEB)
76 Patision Str., 10434 Athens, Greece
{pathan, gstamoul}@aueb.gr

Abstract. We analyze a mechanism that provides strong incentives for the submission of truthful feedback in virtual communities where services are exchanged on a peer-to-peer basis. Lying peers are punished with a severity that is exponential to their frequency of lying. We had first introduced and evaluated experimentally the mechanism in [1]. In this paper, we develop a Markov-chain model of the mechanism. Based on this, we prove that, when the mechanism is employed, the system evolves to a beneficial steady-state operation even in the case of a dynamically renewed population. Furthermore, we develop a procedure for the efficient selection of the parameters of the mechanism for any peer-to-peer system; this procedure is based on ergodic arguments. Simulation experiments reveal that the procedure is indeed accurate, as well as effective regarding the incentives provided to participants for submitting truthful feedback.

1 Introduction

Virtual communities for the exchange of files, services, knowledge or opinions possibly on a peer-to-peer basis have already been widely developed. In the absence of any proper accounting about who is offering value to others in such communities, there is opportunity for free-riding and for malicious actions against other members. Revelation of hidden information on the quality of the exchanged good and on the trustworthiness of the community members is necessary. For, otherwise, such virtual environments may offer low value and eventually collapse. Reputation on the basis of ratings can be a proper means for achieving accountability. However, reputation mechanisms are vulnerable to *false* or *strategic voting (rating)*. For example, a particular peer may benefit by submitting unjustified positive ratings for his friends or his collaborators, and/or by submitting unfair negative ratings for his competitors. This problem is further augmented in case of pseudo-spoofing, i.e. use of multiple false identities, which may arise in virtual environments, especially peer-to-peer systems. In [1], we proposed a mechanism for providing incentives for credible reporting of feedback information in a peer-to-peer system. The mechanism was combined with

* The present work was partly funded by the IST project EuroNGI (IST-2003-507613).

Z. Despotovic, S. Joseph, and C. Sartori (Eds.): AP2PC 2005, LNAI 4118, pp. 1–15, 2006.

reputation-based policies that we introduced in [2]. These determine the pairs of peers that are eligible to transact, in order incentives to peers for offering better services to others to be provided as well. According to the mechanism both transacting peers (rather than just the client) submit ratings on the performance of their mutual transaction. If these ratings are in *disagreement*, then *both* transacting peers are punished, since such an occasion is a sign that one of them is lying, yet the system cannot tell which one. When under punishment, a peer is not allowed to transact with others. The severity (i.e. duration) of each peer's punishment is determined by his corresponding non-credibility metric; this is maintained by the mechanism and evolves according to the peer's record. Simulation experiments in [1] showed clearly that the combination of the mechanism with reputation-based policies detects and isolates liar peers effectively, while rendering lying costly even in dynamically evolving peer-to-peer systems. Also, the efficiency losses induced to sincere peers by the presence of large subsets of the population of peers that provide their ratings either falsely or according to various unfair strategies are diminished. As explained in [1], this mechanism can be implemented in practical cases of peer-to-peer systems.

In this paper, we analytically study the standalone effectiveness of the mechanism of [1] (i.e. without being combined with reputation-based policies) in providing incentives for truthful reporting. We define a Markov-chain model in order to study the steady-state effect of the credibility mechanism in punishing liar peers. We also develop an optimization procedure for the determination of the proper parameters of the credibility mechanism employed to a dynamically renewed peer-to-peer system, so as to maximize the effectiveness of the mechanism in punishing lying and minimize the cost induced to sincere peers by potential unfair punishments thereof due to the mechanism. This optimization procedure is based on ergodic arguments. We evaluate our Markovian model and our optimization procedure by simulation experiments that show the accuracy and the effectiveness of the approach. The results scale for realistic population sizes of peer-to-peer systems thus making both our mechanism and our approach for selecting its parameters applicable in practical cases.

There is significant related work in the literature. Dellarocas deals in [3] with the problem of unfair ratings and discriminatory behavior in on-line trading communities. Schillo *et al.* [4] deal separately with behavior and credibility of other agents using the so-called disclosed prisoners' dilemma game with partner selection based on own observations. Damiani *et al.*, in a similar approach [5], extend Gnutella protocol to calculate performance and credibility of other peers based on a peer's own experience and on votes from witnesses. A single trust metric is used for credibility and performance by Yu *et al.* in [6]. Aberer *et al.* [7] present an approach to evaluate trustworthiness (i.e. the combination of credibility and performance) of peers based on the complaints posed for them by other peers following transactions. An approach for providing incentives for truthful reporting of feedback in e-markets has been proposed by Jurca and Faltings in [8]. This approach, similarly to ours, employs disagreement in feedback messages for discovering potential lying. Detailed comparison of our credibility mechanism with these works has been done in [1]. However, these approaches (including [1]) mostly resort to simulation for the purpose of evaluation of their mechanisms. Moreover, they do not deal with large fractions of collaborated liar peers, as opposed to both [1] and the present work.

The remainder of this paper is organized as follows: in Section 2, we overview our credibility mechanism. In Section 3, we describe the Markov-chain model of a peer-to-peer system that employs our credibility mechanism. In Section 4, we present our procedure for the optimization of the parameters of the credibility mechanism for a peer-to-peer system. In Section 5, we evaluate our Markov-chain model and our optimization procedure by simulation experiments. Finally, in Section 6, we provide some concluding remarks.

2   The Credibility Mechanism

Consider a peer-to-peer system for exchanging services that employs a distributed reputation system for performance. Time is assumed to be slotted. For simplicity, we assume that the minimum time interval between two successive service requests by the same peer equals one time slot. Following a transaction, the client peer sends feedback rating his offered performance. For example, he may rate the transaction as "successful" (i.e. high offered performance) or as "unsuccessful" (i.e. low offered performance). The feedback messages are useful only if their content is *true*. Unfortunately, peers actually have the incentive of strategic rating of others' performance, since they can thus hide their poor performance, improve their reputation, and possibly take advantage of others. Thus, a proper mechanism should make lying costly or at least unprofitable. "Punishing liars" is a known recipe [9], [10], but two questions arise: How can lying peers be discovered? How can they be punished in a peer-to-peer system, where there is no central control?

Under our approach peers submit ratings' feedback according to the following rules: i) after a transaction, *both* peers involved have to send one feedback message each, and ii) besides rating (i.e. voting) the transaction as successful or not, each feedback message *also* contains a quantifiable performance metric, e.g. the number of transferred bytes of useful content. We assume that the observed performance is with high probability the same with that actually offered. (The opposite may only occur due to unexpected events during a transaction like network congestion etc.) Thus, if feedback messages for a transaction *disagree* (either in their performance metric or in their vote), then, with high probability, at least one of the transacted peers is lying and has to be somehow *punished*, in order for the right incentives to be provided. However, the system cannot tell which of the peers does lie, and consequently whom to believe and whom to punish. Thus, according to our approach, *both* peers are punished in this case. This idea was initially introduced in [9]. However, by simply applying it, a sincere peer is often punished unfairly.

Therefore, we need a complete mechanism specifying how to punish peers in such an uncontrolled system and how to limit potential unfairness. To this end, we introduce for each peer: i) the *non-credibility* metric ncr, which corresponds to reputation for non-credibility, and ii) a binary *punishment state* variable, declaring whether the peer is "under punishment" (if the variable is "true") or not (if the variable is "false"). For each peer, both ncr and punishment state are public information, and they are appropriately stored so that they are available to other peers. (See [1] for a discussion on practical implementation.) Upon entering the peer-to-peer system, each peer is assigned a positive non-credibility value ncr_0, while he is not under punishment. (Note that the lower the value of ncr the better.) This choice of ncr_0 limits the incentive for name changes after a disagreement. The flowchart of the credibility mechanism is depicted in Figure 1. In particular, after a transaction between two not punished peers i, j their feedback messages f_i, f_j are sent as input to the mechanism: Upon *disagreement* (i.e. if $f_i \neq f_j$), the non-credibility values of the transacted peers are both increased by x while both get punished. The duration of a peer's punishment equals b_{ncr}, i.e. is exponential in his non-credibility, with a base $b > 1$. Upon *agreement* (i.e. if $f_i = f_j$), the non-credibility values of the transacted peers are decreased (i.e. improved) by d, where $0 < d \leq x$, without ever dropping below 0. In the rest of the paper, without loss of generality, we take $x = 1$. The common feedback is forwarded to the system computing reputation for performance.

Decrease of non-credibility in cases of agreement serves as a rehabilitation mechanism. This is crucial for the efficient operation of the credibility mechanism, because, as already mentioned, upon disagreement in reports, most probably one peer is unfairly punished. The value of d determines the speed of restoring a non-credible reporting behavior. We employ additive increase/decrease of the non-credibility values for simplicity. Other approaches such as additive increase/multiplicative decrease are also possible.

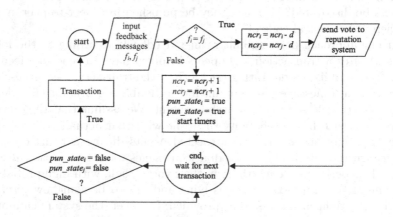

Fig. 1. The credibility mechanism

Punishing peers is not an easy task to employ in the absence of any control mechanism, particularly if peers have full control over their part of peer-to-peer middleware. In our mechanism, a punishment amounts to loss of value offered by other peers. That is, a peer under punishment does *not* transact with others during his punishment period, while his ratings for such transactions are *not* taken into account. The latter measure provides incentives for peers to abide with the former one! Indeed, first, note that sincere peers under punishment are not expected to be willing to offer services as they would be subject to strategic voting without being able to disagree. On the other hand, liar punished peers collaborated with other liar peers that strategically vote them (i.e. always positively) can raise their reputation anyway, thus having no incentives to perform well during their punishment. Thus, no peer has any incentives to *ask* for services from a punished peer except for strategic voting. Moreover, no peer has any incentive to perform well when offering services to a punished peer, because the corresponding feedback is not taken into account. Therefore, it is beneficial for the system to *prohibit* transaction with punished peers by rule. To this end, if a peer transacts with a punished one, then both of the transacting peers are punished as if they were involved in a new disagreement. Thus, the non-credibility value of a peer remains unchanged during his punishment period unless he transacts with other peers; in such a case it is further increased.

Peers should have the incentive to submit feedback, despite the risk of disagreement and subsequent punishment. Indeed, after a transaction that failed peers may not be willing to report the failure at all. Thus, to provide peers with the incentive to submit their feedback, our mechanism punishes both peers involved in a transaction if only one of them submits feedback. This also prevents unilateral submission of feedback messages for non-existing transactions. Note also that, since the proposed mechanism improves the long-term efficiency of the sincere peers, only liar peers are expected to have incentives to avoid submitting feedback. Yet applying the reasoning of [11] to our case, we expect that under certain circumstances, the existence of our mechanism will lead liar peers to give up their strategic behavior since it is not beneficial to them.

3   The Markovian Model Approximating the Mechanism

In this section, we analytically study the *effectiveness* of the proposed mechanism in *equilibrium* for providing incentives to peers for truthful reporting. For this purpose, we define a discrete-time Markov-chain model of a peer-to-peer system where the credibility mechanism is employed. Then, we derive the *steady-state* distribution of the punishment state of sincere and liar peers of the modeled peer-to-peer system. Modeling of time is different than that introduced in Section 2. In particular, for the purpose of specifying and analyzing this Markov chain, we define as time step of our discrete-time model the interval between two successive service requests. We assume that in this interval at most *one* transaction takes place. Thus, transition from one state to another can *only* happen after a transaction between two peers. This is very convenient for analyzing the Markov-chain model and studying the performance of the original system defined in Section 2. Performance measures can be easily translated from the new "transaction units" to actual time slots; see Section 4. Note that at the beginning of each time step, a peer is randomly selected to be the client of the only transaction that takes place in this step.

The total populations of sincere and liar peers in the peer-to-peer system modelled as a Markov chain are S_0 and L_0 respectively. Consider that a state is a snapshot of the system where state variables are the number of not punished sincere peers s, the number of not punished liar peers l, and the number of peers under punishment k. Clearly, this Markov chain has $(S_0 + 1)(L_0 + 1)$ different states. Observe also that state variable k can be computed by the formula $k = S_0 - s + L_0 - l$, but k is used for readability reasons. Let q be the probability that a requested service is found at a certain peer and r to be the probability that a peer asks for a service. Recall that credibility values and punishment state are *public* information, and that not punished peers are not allowed to transact with punished peers. The probability that a selected client peer finds a requested service is given by:

$$y = r(1 - (1 - q)^{l+s-1})$$ (1)

A client sincere peer is punished if he finds his service at a liar peer. The probability PS of this event is given by:

$$P_S = \frac{l}{s + l - 1}y$$ (2)

A client liar peer is punished if he interacts with a sincere peer plus or with another liar peer that is not collaborated with. We assume that the probability of each given pair of liars to be collaborated with each other equals , which is fixed. Thus, the probability of punishment for a client liar peer is given by the formula below:

$$P_L = \frac{s}{s + l - 1}y + \frac{l - 1}{s + l - 1}ya$$ (3)

If no liars are collaborated with each other, then $a = 1$, while for all liars being collaborated with each other $a = 0$. In the analysis that follows we study the case where all liar peers are collaborated with each other, which is the hardest one for the mechanism to deal with.

Recall that at the beginning of each time step, a peer is randomly selected to be the client of the only transaction to take place. The probability P_T that the two peers of a transaction are punished, i.e. they disagree in their feedback messages is given by:

$$P_T = \frac{s}{s + l}P_S + \frac{l}{s + l}P_L$$ (4)

For modeling purposes, we assume that during a time step, a sincere (resp. liar) peer that is under punishment can be "rehabilitated", i.e. stop being under punishment in the next step, with probability P_{RHS} (resp. P_{RHL}). Thus, when there are $k = S_0 - s + L_0 - l$ peers under punishment in the current state, the average number of rehabilitated peers in the next state is $(S_0 - s)P_{RHS} + (L_0 - l)P_{RHL}$. Next, we relate the Markovian model with the original mechanism of Section 2.

Suppose that the peer-to-peer system is currently in state (s, l, k), i.e. there are s not punished sincere and l not punished liar peers, while k peers are under punishment. Then, in the next time step (i.e. after a transaction), the system may move to various states with the transition probabilities given in the Table 1. Term A corresponds to the transition arising when the transacting peer are punished, while term B corresponds to the transition arising when they are not punished. Both terms also involve the probability of rehabilitation of the number of liar and sincere peers necessary for the transaction to happen.

Table 1. Formula for transition probability from current state (s, l, k) to another

Transition Probability
$Probability[(s, l, k) \rightarrow (s - 1 + i, l - 1 + j, k + 2 - i - j) = A + B$, where

$$A = \begin{cases} P_T \binom{S_0 - s}{i} P_{RHS}{}^i (1 - P_{RHS})^{S_0 - s - i} \binom{L_0 - l}{j} P_{RHL}{}^j \cdot \\ (1 - P_{RHL})^{L_0 - l - j}, \text{ for } 0 \leq i \leq S_0 - s \text{ and } 0 \leq j \leq L_0 - l \\ 0, \text{ otherwise} \end{cases}$$

$$B = \begin{cases} (1 - P_T) \binom{S_0 - s}{i - 1} P_{RHS}{}^{i-1} (1 - P_{RHS})^{S_0 - s - i + 1} \binom{L_0 - l}{j - 1} P_{RHL}{}^{j-1} \cdot \\ (1 - P_{RHL})^{L_0 - l - j + 1}, \text{ for } 1 \leq i \leq S_0 - s + 1 \text{ and } 1 \leq j \leq L_0 - l + 1 \\ 0, \text{ otherwise} \end{cases}$$

Under the Markovian model, the distribution of the punishment period is geometric; i.e. the duration of the punishment period is independent of the peer's past history. Clearly, this is only an approximation of the behavior of our credibility mechanism as described in Section 2, which is very complicated to model accurately and has a huge state-space. Indeed, recall that a peer upon disagreement is punished for a time period that is exponential to his non-credibility value, which should be maintained as part of the state for all peers! However, as the results of Section 5 reveal, this approximation is indicative of the performance of the actual mechanism provided that rehabilitation probabilities are successfully selected. Indeed, let us denote as c the period of conviction for a peer with a certain punishment record. Then, for a geometric-distribution approximation of this period, the probability of rehabilitation of this peer in the next state should be estimated as $1/c$. The probabilities P_{RHS} and P_{RHL} that lead to the same expected punishment time per type of peer (throughout a peer's lifetime) depend on the parameters b, ncr_0, and d of the credibility mechanism. All these parameters can be inter-related by means of the optimization procedure presented in Section 5. Thus, for given b, ncr_0, and d, appropriate values of P_{RHS} and P_{RHL} can be derived that render the Markov-chain model a good approximation of the evaluation of the actual systems. The steady state distribution of the model is depicted in Figure 2a for a certain peer-to-peer system with $S_0 = 30$, $L_0 = 20$, $r = 0.5$, $q = 0.1$ and rehabilitation probabilities $P_{RHS} = 0.1$ and $P_{RHL} = 0.0024$. As already discussed, these values of P_{RHS} and P_{RHL} result from the proper selection of the parameters of the credibility mechanism according to the procedure described in Section 4. In the peer-to-peer system of Figure 2a, sincere peers are almost never under punishment during their lifetime, while liar peers are under punishment almost all of their lifetime. Thus, the credibility mechanism is very effective in expelling liar peers from the peer-to-peer system if its parameters are properly selected.

4   The Procedure for Optimizing the Mechanism

As shown in Figure 2, the credibility mechanism is capable of providing the right incentives to peers for truthful reporting of feedback. However, this result applies for certain rehabilitation probabilities (essentially for certain expected punishment periods) that are determined by the parameters of the mechanism (i.e. initial non-credibility ncr_0, the base b of the exponential punishment, and the restoration factor d). These parameters have to be properly selected on the basis of the peer-to-peer system's, i.e. peers' lifetime, service availability, service request probability etc. in order lying to be effectively punished without inducing an unacceptable overhead for sincere peers. In this section, we propose a methodology for the calculation of the proper parameters of the mechanism for any peer-to-peer environment. We specify two *objectives* when employing the credibility mechanism in a peer-to-peer system:

- Objective 1: Sincere peers must *not* be punished more than *once* during their lifetime.
- Objective 2: Liar peers must *always* be punished when they transact with other sincere peers.

Specifically, consider the Markov-chain model of peer-to-peer system described in the previous section. Recall that we have defined as the time step of our discrete time Markov chain the duration of a transaction. The expected value of this is henceforth referred to as transaction unit. Furthermore, recall that, for the peer-to-peer system originally defined in Section 2, we assume that time is slotted, while the population of the peer-to-peer system is dynamically *renewed*, and S_0, L_0 are kept constant. Moreover, each time slot equals the minimum time interval between two successive service requests by the same peer. Next, we explain how we can inter-relate the two aforementioned systems. We denote as $t_{lifetime}$ the mean lifetime of a peer in time slots. We also denote as t_s (resp. t_l) the mean number of time slots that a sincere peer is not under punishment during his lifetime, when our credibility mechanism is employed in the peer-to-peer system. Thus, $S_0(t_s/t_{lifetime})$ (resp. $L_0(t_l/t_{lifetime})$) is the mean number of sincere (resp. liar) peers not under punishment at a certain time slot. Recalling that y is the probability to find a requested service, then the mean total number N_{trans} of transactions per time slot is given by the following equation:

$$N_{trans} = y \frac{t_s S_0 + t_l L_0}{t_{lifetime}} \tag{5}$$

Furthermore, we denote as n_s and n_l the mean numbers of transaction periods that a sincere and a liar peer respectively are not under punishment during their lifetime. Therefore, $n_s = N_{trans} \cdot t_s$, $n_l = N_{trans} \cdot t_l$ and $n_{lifetime} = t_{lifetime} \cdot N_{trans}$. Recall now that according to the Markov model, the distribution of each punishment period is geometric with expected value equal to $1/P_{RHS}$ for sincere peers and $1/P_{RHL}$ for liar peers. Using ergodic arguments, Objectives 1 and 2 lead to the following equations:

$$\frac{1}{P_{RHS}} = t_{lifetime} - t_s = \frac{n_{lifetime} - n_s}{N_{trans}} \tag{6}$$

$$\frac{1}{P_{RHL}} = \frac{n_{lifetime} - n_l}{yt_l \frac{t_s S_0}{t_s S_0 + t_l L_0}} = \frac{n_{lifetime} - n_l}{yn_l \frac{n_s S_0}{n_s S_0 + n_l L_0}} N_{trans} \tag{7}$$

Indeed, Objective 1 amounts to equation (6), which implies that the expected punishment time for sincere peers equals the mean duration (in transaction periods) of the one and only punishment during their lifetime. Objective 2 amounts to equation (7), which implies that the expected punishment time for liar peers equals the mean punishment time of a liar peer in transaction periods divided by the mean number of time slots where: (i) he is not under punishment, and (ii) he gets punished upon transaction with a sincere peer. The $t_s S_0/(t_s S_0 + t_l L_0)$ in the dominator of equation (7) expresses the percentage of *unpunished peers* that are sincere. Note that equations (6) and (7) express the most conservative bounds arising from Objectives 1 and 2 for the mean punishment periods of a sincere and a liar peer respectively. For example, equation (6) expresses the mean duration of one complete punishment period, while according to Objective 1 sincere peers are not punished more than once. Equation (6) (resp. (7)) involves n_s (resp. n_l), which determines the mean fraction of a sincere (resp. liar) peer's lifetime that he is not under punishment, namely $n_s/n_{lifetime}$ (resp. $n_l/n_{lifetime}$). In equations (6) and (7), the values of these fractions are treated as inputs. However, these values actually arise as a result of the operation of the credibility mechanism. Thus, the input values in equations (6) and (7) have to be *consistent* with those resulting due to the mechanism. Therefore, in order to determine the values of n_s, n_l that render the objectives feasible a *fixed-point* approach is followed:

1. Initially, we take that $n_s = \min\{0.95 \cdot n_{lifetime}, 10\}$ and $n_l = \min\{0.05 \cdot n_{lifetime}, 1\}$.
2. We calculate the mean fraction of a peer's lifetime that he is not under punishment, which equals $n_s/n_{lifetime}$ for sincere and $n_l/n_{lifetime}$ for liar peers.
3. From equations (6) and (7) we calculate P_{RHL} and P_{RHS}. These are employed in the Markov-chain model and the steady-state distribution of the punishment state is calculated.

4. Then, the mean fraction of a peer's lifetime that he is not under punishment is re-calculated for sincere and liar peers based on the steady state probabilities, i.e. $\acute{n}_s/n_{lifetime}$ for sincere and $\acute{n}_l/n_{lifetime}$ for liar peers.
5. If a convergence criterion is met, e.g. $|\acute{n}_s - n_s| < \epsilon$ and $|\acute{n}_l - n_l| < \epsilon$, then a fixed point has been reached, and the proper values of n_s, n_l have been found for this peer-to-peer system. Otherwise, we set $n_s = (1 - \delta)n_s + \delta\acute{n}_s$ and $n_l = (1 - \delta)n_l + \delta\acute{n}_l$, where $\delta \in (0.5, 1)$ is a relaxation parameter, and the control is transferred back to step 2.

Having determined the values of ns and nl that give rise to Objectives 1 and 2, the proper parameters of the credibility mechanism have also to be derived. The expected value of total punishment period in time slots for a liar peer that is punished in all of his transactions is at most $E[b^{ncr_0}(1 + b^2 + .. + b^v)]$, where v is the number of transactions. This is approximated as $b^{ncr_0}(1 + b^2 + .. + b^{y \cdot t_l})$, since $E[v] = y \cdot t_l$, which is henceforth treated as integer for simplicity. The total punishment period for a liar peer should be equal to the mean total punishment time for that peer $t_{lifetime} - t_l$, see equality (8). (Note that this is a bound because the last punishment period may not be fulfilled until the end of the lifetime of the peer. However, again we take the equality, as it is the most conservative relation.) Similarly, the total expected punishment time of a sincere peer is taken as $b^{ncr_0 - d \cdot rh}$ (see equation (9)). rh is the expected number of time slots where transactions are conducted by a sincere peer until his one and only punishment (see equation (10)) and d is the restoration factor; thus $rh \cdot d$ is the decrease in the sincere peer's non-credibility value until his punishment. Note that the relations for b and ncr_0 involve d as a parameter. Instead of setting one more objective and devise one more equation in order to determine d, we take $d = 0.5$ for illustrative purposes. This is a meaningful choice for the restoration of a disagreement to require two agreements. Therefore, b, ncr_0 (and rh) can be determined by the following equations.

$$t_{lifetime} - t_l = b^{ncr_0}\frac{b^{y t_l} - 1}{b - 1} \tag{8}$$

$$b^{ncr_0 - d \cdot rh} = t_{lifetime} - t_s \tag{9}$$

$$rh = \frac{y(\frac{1}{P_s} - 1)}{N_{trans}} \tag{10}$$

5   Results

5.1   The Simulation Model

In order to evaluate the optimization procedure, we apply the calculated parameters of the credibility mechanism in a simulated peer-to-peer environment where the mechanism is employed. Specifically, we consider a peer-to-peer system employing the credibility mechanism where services of a certain kind are exchanged among peers. Each peer employs a reporting strategy regarding the sincerity of his feedback: he is either (*always*) *sincere* or *liar*. All liars follow the destructive strategy defined in [1] and they are collaborated to each other. According to the *destructive* strategy, liar peers maliciously send reverse feedback about the outcome of their transaction. The reporting types (i.e. lying strategies) of peers are *private* information, i.e. only the peer himself knows whether he is liar or sincere. Time is assumed to be slotted. The duration of the time slot is of the same order of magnitude as the average interval between two successive service requests. At each slot, every peer requests a service with a certain probability $r = 0.5$. Service availability is Uniform with probability q to find a service at a particular peer. A peer can serve only one peer per slot due to his limited resources. Furthermore, the population of peers is assumed to be *renewed* according to a Poisson process with mean rate λ peers/time slot. That is, each peer is assumed to live in the peer-to-peer system for a period determined according to the exponential distribution with mean N/λ, where N is the total size of the population. When a peer leaves the system, a new entrant of the *same type* takes his place. After a transaction each of the peers involved sends feedback to the credibility mechanism as explained in Section 2. The non-credibility values are increased upon disagreement with his transacted peer in their feedback by 1 and decreased upon agreement by $d = 0.5$. In the experiments conducted, we assess the *incentives* offered for truthful reporting measuring the mean fraction of punishment time over lifetime per peer of each reporting type.

5.2   Assessment of the Optimization Procedure and the Markovian Model

In this subsection, we assess the accuracy of the optimization procedure of the parameters of the credibility mechanism. For various peer-to-peer systems with different characteristics (S_0, L_0, r, q, peers' lifetime) we employ the optimization procedure in order to calculate the proper values of parameters b and ncr_0 of the credibility mechanism. Then, we employ the Markovian model to derive the probability that a peer of a certain type is not punished at equilibrium, denoted as PM_S and PM_L for sincere and liar peers respectively. Then, we run simulations, according to the model of Subsection 5.1, using the optimized parameters b and ncr_0 for each of these systems in order to find the mean fraction of the lifetime per peer of a certain type that he is not punished, denoted as PS_S and PS_L for sincere and liar peers respectively. Due to ergodicity, we expected PM_S and PM_L to be roughly equal to PS_S and PS_L respectively. Indeed, as depicted in Table 2, their maximum absolute difference for sincere peers (i.e. $|PS_S - PM_S|$) is 0.03 and for liar peers (i.e. $|PS_L - PM_L|$) is 0.05. Thus, although approximate, the optimization procedure is rather effective in calculating the proper parameters of the credibility mechanism. Furthermore, the Markov model is an accurate proxy of the simulated environment, since the fractions of lifetime under punishment for each type of peers in the steady state also arise in the corresponding simulated environment with the optimized parameters b and ncr_0.

Next, we study how the optimized parameters scale for larger systems (i.e. when $S_0 + L_0$ increases). As shown in Table 3, b and ncr_0 remain roughly the same as the population increases and for different fractions of sincere and liar peers, keeping the other characteristics of the system constant. Thus, the parameters b and ncr_0 of the credibility mechanism are not affected by the mixture of reporting types in the population. Running additional simulations, we find that the effectiveness of these punishment parameters in providing incentives for truthful reporting is maintained for much larger systems with the same *lifetime*, r and q parameters, as shown in Table 4.

Table 2. Proper punishment parameters for various systems

lifetime	Q	r	S_0	L_0	b	ncr_0	PM_S	PS_L	PM_L	PS_L
1000	0.1	0.5	30	20	4.23	1.66	0.997	0.989	0.011	0.004
150	0.5	0.5	30	25	1.939	3.53	0.982	0.956	0.071	0.021
150	0.1	0.8	30	10	1.22	11.36	0.992	0.969	0.048	0.041
150	0.1	0.5	50	45	1.939	3.5	0.99	0.961	0.075	0.03
150	0.1	0.5	30	25	1.939	3.53	0.982	0.956	0.074	0.024
150	0.1	0.5	100	50	1.939	3.5	0.985	0.974	0.078	0.03

Table 3. Proper b and ncr_0 parameters as the peer-to-peer system scales up for larger systems and for different relative fractions S_0/L_0, keeping constant $lifetime = 150$, $q = 0.1$ and $r = 0.5$

S_0/L_0	$S_0 + L_0$	b	ncr_0	PM_S	PS_L	PM_L	PS_L
3/2	50	1.939	3.54	0.985	0.963	0.075	0.029
3/2	75	1.939	3.52	0.99	0.97	0.074	0.027
2	30	1.939	3.6	0.982	0.974	0.075	0.031
2	150	1.939	3.5	0.985	0.974	0.078	0.03
3	40	1.939	3.59	0.992	0.982	0.075	0.028
3	60	1.939	3.55	0.994	0.984	0.0725	0.027

As depicted in Figure 2, the optimization procedure and the Markov model are both *very accurate* in the estimation of the proper parameters of punishment and *very effective* in deriving the punishment parameters that render the mechanism very efficient. Next, we examine how the rest of the characteristics of the peer-to-peer system affect punishment parameters. The probability q to find a certain service at a specific peer determines the service availability and affects the number of transactions conducted per time slot. Provided that there is only small probability for a requested service not to be found at all in the peer-to-peer system, then q essentially does *not* affect parameters b and ncr_0 (see Table 2). Furthermore, the rate of transactions (that depends on service request probability r) is important in order for lying to be revealed and properly

Table 4. The punishment parameters $b = 1.939$ and $ncr_0 = 3.5$ remain effective in providing incentives for truthful reporting as the <u>simulated</u> peer-to-peer system scales up, when $lifetime = 150$, $q = 1$ and $r = 0.5$

S_0	L_0	PM_S	PS_L
500	100	0.973	0.038
600	400	0.9651	0.036
900	600	0.9643	0.042

Table 5. The impact of service request probability to punishment parameters when $lifetime = 150$, $q = 0.1$, $S_0 = 30$ and $L_0 = 20$

r	b	ncr_0
0.2	13	1.09
0.5	1.939	3.54
0.8	1.22	11.33

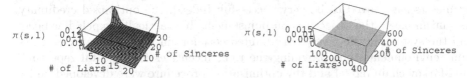

Fig. 2. The Markov model (a) is accurate as it approximates simulation results (b). The optimization procedure is successful as it finds punishment parameters that lead to a beneficial steady state. $q = 0.1$, $r = 0.5$, $b = 1.939$, $ncr_0 = 3.5$, $lifetime = 150$.

Table 6. The impact of of lifetime to punishment parameters when $r = 0.5$, $q = 0.1$, $S_0 = 30$, $L_0 = 10$

$lifetime$	b	ncr_0
50	11.17	0.67
150	1.94	3.59
300	2.63	2.49
500	3.24	2.07

punished. The rate of transactions has a considerable impact on the calculation of the proper punishment parameters, as demonstrated in Table 5. Notice that decreasing r results in higher b and lower ncr_0, as expected for inducing heavier punishment to liar peers since their transactions are now less frequent.

Another important aspect of the peer-to-peer system that affects the calculation of proper punishment parameters is the renewal rate of the population. In fact, as shown in Table 6, if peers are short-lived, then the value of b should be large and the value of ncr_0 should be relatively small. Indeed, for a liar peer, the most likely case is to be punished early enough and only once, due to his short lifetime; the aforementioned values of b and ncr_0 render this punishment severe enough. On the other hand, for long-lived peers the punishment parameters adjust smoothly to punish liar peers progressively for all of their longer lifetime. Note that the optimization procedure computes always the same punishment parameters b and ncr_0 for a peer-to-peer system with specific characteristics.

6   Conclusions

In this paper, we have studied the credibility mechanism that we first proposed in [1]. This mechanism provides incentives for truthful reporting of ratings' information in peer-to-peer systems. The credibility mechanism attains this objective by discovering and punishing liar peers. Also, we modeled the employment of the credibility mechanism in a peer-to-peer system as a Markov-chain. Although approximate, this Markov-chain model is rather accurate. It has proved to be a *very useful tool* for tuning the parameters of the mechanism in an actual system by means of the fixed-point optimization procedure that was also proposed in this paper. Furthermore, our approach for finding the appropriate punishment parameters has proved to be very successful: Indeed, the optimized credibility mechanism meets the objectives on punishment. It practically expels liar peers from the system at effectively very limited cost for sincere peers even in a dynamic environment, thus providing the right incentives for truthful reporting. The Markov-chain model and the optimization procedure were developed under the assumption of a particular strategy for lying peers. Incorporation of different lying strategies in our model is left for future research.

References

1. Papaioannou, T.G., Stamoulis, G.D.: An Incentives' Mechanism Promoting Truthful Feedback in Peer-to-Peer Systems. In: Proceedings of the 5th IEEE/ACM International Symposium in Cluster Computing and the Grid, Cardiff, UK (2005)
2. Papaioannou, T.G., Stamoulis, G.D.: Effective Use of Reputation in Peer-to-Peer Environments. In: Proceedings of the 4th IEEE/ACM International Symposium in Cluster Computing and the Grid, Chicago, Illinois, USA (2004)
3. Dellarocas, C.: Immunizing Online Reputation Reporting Systems Against Unfair Ratings and Discriminatory Behavior. In: Proceedings of the 2nd ACM Conference on Electronic Commerce, Minneapolis, MN, USA (2000)
4. Schillo, M., Funk, P., Rovatsos, M.: Using Trust for Detecting Deceitful Agents in Artificial Societies. Applied Artificial Intelligence **14** (2000) 825–848
5. Damiani, E., di Vimercati, S.D.C., Paraboschi, S., Samarati, P.: Managing and Sharing Servents' Reputations in P2P Systems. IEEE Transactions on Knowledge and Data Engineering **15** (2003) 840–854
6. Yu, B., Singh, M.P.: Distributed Reputation Management for Electronic Commerce. Computational Intelligence **18** (2002) 535–549
7. Aberer, K., Despotovic, Z.: Managing Trust in a Peer-to-Peer Information System. In: Proceedings of the 10th International Conference on Information and Knowledge Management, New York, NY, USA (2001)

8. Jurca, R., Faltings, B.: Eliciting Truthful Feedback for Binary Reputation Mechanisms. In: Proceedings of IEEE/WIC/ACM International Conference on Web Intelligence, Beijing, China (2004)
9. Antoniadis, P., Courcoubetis, C., Mason, R., Papaioannou, T.G., Stamoulis, G.D., Weber, R.: Results of peer-to-peer market models. (2004) Project IST MMAPPS: Deliverable 8. Available at: http://www.tik.ee.ethz.ch/~mmapps/www.mmapps.org/results/main.html.
10. Feldman, M., Papadimitriou, C., Chuang, J., Stoica, I.: Free-riding and whitewashing in peer-to-peer systems. In: Proceedings of the ACM SIGCOMM Workshop on Practice and Theory of Incentives in Networked Systems, Portland, Oregon, USA (2004)
11. Fowler, J.H.: Altruistic Punishment and the Origin of Cooperation. Proceedings of the National Academy of Sciences of the United States of America **102** (2005) 7047–7049

A New View on Normativeness
in Distributed Reputation Systems
Beyond Behavioral Beliefs[*]

Philipp Obreiter[1] and Birgitta König-Ries[2]

[1] Institute for Program Structures and Data Organization
Universität Karlsruhe (TH), 76128 Karlsruhe, Germany
obreiter@ipd.uni-karlsruhe.de
[2] Institute of Computer Science
Friedrich-Schiller-Universität Jena, 07743 Jena, Germany
koenig@informatik.uni-jena.de

Abstract. Autonomous entities in artificial societies are only willing to cooperate with entities they trust. Reputation systems keep track of the entities' behavior
and, thus, are a widely used means to support trust formation. In a P2P network,
the reputation system needs to be distributed to the individual entities. In previous
work, we have shown that some of the limitations of distributed reputation systems can be overcome by making use of hard evidence. In this paper, we take this
idea one step further by deriving beliefs of others' trustworthiness from one's
own experiences and the available hard evidence. For this purpose, we justify
why a self-interested autonomous entity may choose to behave according to the
norms of the system designer. As a consequence, the proposed belief model does
not only incorporate behavioral beliefs but also beliefs regarding the normativeness of an entity. We prescribe how beliefs are revised if new evidence becomes
available. The introduced models for recommendations and belief formation enable us to prove that self-interested entities always issue truthful recommendations regarding transactional behavior. The simulative evaluation shows that a
self-interested entity can be expected to be normative and, thus, to comply with
our system design.

1 Introduction

If you look at computer systems, there is a clear trend away from closed monolithic
systems towards self-organizing artificial societies composed of autonomous entities
with no central control and no commonly trusted unit. Examples are peer-to-peer systems, open multi-agent systems, and ad hoc networks. All these systems have a number
of characteristics in common: In order to achieve their individual goal, it is necessary
for the entities in the system to cooperate. However, due to their autonomy, on the one
hand, entities will only cooperate, if it is beneficial to them, on the other hand, entities

---

[*] The work done for this paper is funded by the German Research Community (DFG) in the
context of the priority program (SPP) no. 1140. The authors would like to thank Michael
Klein, Jens Nimis and Sokshee Goh for their comments on this paper. In addition, we are
grateful for Peter Reiher's comments on the legal obstacles for tampering software.

Z. Despotovic, S. Joseph, and C. Sartori (Eds.): AP2PC 2005, LNAI 4118, pp. 16–29, 2006.

are able to cheat in the course of a cooperation. In order to avoid being cheated on, an entity will only cooperate with entities it trusts.

Distributed reputation systems are a commonly suggested means to support trust formation [1, 2, 3, 4]. They allow for the exchange of information about certain entities' behavior and make it thus possible to base trusting decisions not only on one's own prior experience with that entity but also on others' experiences. The major challenge for the design of distributed reputation systems consists of accurately estimating others' behavior based on the information at hands. In previous work [5], we have argued that some of the exchanged information should be non-repudiable (and, thus, become *hard evidence*) in order to improve the accuracy of the estimation. Other authors [4] propose the inclusion of *norms* for the same purpose. However, existing distributed reputation systems cannot make use of the additional information provided by hard evidence and norms. For the most part, this is due to their ignorance of non-repudiability and their fixation on behavioral information. In this paper, we make up for these deficiencies by redesigning distributed reputation systems. We mainly contribute (1) by justifying the consideration of norms for systems of self-interested autonomous entities, and (2) by providing a multi-layered *belief model* that derives the belief of others' normativeness from own experiences and hard evidence.

The remainder of this paper is structured as follows: In Section 2, we extend the basic system model by considering hard evidence and norms. In Section 3, we show that existing approaches fail to exploit relevant information for the formation of beliefs. Based on this analysis, we make up for this deficiency by proposing a novel belief model in Section 4. We evaluate the properties of the redesigned distributed reputation system in Section 5 and, finally, conclude the paper in Section 6.

2 System Model

In this section, we present the system model that is assumed for the remainder of this paper. For this purpose, we describe the basic system model and extend it in two directions: (1) Based on the ideas of our previous work [5], non-repudiability is proposed as a means of acquiring hard evidence. In this context, a recommendation model based on hard evidence is described. (2) We suggest that system design should make use of norms and provide a justification of this idea. The justification is valid even for systems that consist of self-interested autonomous entities.

2.1 Basic System Model

The system consists of *entities* that may enter into *transactions* at any time. Each transaction occurs between a pair of entities (*transaction peers*). Each transaction peer executes an *action* on behalf of the transaction partner[1] who is able to check whether the action has been executed correctly. The autonomy of the entities implies that an entity may *defect* by failing to execute its action. Take for example two entities of a

---

[1] This assumption of mutually beneficial transactions may be relaxed by making use of non-repudiable promises [6].

P2P network that agree on exchanging a pair of documents. After having received the document of the transaction partner, a transaction peer may defect by refusing to transmit its promised document. The *reputation system* keeps track of defections in order to caution the entities about the defectors. In the absence of a central component, the reputation system is distributed to the entities themselves. More specifically, each entity runs a *local instance* of the reputation system. As a prerequisite for the operation of a distributed reputation system, the entities have to be able to send *authenticated messages*. This means that the recipient of a message knows which entity has sent it. For this purpose, each entity has a unique and unalterable *identity*. The local instances of the reputation system may cooperate by exchanging *recommendations*. The issuer of a recommendation (*recommender*) communicates information regarding a certain entity (*recommendee*) to the *recipient* of the recommendation.

2.2 Evidential Extension of the System Model: Non-repudiability and Hard Evidence

In our previous work [5], we have pointed out that distributed reputation systems should make use of non-repudiability. In the following, we recapitulate this idea and extend the system model accordingly.

Each entity is able to issue *non-repudiable* tokens and verify the validity of the non-repudiable tokens that have been issued by others. By this means, the issuer of such a token is able to non-repudiably commit to a statement. The token itself provides *hard evidence* of this commitment. Hence, we refer to non-repudiable tokens as hard evidence in the remainder of this paper. As we have pointed out in [5], presuming a means of non-repudiability is practically not a stronger assumption than presuming a means of authenticating messages.

According to the basic system model, a transaction consists of the exchange of repudiable actions between the transaction peers. This transactional model is extended as follows: The transaction peers exchange a pair of non-repudiable tokens before and after the proper transaction. First, each transaction peer commits to the imminent transaction and its terms by issuing a *contract* to its transaction partner. After the exchange of actions, each transaction peer issues a *receipt* and, thus, confirms that its transaction partner has complied with the transaction terms as promised. In the absence of a trusted third party, defections are still possible by retaining one's own contract, action or receipt.

The availability of contracts and receipts leads to a redefinition of the recommendation model. It dispenses with (potentially fake) reports of beliefs. Instead of that, a recommendation consists of hard evidence and is required to be non-repudiable. By this means, a recommender is forced to commit to the content of his recommendations. We distinguish between three types of recommendations: (1) *Disrecommendations:* The perception of cooperation is documented by a receipt. In a disrecommendation, an entity commits to such a perception. A disrecommendation is required to be non-repudiable so that its recipient has hard evidence of such commitment. Furthermore, we apply the policy that, in order to be valid, a disrecommendation has to enclose the contract of the entity that reportedly defected [5]. By this means, disrecommendations are always based on transactions that actually took place. (2) *Self-recommendations:* Each entity may disseminate its receipts by issuing self-recommendations [7]. (3) *Inconsistency proofs:* An inconsistency proof can be furnished if an entity issues non-repudiable commitments that are mutually incompatible. This is the case if an entity issues both a receipt and a disrecommendation regarding the same transaction.

2.3 Normative Extension of the System Model: Justification and Norm Design

In the past, it has been proposed to include norms into the design of distributed reputation systems [4]. However, the authors fail to justify why a self-interested autonomous entity could possibly decide to abide with norms that are detrimental to itself. In the following, we provide such a justification. Furthermore, we provide a thorough discussion of how norms should be designed. In addition, we define the type of an entity based on its normativeness.

System design and autonomy. According to the basic system model, each entity is *autonomous* and, thus, cannot be forced to behave in a certain way. Instead of that, each entity is only controlled by its human principal. For example, in a P2P system like KaZaA, a piece of software constitutes the entity and the user owning the hardware represents the human principal. If the user is not pleased with the performance of the software, he can remove or tamper it. The user does not have to be an expert for doing so if he has access to a tampered version of the software that meets his demands.

What are the consequences if each entity can be arbitrarily tampered? The system designer conceives a set of algorithms that should be run by the participants of the system. Traditionally, it is argued, that, if any part of the algorithms is not *incentive compatible*, the designer has to expect that the entities are tampered. Therefore, incentive compatibility of any behavior becomes the key criterion of system design (e.g., [8]). However, this is not completely true.

Tampering costs and compliance costs. In the following, we argue that – contrary to popular belief – tampering does incur some costs (*tampering costs*) and that, as a consequence, system design is disburdened of some difficulties.

A human principal may tamper his entity either by *creating* a tampered version of the software or by *adopting* the tampered version of others. Both options violate laws for a couple of reasons: (1) Tampering includes re-engineering of the software. In the US, this is explicitly forbidden by the Digital Millennium Copyright Act if the software is protected by a technical means [9]. (2) A tempered version represents a derived work. Hence, its creation or distribution infringes copyright law. This also applies the adoption of a tampered version since it incurs downloading and, thus, duplicating the derived work [10]. (3) Contractual law is violated, too, if the system designer protects his software by an adequate licence. In contrary to the US, such contractual protection is forbidden in the EU by the Software Directive §6.1 [11]. Still, the system designer could demand that the users agree with a licence regarding the identities that he assigns to them. According to that additional licence, identities may only be used in connection with the original software. By this means, the use of tampered versions infringes contractual law even in the EU.

Furthermore, there are tampering costs that are specific to the creation or adoption of tampered versions: The creation of a tampered version requires expert skills and is rendered even more costly by the means of code obfuscation [12]. On the other hand, the adoption of a tampered version exposes the user to risks due to the intransparency of its behavior. It could perform worse than the original version or even be a trojan. Consequently, tampering one's own entity always incurs costs.

We do not claim that these costs are prohibitive. Rather, we argue that system design should make use of these tampering costs, even if they are small. This means that system design could foresee some behavior that is not fully incentive compatible. As a result, complying with the system design also incurs some costs (*compliance costs*). It is clear that entities are tampered whenever these compliance costs exceed the tampering costs. For this purpose, system design has to keep the compliance costs as marginal as possible. This rules out systems in which the participants are designed to behave altruistically[2]. However, it makes sense to design a system in which proposed behavior may be not fully incentive compatible under infrequent circumstances.

Norm design. A norm refers to a non-enforceable rule given by the system designer (i.e., r-norms [13]). We propose to incorporate *norms* into the design of distributed reputation systems. The presence of norms leads us to defining the *type* of entities based on their normativeness: An entity's type is *normative* if the entity always complies with the norms. Hence, normative entities adhere to the original system software. Contrarily, its type is *strategic* if it decides whether to comply depending on the circumstances. Therefore, strategic entities run a tampered version of the system software. In the following, we discuss which norms should be included into the design of the system.

Norm design has to reconcile two conflicting demands. **(D1)** Norms should prescribe cooperative behavior in order to allow a population of norm compliant entities to perform well. **(D2)** Norms have to be self-enforcing by rendering norm compliance incentive compatible. If norms are not sufficiently self-enforcing, the compliance costs surpass tampering costs so that entities are tampered and deviate from the norm. In order to obtain self-enforcing norms, we propose to orientate norm design towards two maxims. **(D2a)** The only means of being perceived as *normative* entity is to actually abide with the norms. For this purpose, behavior that is prescribed in a norm has to be highly perceptible by others. **(D2b)** Each entity wants to be perceived as normative entity, i.e., as an entity that always complies with the norms. The maxims create a momentum towards self-interested norm compliance.

We propose two norms: **(N1)** *Never defect* in a transaction after having agreed on participating in it. **(N2)** *Never* issue *inconsistent* statement about the same issue. These norms meet the above demands of norm design: **(D1)** Both norms prescribe cooperative behavior. **(D2a)** Compliance with norm (N1) is perceptible to the transaction partner. Furthermore, compliance with norm (N2) has the potential of being fully perceptible by any entity if statements are required to be non-repudiable. **(D2b)** Since a transaction represents a win-win situation, each entity desires to participate in as much transactions as possible. For the choice of transaction partners, an entity prefers those entities that

---

[2] For example, the reputation mechanism of KaZaA has been hacked because it presumes that each entity truthfully calculates and disseminates its reputation.

are least likely to defect. Normative entities abide with norm (N1). Hence, entities want to be perceived as normative in order to be preferred as transaction partners. By an analogous argumentation for norm (N2), we obtain that each entity wants to be perceived as normative so that its statements are given more weight.

3   Exploiting Information for the Formation of Beliefs

In the previous section, the system model has been extended in order to account for hard evidence and norms. In this section, we point out that a distributed reputation system should exploit additional information that arises from these extensions. Furthermore, we discuss behavioral beliefs and show that their formation is the ultimate goal of a distributed reputation system. Based on these preconsiderations, we review existing distributed reputation systems.

3.1   Information and Behavioral Beliefs

An entity runs a local instance of the distributed reputation system in order to obtain support for its trusting decisions. In the following, we take a closer look at the general set-up for the provision of such support. The treatment is divided into two steps. First, we examine which type of information is available as input to a local instance of the reputation system. Second, we show that behavioral beliefs are required as output in order to support trusting decisions.

Information. The most obvious source of information are first-hand experiences. In the course of a transaction, the transaction partner may cooperate or defect. Since norm (N1) prescribes "never defect", these two cases correspond to normative and non-normative behavior respectively. In the following, we denote normative behavior by entity Y with $N_Y^{(b)}$ and non-normative (strategic) behavior with $S_Y^{(b)}$. Therefore, first hand experiences regarding entity Y consist of a sequence of $N_Y^{(b)}$ and $S_Y^{(b)}$. An entity has to consider the first hand experiences made by others that are communicated in recommendations. The recommendation model of Section 2.2 ensures that the contents of the recommendation relates to transactions and conflicts that actually occurred. Furthermore, transactional behavior is context-dependent [14]. This means that, even if an entity always behaves well in a specific context (e.g., low value transactions), it could still misbehave in other contexts. Hence, an entity should make use of *context information* in order to assess transactional behavior.

Behavioral beliefs. The decision whether to participate in a transaction represents a trusting decision. In order to make this decision, an entity has to predict the likely behavior of the potential transaction partner (say Y). Such a prediction has to cope with two types of uncertainty [15]: *Aleatory uncertainty* (or stochastic uncertainty) results from the fact that the transaction partner may behave in random ways. This means that there exists an intrinsic probability $p(N_Y^{(b)})$ that Y behaves cooperatively in the forthcoming transaction. In contrast, *epistemic uncertainty* (or subjective uncertainty) ensues from the lack of knowledge about the transaction partner. Therefore, the probability has to be estimated according to one's own current beliefs [16]. We denote such subjective estimate by entity X with $p_X(N_Y^{(b)})$. Since the estimate is based on X's beliefs and regards Y's behavior, we refer to it as *behavioral belief* of X regarding Y.

We elaborate on three important issues of behavioral beliefs. First, a behavioral belief is a probabilistic belief due to the aleatory uncertainty. Second, a behavioral belief is fallible due to the epistemic uncertainty. Therefore, it might be necessary to revise it if new information becomes available. Third, the probabilistic interpretation of behavioral beliefs provides for a straightforward means of making trusting decisions. More specifically, an entity decides to participate in a transaction if its expected utility is positive [2].

3.2   From Information to Behavioral Beliefs: Existing Approaches

In the following, we analyze how existing approaches of distributed reputation systems derive behavioral beliefs from the information at hand. We focus our analysis in two directions: **(1)** We do not consider approaches that make use of a central component in order to manage reputation (e.g., [17]) or foresee side-payments (e.g., [8]). **(2)** An approach is not taken into account if it does not provide for probabilistic estimations of behavior. This is because such estimations are a prerequisite for utilitarian decision making. Examples of approaches that fail to fulfill this requirement are [3].

The approaches of [1, 2] presume that the inert probability $p(N_Y^{(b)})$ of cooperative behavior by Y is the same for each transaction of Y. In such a case, Y's behavior follows a Bernoulli distribution of $N_Y^{(b)}$ and $S_Y^{(b)}$. Based on this assumption, the beta function is proposed as probability density function regarding $p(N_Y^{(b)})$ [1]. By this means, both aleatory and epistemic uncertainty are taken into account. Furthermore, first hand experiences can be directly integrated into the parameters of the beta function. However, this approach lacks a theoretically founded means of integrating others' first-hand experiences. Therefore, the maximum likelihood estimation of $p(N_Y^{(b)})$ is suggested in [2]. This provides a straightforward means of integrating others' first-hand experiences.

We argue that behavioral approaches suffer from three deficiencies: **(1)** The consideration of others' first-hand experiences is solely based on plausibility and dispenses with hard evidence. According to [5], this yields several limitations. **(2)** The approaches do not allow for the integration of type information. Even if entity Y was known to be normative, the probability $p(N_Y^{(b)})$ is not necessarily 1 since the entity could defect unintendedly. The other way round, a strategic entity Y does not have to defect in every transaction. **(3)** The approaches are based on the assumption that the inert probability of cooperative behavior is the same for each transaction. This inhibits the use of context information. Therefore, it has been proposed to provide separate behavioral beliefs for a set of potentially interrelated context categories [18]. Yet, the definition of the categories' granularity is difficult because it has to trade off the imprecision of aggregating contexts with the overhead of managing several separate behavioral beliefs for each entity.

4   The Multi-layered Belief Model and Belief Revision

Existing approaches apply too narrow models of beliefs that cannot exploit the information at hands. Therefore, in this section, we redesign the belief model by proposing several novel concepts: (1) Type beliefs are modelled such that epistemic uncertainty is taken into account. (2) Beliefs regarding type and behavior are interrelated by a multi-layered mapping. It explicitly models context-dependent norm abidance and unintended defection. (3) The revision strategy of type beliefs is able to take any relevant information (including behavioral information) into account.

4.1   The Belief Model

Apart from behavioral beliefs, we propose to make use of beliefs regarding an entity's type and intentions. In addition, we interrelate beliefs by suggesting the mappings type-to-intention and intention-to-behavior. The ensuing three layers of beliefs are illustrated in Figure 1.

Type beliefs and intention beliefs. In order to capture epistemic uncertainty, we model a belief regarding an entity's type as a probabilistic belief. For this purpose, we introduce some further notation: We denote the fact that entity Y is normative/strategic with $N_Y^{(t)}$ and $S_Y^{(t)}$ respectively (the superscript (t) refers to Y's type). Thus, the *type belief* of entity X regarding entity Y is the subjective probability $p_X(N_Y^{(t)})$. According to Section 2.3, an entity is either normative or strategic. Hence, there is no aleatory uncertainty about an entity's type. Consequently, a type belief may be expressed as a simple probability. Contrarily, the existing behavioral approaches have to make use of probability density functions in order to account for both aleatory and epistemic uncertainty.

In order to interrelate type beliefs and behavioral beliefs, we introduce an intermediate kind of belief regarding intentions. Entity Y may intend to abide with norm (N1) by refraining from defection. We denote this fact with $N_Y^{(i)}$. If Y intends to break the norm by defecting, its intention is strategic (denoted with $S_Y^{(i)}$). Thus, an *intention belief*[3] of X regarding Y is the subjective probability $p_X(N_Y^{(i)})$.

Type-to-intention mapping. An entity's intention is derived from its type. Normative entities always intend to abide with the norms, hence $p_X(N_Y^{(i)}|N_Y^{(t)}) = 1$. However, strategic entities abide with the norms only if they want to. Their decision of norm abidance is based on the context γ of the transaction. In the following, we denote the subjective probability $p_X(N_Y^{(i)}|S_Y^{(t)}, \gamma)$ that a strategic entity intends norm abidance with $p_X^{(n)}(\gamma)$. If the transaction value v is the main driving force of context-dependent behavior, a simple estimate of this probability is $e^{-\kappa v}$ with some positive parameter κ. This type-to-intention mapping incorporates context-dependence more seamlessly than the existing behavioral approaches. This is because it solves their conflict between imprecision of aggregating contexts and overhead of separate context categories.

---

[3] This definition is compatible to the BDI-architecture [19]. It refers to X's beliefs regarding Y's intention.

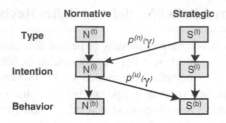

Fig. 1. Derivation of behavioral beliefs from type beliefs

Intention-to-behavior mapping. An entity's behavior is derived from its intention. The intention to abide with the norms is a prerequisite for actually abiding with them, hence $p_X(N_Y^{(b)}|S_Y^{(i)},\gamma) = 0$. However, norms can be broken unintendedly. The probability of unintended defection depends on the context of the transaction. For instance, partitioning is more likely to occur in long running transactions. Therefore, we have to estimate the conditional probability $p_X(S_Y^{(b)}|N_Y^{(i)},\gamma)$ that we denote with $p_X^{(u)}(\gamma)$ in the following.

The estimation of unintended defection is considerably easier than the one of strategic norm abidance. This is because unintended defection is due to the transaction's environment (i.e., nature [20]) that behaves non-strategically. Hence, it suffices to be able to estimate the probability of partitioning and node failure in order to estimate the subjective probability $p_X^{(u)}(\gamma)$ appropriately. In such a case, this probability only contains aleatory uncertainty.

4.2   The Belief Revision

The belief state of an entity consists of its type beliefs regarding the entities it is acquainted with. Whenever previously unknown information becomes available, type beliefs have to be revised. In the following, we provide a probabilistically sound means of such belief revision.

Let us assume that entity X perceives *cooperation* or *defection* of its transaction partner Y for the transaction context γ. In such a case, X's type belief regarding Y is revised according to Bayes' formula. The required conditional probabilities are derived from the formulas of Section 4.1. For perceived cooperation ($N_Y^{(b)}$), belief revision is as follows[4]:

$$p_X(N_Y^{(t)}|N_Y^{(b)},\gamma) = \frac{p_X(N_Y^{(t)}) \cdot p_X(N_Y^{(b)}|N_Y^{(t)},\gamma)}{p_X(N_Y^{(b)}|\gamma)} \qquad (1)$$

Disrecommendations are considered as follows: If entity Y disrecommends entity Z, we have to presume that Y or Z defected, i.e., $S_{YZ}^{(b)}$ occurred. We cannot infer that Z defected since Y could have disrecommended after having defected itself. Upon

---

[4] The formula of perceived defection is obtained by replacing $N_Y^{(b)}$ with $S_Y^{(b)}$.

receival of such a disrecommendation, we revise the beliefs regarding Z based on Bayes' formula:

$$p_X(N_Z^{(t)}|S_{YZ}^{(b)},\gamma) = \frac{p_X(N_Z^{(t)}) \cdot p_X(S_{YZ}^{(b)}|N_Z^{(t)},\gamma)}{p_X(S_{YZ}^{(b)},\gamma)} \qquad (2)$$

The belief regarding Y cannot be revised because, otherwise, the issuance of disrecommendations is not incentive compatible any more. Hence, the belief regarding Y is only revised if it is disrecommended by Z. This is no restriction since Z possesses the contract that is needed for issuing a disrecommendation.

Belief revision due to a *self-recommendation* leads to rehabilitation: A prior disrecommendation could be refuted by the receipt that is enclosed in the self-recommendation. In such a case, an inconsistency proof regarding the disrecommender Y becomes available. Before updating the beliefs regarding Y, the disrecommendee (and self-recommender) Z has to be rehabilitated from its downgrading of equation (2). This is done by inverting the equation based on the present type belief regarding Y.

An *inconsistency proof* evinces that an entity is tampered. If such proof regarding entity Y is available, the entity is believed to be certainly strategic, i.e., $p_X(N_Y^{(t)}) = 0$.

5 Evaluation

The previous sections have shown how a distributed reputation system has to be redesigned in order to account for hard evidence and norms. In this section, we discuss and evaluate two issues that ensue from the redesign: (1) We analyze under which circumstances strategic entities disrecommend. The analysis shows that defective behavior always leads to disrecommendations. (2) We determine simultaneously the costs that normative entities have to bear in order to comply with the norms. By this means, we evaluate to which degree the system's norms are self-enforcing.

5.1 The Disrecommendation Game

The motivation of discussing disrecommendation behavior is twofold. On the one hand, most existing approaches fail to provide a means for rendering the issuance of disrecommendations individually rational. We show that our system provides for such a means and, thus, guarantees that defective behavior of strategic entities is widely perceived as such. On the other hand, the analysis clarifies the relationship between the two novel concepts of our approach, i.e., the belief model and the recommendation model.

The analysis of disrecommendation behavior is based on the following situation. Let us assume that, during a transaction between entity Y and Z, a transaction peer defected by failing to execute its action. In such a case, both entities possess a contract but lack a receipt of the transaction and, thus, are able to mutually disrecommend. However, a strategic Y or Z only chooses to disrecommend if it is in its interests to do so. In the following, we provide a game-theoretic analysis of this situation.

According to Section 2.2 and 4.2, Y is only able to disrecommend Z to a third party X if X requested from Y such a disrecommendation. Upon receival of this disrecommendation, X revises its type belief $p_X(N_Z^{(t)})$ regarding Z. More specifically, the belief

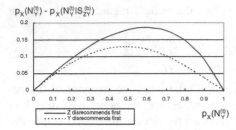

$p_X(N_Y^{(t)}) - p_X(N_Y^{(t)}|S_{ZY}^{(b)})$

- - - Z disrecommends first
····· Y disrecommends first

$p_X(N_Y^{(t)})$

		Z	
		no DR	DR
Y	no DR	$(0,0)$	$(-c_d,-c_i)$
	DR	$(-c_i,-c_d)$	$(-c_i-c_d+\frac{b_f}{2},-c_i-c_d+\frac{b_f}{2})$

Fig. 2. (a) Impact of disrecommending first and (b) the Disrecommendation Game

regarding Z's normativeness is degraded since it could be the originator of the defection. As a result of the degradation, X becomes less willing to transact with Z. Hence, the fact of being disrecommended incurs some costs c_d for Z. On the other hand, Y has to bear the costs c_i of issuing the non-repudiable disrecommendation and handing it over to X. Consequently, the disrecommendation appears to be detrimental for both the Y and Z. However, the prescription of belief revision provides a counterweight for the costs of disrecommending. If Y knew that Z subsequently disrecommends it to X, it could preemptively decrease X's type belief regarding Z by disrecommending Z first. By this means, the impact of Z's disrecommendation is decreased. Figure 2(a) illustrates[5] these considerations. It interrelates X's prior type belief regarding Y (*x-axis*) with the relative degradation of the type belief after having considered Z's disrecommendation (*y-axis*). The impact of Z's disrecommendation is considerably lower if Y disrecommends Z first. We conclude that being the first to disrecommend provides for a comparative benefit b_f. For virtually every application area of our system model (e.g., P2P systems), the synergies of inter-entity transactions outweigh by far the overhead of issuing a non-repudiable token. Therefore, we presume that the comparative benefit b_f of disrecommending first largely exceeds the costs c_i of issuing a disrecommendation.

We summarize these considerations in the *disrecommendation game*. Its normal form is shown in Figure 2(b). If both Y and Z choose to disrecommend (DR), they are equally likely to disrecommend first. Therefore, their expected comparative benefit of disrecommending first is $\frac{b_f}{2}$. If this benefit is higher than the disrecommendation costs c_i, we obtain a coordination game. This means that Y would decide to do as Z if it knew how Z decides and vice versa. More technically speaking [20], there are two stable equilibria in pure strategies, i.e., (DR, DR) and $(\neg DR, \neg DR)$. Furthermore, the equilibrium in mixed strategies consists of Y and Z disrecommending with the probability $\frac{2c_i}{b_f}$. This equilibrium is unstable since, whenever Y deviates from this equilibrium strategy by increasing (decreasing) the probability of disrecommending, Z decides to always (never) disrecommend.

The derivation of equilibrium strategies is based on the assumption that Y and Z behave rationally. This is the case if both Y and Z are strategic entities. However, according to the prescription of Section 2.2, normative entities always disrecommend. This raises the question how a strategic Y would decide depending on its type belief

---

[5] The illustration is based on $p^{(n)}(\gamma) = 30\%$, $p^{(u)}(\gamma) = 5\%$ and the prior belief $p_X(N_Z^{(t)}) = 50\%$.

$p_Y(N_Z^{(t)})$ regarding Z. The probability $p_Y(N_Z^{(t)})$ provides a lower bound of the probability that Z decides to disrecommend. Hence, we derive $p_Y(N_Z^{(t)}) > \frac{2c_i}{b_f}$ as a sufficient condition that a strategic Y always disrecommends. Due to $b_f \gg c_i$, this condition is fulfilled for virtually every belief of Y. Consequently, *strategic entities decide to disrecommend under most circumstances.*

The desirable outcome of above analysis is based on the two key concepts of our approach. On the one hand, the *recommendation model* ensures that disrecommendations are only possible for transactions in which a defection actually occurred. By this means, the disrecommendation game is only played by a pair of entities that had a conflict during their transaction. On the other hand, the *belief model* is exploited twice. First, the prescription of *belief revision* yields the comparative benefit of disrecommending first and minimal disrecommendation costs. Second, the solution of the disrecommendation game is based on the presence of *normative* entities that are pre-committed to norm abidance.

5.2   Simulative Quantification of the Compliance Costs

According to Section 2.3, an entity decides to remain normative as long as the costs of complying with the norms do not exceed the costs of tampering the original system software. In the following, we simulatively quantify the compliance costs in order to assess under which circumstances normativeness is a rational choice.

We have implemented our approach in DIANEmu [21]. The most important aspects of the simulation setting are as follows[6]: (1) *Benchmark:* The system consists of 100 entities. The number of normative entities varies between 20% and 95%. No a priori knowledge exists among the entities. Each entity obtains between 5 and 25 opportunities to choose its transaction partner among 2 entities. The transaction value is distributed uniformly in $[0.5, 1.5]$. The probability of unintended defection by any peer is 5%. (2) *Configuration of normative entities:* The estimation of the conditional probabilities are set by $\kappa = 0.5$ and $p_X^{(u)}(\gamma) = 0.05$. (3) *Configuration of strategic entities:* A strategic entity defects if its transaction partner executes its action first. In such cases, the defected transaction partner is disrecommended whenever possible. (4) *Metric:* The compliance costs are defined as the difference between the average utility of strategic and normative entities.

Figure 3 shows the simulation results. It appears that the compliance costs tend to decrease for an increasing number of transactions or an increasing ratio of normative entities. We interpret the results by making three quantitative conclusions: (1) Irrespective of the setting, the compliance costs never exceed 6, which is the equivalent value of defecting in 6 transactions. Therefore, a human principal runs the original version of the system software if his tampering costs outweigh the benefits of defecting 6 times. (2) Irrespective of the number of transactions, the compliance costs become negative for a sufficient high ratio of normative entities. In such cases, an average normative entity outperforms an average strategic entity. Since tampering costs are non-negative,

---

[6] Due to space limitations, we describe the setting in detail in a technical appendix. It is available at *http://www.ipd.uka.de/~obreiter/iTrust05techApp.pdf*

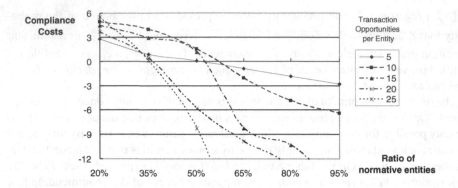

Fig. 3. The costs of complying with the norms

the system becomes completely normative if the ratio of normative entities exceeds a certain threshold (between 35% and 60% depending on the number of transactions). (3) Based on the first two points, we are able to interpret the overall system's dynamics: A fully normative system is in an equilibrium state. The equilibrium is very stable since norms are self-enforcing unless 40% of the entities (or even 80% for tampering costs beyond 6) are irrationally tampered.

6 Conclusion

Distributed reputation systems provide a means for restricting misbehavior in self-organizing systems of autonomous entities. Previous work has suggested the inclusion of hard evidence and norms into distributed reputation systems. In this paper, we have justified why system design should make use of norms. The presence of norms has led us to the distinction of *normative* and *strategic* entities. We have shown that existing distributed reputation systems cannot make use of the additional information provided by hard evidence and norms. We have made up for these deficiencies by redesigning distributed reputation systems. For the integration of hard evidence, we have suggested a novel *recommendation model* that is built on three types of recommendations. Furthermore, we have provided a multi-layered *belief model* that incorporates type beliefs. By this means, we are able to capture different types of informational input. We have considered in detail the mapping of type beliefs to behavioral beliefs and the revision of type beliefs based on behavioral information. The analysis of the disrecommendation game has shown that all entities issue disrecommendations regarding transactional behavior whenever they are able to do so. Finally, we have demonstrated simulatively that cooperative behavior is self-enforcing if the ratio of normative entities is at least moderate.

In the future, we aim at integrating a means of bailing for another entity's normativeness [7]. In this context, we will investigate how the availability of hard evidence regarding such bails influences belief formation and self-recommendations. Furthermore, we plan to compare simulatively the properties of our system with other existing distributed reputation systems.

References

1. Buchegger, S., Boudec, J.Y.L.: A robust reputation system for P2P and mobile ad-hoc networks. In: Second Workshop on the Economics of Peer-to-Peer Systems. (2004)
2. Despotovic, Z., Aberer, K.: A probabilistic approach to predict peers' performance in P2P networks. In: 8th Intl Workshop on Cooperative Information Agents (CIA'04). (2004)
3. Kamvar, S.D., Schlosser, M.T., Garcia-Molina, H.: The EigenTrust algorithm for reputation management in P2P networks. In: WWW2003. (2003)
4. Castelfranchi, C., Conte, R., Paolucci, M.: Normative reputation and the costs of compliance. Journal of Artificial Societies and Social Simulation 1 (1998)
5. Obreiter, P.: A case for evidence-aware distributed reputation systems. In: Second International Conference on Trust Management (iTrust'04), Oxford, UK, Springer LNCS 2995 (2004) 33–47
6. Obreiter, P., Nimis, J.: A taxonomy of incentive patterns - the design space of incentives for cooperation. In: Second Intl. Workshop on Agents and Peer-to-Peer Computing (AP2PC'03), Springer LNCS 2872, Melbourne, Australia (2003)
7. Obreiter, P., Fähnrich, S., Nimis, J.: How social structure improves distributed reputation systems - three hypotheses. In: Third Intl. Workshop on Agents and Peer-to-Peer Computing (AP2PC'04), To appear in post-proceedings, New York (2004)
8. Jurca, R., Faltings, B.: Towards incentive-compatible reputation management. In et al., R.F., ed.: AAMAS'02-Workshop on Deception, Fraud and Trust in Agent Societies, Springer LNAI 2631 (2003)
9. Jones, P.: Software, reverse engineering and the law (2005) http://lwn.net/Articles/134642/.
10. Hoffman, I.: Derivative works (2002) http://www.ivanhoffman.com/derivative2.html.
11. Council of the European Communities: Software directive – council directive on the legal protection of computer programs (91/250/EEC) (1991)
12. Linn, C., Debray, S.: Obfuscation of executable code to improve resistance to static disassembly. In: Proceedings of the 10th ACM Conference on Computer and Communication Security. (2003) 290–299
13. Tuomela, R.: The Importance of Us: A Philosophical Study of Basic Social Norms. Stanford University Press, Stanford, California (1995)
14. Mui, L., Halberstadt, A., Mohtashemi, M.: Notions of reputation in multi-agents systems: A review. In: Proceedings of the First International Joint Conference on Autonomous Agents and Multiagent Systems (AAMAS'02), Bologna, Italy (2002)
15. Helton, J.: Uncertainty and sensitivity analysis in the presence of stochastic and subjective uncertainty. Journal of Statistical Computation and Simulation 57 (1997) 3–76
16. Bacchus, F.: Probabilistic belief logics. In: Proceedings of European Conference on Artificial Intelligence (ECAI-90). (1990) 59–64
17. Josang, A., Ismail, R.: The beta reputation system. In: 15th Bled Conference on Electronic Commerce, Bled, Slovenia (2002)
18. Kinateder, M., Rothermel, K.: Architecture and algorithms for a distributed reputation system. In Nixon, P., Terzis, S., eds.: Proc. Of the First Intl. Conf. On Trust Management (iTrust), Heraklion, Greece, Springer LNCS 2692 (2003) 1–16
19. Rao, A.S., Georgeff, M.P.: Modeling rational agents within a BDI-architecture. In Allen, J., Fikes, R., Sandewall, E., eds.: 2nd Intl Conference on Principles of Knowledge Representation and Reasoning, Morgan Kaufmann, CA, USA (1991) 473–484
20. Rasmusen, E.: Games and Information : An Introduction to Game Theory. Oxford Blackwell (1989)
21. Klein, M.: DIANEmu – a java-based generic simulation environment for distributed protocols. Technical Report 2003-7, Universität Karlsruhe, Faculty of Informatics (2003)

A Trust Management Scheme in Structured P2P Systems

So Young Lee, O-Hoon Kwon, Jong Kim, and Sung Je Hong

Department of Computer Science & Engineering,
Pohang University of Science and Technology
{soyoung, dolphin, jkim, sjhong}@postech.ac.kr

Abstract. Since there is no method to verify the trustworthiness of shared files in P2P file sharing systems, malicious peers can spread untrustworthy files to the system. In order to prevent untrustworthy files from spreading, we propose an effective trust management scheme using peer reputation and file reputation together in a DHT-based structured P2P systems. Simulation results show that the proposed scheme effectively restrains the spreading of untrustworthy files even in cases where malicious peers change their identities. Simulation results show that the overall message cost for managing trust data is relatively low. We also propose a replication scheme so as to avoid the loss or corruption of trust data.

1 Introduction

In P2P systems, since no peer has the power or responsibility to monitor and restrain the others' behavior, there is no method to verify the trustworthiness of shared files. Therefore, malicious peers can spread untrustworthy files such as fake files that cheat their contents and corrupted files that infect systems or leave back doors in systems with viruses like the VBS.Gnutella [4] in Gnutella and W32.Supova.Worm [5] in Kazaa. In order to prevent these files from spreading without the help of any powerful central authorities, it is necessary that peers themselves judge the reliability of other peers based on their experience and share the judgments with all other participants. One way to help the peers share their experience is through the use of a reputation system. Generally, a reputation system receives, aggregates, and provides feedbacks about participants' past behavior. The feedbacks help participants decide whom to trust, encourage trustworthy behavior and deter dishonest people from participation [12]. One successful example of a reputation system is eBay [1]. In eBay, since individuals as well as companies can sell products, there exist many unknown entities. People who purchased products before can leave feedback about the seller so that others can refer to their opinion. A P2P reputation system is similar to the eBay reference system, but there are some design considerations that are different from general reputation systems [10].

Change of Identity. In the real world, changing someone's identity is very complicated since the identity is strongly connected with the owner. In P2P

Z. Despotovic, S. Joseph, and C. Sartori (Eds.): AP2PC 2005, LNAI 4118, pp. 30–43, 2006.

systems, however, the identifier of a peer has no relation with its owner and there is no restriction to change. For this reason a participant with a low reputation can change its identifier and rejoin the system as a newcomer. If the reputation information is only recorded based on an easily changeable identifier, it is hard to prevent malicious peers from feigning innocence. In this paper we use the reputation information of files which is more difficult to change than that of peers. By using file reputation information, we can preclude a malicious peer from spreading an identical untrustworthy file again just by changing its identifier and rejoining the system.

Storage of the reputation information. An important consideration for a P2P reputation management system is where to store the reputation information. There are two choices, local storage or global storage. The reputation system using local storage works as follows. Peer A can store its experience against peer B only in its local storage, and when others ask "What do you know about peer B?", it answers them based on his stored information. It is a very simple and traditional way for people to learn the reputation of others. But, if you want to know someone more objectively, you must ask as many people as possible. This is also applied in the case of using local storage. If a peer wants more objective reputation about another peer, it must ask many peers. This will generate a lot of messages in P2P systems. Whenever reputation information is required an aggregating process must be performed, which produces the overhead of handling many messages. Also, if a peer is not on-line when the reputation information is needed, the information of the peer is not reflected. Thus in this paper we propose to use global storage where others can easily access reputation information and it is still available when an evaluator is not on-line. To manage distributed data more efficiently, we use DHT-based structured P2P networks.

Integrity of the reputation information. The integrity of reputation information will be the most important characteristic that is directly connected with the reliability of the system. A reputation system based on P2P has to guarantee two kinds of integrity. First, the evaluation itself should be reliable. The reputation system should prevent malicious peers from polluting it by giving a positive evaluation to an untrustworthy file or a negative evaluation to a trustworthy file. To prevent this, we confirm whether the evaluator is trustworthy or not before applying the evaluation. Secondly, when the reputation data is stored and retrieved, it should not be altered. The system should keep malicious peers from modifying the reputation information to raise their own reputation or just to subvert the system. Whether a peer stores its own reputation or others, it must give unchanged information to the requester who wants to use it. If some part of the system is forged, it must not affect normal system behavior. To prevent this kind of malicious behavior, we propose a replication scheme.

In this paper, we propose a trust management scheme in DHT-based structured P2P systems. We use the term reputation to mean the trustworthiness of peers and files. The proposed trust management scheme has three characteristics. First, it uses file reputation information as well as peer reputation information.

Second, the system uses a global storage for reputation information. Third, the system uses a replication of reputation information for integrity and availability. Although there are many application areas for P2P such as instant messaging and distributed computing, we just consider file sharing applications which are the most popular.

This paper is organized as follows: We describe the proposed system model in Section 2 and the reputation management protocol in Section 3. We explain a replication scheme for the integrity of the reputation information in Section 4. Then, we show the simulation results in Section 5. Related works and their differences with our work are discussed in Section 6. Finally, we summarize this paper and give concluding remark in Section 7.

2   System Model

In this section, we describe the overall system model and assumptions of our proposed trust management scheme.

2.1   Storing Reputation Information

As we mentioned earlier, we use global storage to store the reputation information. The global storage is virtual and is actually partitioned into several small parts stored in all peers. That is, every peer equally manages some parts of the whole reputation information.

The peer that is responsible for specific reputation information is determined with a hash function with $O(1)$ time. The location of the responsible peer is found using a Distributed Hash Table (DHT) within $O(logN)$ time in the case of Chord [14]. We will explain the proposed system based on Chord [14], which is a very widely cited DHT-based structured P2P networks. Although we use Chord as the base architecture, the proposed reputation scheme can be applied to other DHT-based structured P2P networks.

2.2   Identifiers

Every peer that takes part in the system has a unique identifier ID_{peer} which is the hash value of the peer's IP address or the digest of a public key. In our scheme, each shared file also has two identifiers, a key identifier ID_{key} and a content identifier $ID_{content}$. ID_{key} is generated by hashing the file name and used as a keyword argument name in searching. And additional identifier, $ID_{content}$ is generated by hashing its contents and used to identify files with the same content. Since several versions of files exist with the same keyword, $ID_{content}$ is used to treat these versions differently. In Chord, ID_{peer} is used to determine the position of a peer on the identifier circle and the file indexes that it should take care of. For the reputation management, ID_{peer} is used to determine the file reputation manager and double hash value of ID_{peer}, $Hash$ (ID_{peer}), is used to determine the proper peer reputation manager. Like other DHT-based P2P system, ID_{key} should be one in the same name space with ID_{peer}.

2.3 Roles of Peer

In our scheme, every peer has the following five roles: *File Provider, File Consumer, File Index Manager, File Reputation Manager, Peer Reputation Manager*. Every participant in P2P file sharing system is basically a file provider and a file consumer. Since we assume the use of DHT-based structured P2P networks, every peer is responsible for some part of the file index information. We call this role a file index manager.

The remaining two roles, a file reputation manager and a peer reputation manager, are related to the reputation management. As a file reputation manager and a peer reputation manager, every peer takes care of the reputation informations of files and peers, respectively. In our scheme, the peer that has the role of a file index manager for a given file also takes the role of a file reputation manager. Since two roles are performed by the same peer for a given file, the file index information and the file reputation information can be obtained by one search query. This reduces the number of messages needed to get the reputation of the files. A peer reputation manager manages the reputation information of other peers whose $Hash(ID_{peer})$ matches with its identifier.

2.4 Repositories

Each peer has two separate repositories for reputation management. One is the *file repository* to manage the reputation of files and the other is the *peer repository* to store the reputation of peers. The file repository is organized as a table with attributes (ID_{key}, $ID_{content}$, *file reputation (positive, negative), file owners, description*). The repository stores the information of files including reputation information and the owners using two keys, ID_{key} and $ID_{content}$. The files with same ID_{key} and same $ID_{content}$ share the same row in the table. The file reputation consists of two values: positive reputation which represents the number of evaluations stating the file is trustworthy and negative reputation which represents the number of evaluations stating the file is not trustworthy. By making the same files share the same reputation we can rapidly recognize widely spread identical untrustworthy files and get the reputation information of the files regardless of its owner. Assume that a malicious peer has got a low reputation because of spreading an untrustworthy file X. Although a malicious peer can change its ID_{peer} to hide its low reputation and try to spread the identical untrustworthy file X again, the system can prevent the file from spreading since it already knows that the file is not trustworthy. It also benefits in the case that a newcomer shares a file O which has already received a high reputation. Since the file O is already known trustworthy, we do not need to consider that the provider is trustworthy or not. The table also maintains the list of owners, list of ID_{peer}s that have the file, and optional file descriptions including file name and file size. As the index information and the reputation information exist in the same table, we can obtain the two information together with one search query. Since the file repository is modified from the DHT's file index table by adding a reputation column, our scheme can be applied to other DHTs without a great difficulty.

Table 1. File Repository

ID_{key}	$ID_{content}$	File Reputation $(+,-)$	List of file owners	Description
K_8	F_1	$(30,2)$	N_5,N_{40}	"Music3"
K_{10}	F_4	$(45,0)$	N_{20},N_3	"Music1"
K_{10}	F_{10}	$(10,50)$	N_{19},N_{41}	"Music1"

Table 1 shows an example of file repository of a peer whose ID_{peer} is N_{10}. Different from the original DHT-based system, however, we can see that files F_4 and F_{10} which have same ID_{key}, K_{10}, occupy different rows. The file whose $ID_{content}$ is F_4 that is provided by N_{20} and N_3 has a positive reputation 45 and negative reputation 0. By its reputation, this file is very trustworthy. But, file F_{10} that has the same ID_{key} but different $ID_{content}$ has positive reputation 10 and negative reputation 50, and so it is not trustworthy. The peer repository is also organized as a table with attributes ((Hash (ID_{peer}), positive reputation, negative reputation). It stores the reputation of a peer whose $Hash(ID_{peer})$ matches with its ID_{peer}. In our scheme, the reputation of a peer is the summation of the reputation of files that it has provided. Like the file reputation, it consists of positive reputation and negative reputation. The positive value means how many times trustworthy files the peer has provided and negative value means how many times untrustworthy files it has provided. To prevent repositories from being large, each manager deletes the rows that are not referenced or updated in a pre-determined interval (e.g., 1 month).

3   The Reputation Management Protocol

We explain how our proposed scheme works based on the steps of file sharing system. These steps consists of the following phases: *Join and Publish, Query and Response, Download and Evaluation, Update Repositories.*

3.1   Join and Publish

In this phase, a peer joins the system and publishes its files to the system. When a peer joins the system, peer identifier ID_{peer} is assigned and each shared file gets two identifiers such as ID_{key} and $ID_{content}$. A peer publishes its file by sending publish messages to the file reputation manager: *Publish (ID_{key}, $ID_{content}$, ID_{peer}, description)*. The file reputation manager received the publish message updates its file repository. If the repository does not contain the information of published file, the manager adds a new row to its repository and assigns the initial reputation values, positive value 0 and negative value 0. If the information already exists in the repository, the manager just adds the ID_{peer} value to the list of owner.

As shown in Figure 1, peers N_{10} and N_{20} both publish a file whose name is same as "Music1" but whose contents are different. Since the two files have the same name they are assigned the same ID_{key} and published to the same file reputation

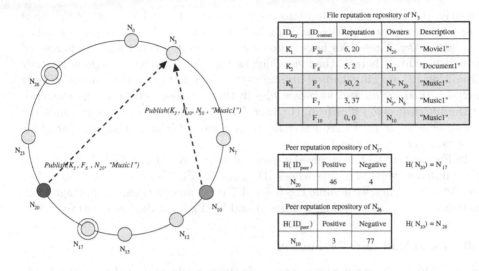

Fig. 1. Join and Publish

manager N_3. The manager N_3 updates its repository using the received message. The file of N_{10} is a newly appeared one because no entry matches its two identifiers, K_3 and F_{10}. Thus, N_3 adds a new row with reputation value (0,0) and file owner N_{10}. Whereas, the file of N_{20} with K_3 and F_6 already exists in the repository. Its reputation is positive 30, negative 2 and the other peer N_7 also has the identical file. In this case, N_3 just adds N_{20} to the list of owner.

3.2 Query and Response

In this phase, a peer sends a search query to find a desired file and receives a filtered response from the manager. The peer searches the file by sending a query message to the appropriate file reputation manager: *Query (ID_{key})*. The file reputation manager that received the query message makes a response through the following procedure. The manager retrieves candidates that have the same ID_{key} from its repository. The candidates are classified into 3 levels by their file reputation: *trustworthy, unknown, untrustworthy*. The reputation level of each file is decided by the following two conditions.

$$|Positive| + |Negative| >= T \qquad (1)$$

$$\frac{Positive}{|Positive| + |Negative|} >= P \qquad (2)$$

The two parameters, T and P, are system-wide parameters. The parameter T is a data confidence threshold, which represents the minimum number of evaluations required and P is a trust threshold, which represents the ratio of positive evaluations. The files that do not satisfy Condition (1) are classified as *unknown*.

Namely, the number of evaluations are not enough to decide whether the file is trustworthy or not. The files which satisfy Conditions (1) and (2) are classified as *trustworthy*. These files have been evaluated enough times and are perceived as trustworthy. Whereas, the files which satisfy Condition (1) but do not satisfy Condition (2) are classified as *untrustworthy*. The file reputation manager only includes *trustworthy* and *unknown* files in the response and hides the existence of the *untrustworthy* files from the user. The file reputation manager sends the response message to the requester:*Response (list of {ID_{key}, $ID_{content}$, list of file owners, level, description}).*

In Figure 1, if N_3 has received a query to search K_3, it can find that there are three different version of files whose $ID_{content}$ are F_6, F_7 and F_{10} with same key identifier K_3. When we assume P is 0.8 and T is 10, among them the manager only includes file F_{10} (classified as *unknown*) and file F_6 (classified as *trustworthy*).

3.3   Download and Evaluation

In this phase, a peer selects, downloads, uses a file and evaluates the trustworthiness of the provider and the file. The peer received the *Response* selects one among the files in the *Response*. When the peer selects a file whose level is *trustworthy*, it randomly selects one of its providers. When it chooses a file whose level is *unknown*, it estimates the file reputation by referencing its owner's reputation. To keep malicious peers from modifying untrustworthy files and republishing them as new, the peer queries the reputation of the owners. If the file is provided by several owners, the peer can take an average value, a maximum value or a minimum value of several file owner's reputation as the file reputation. If the reputation of the file owner is low, the file is excluded from the selection.

After downloading and using the selected file the peer evaluates its trustworthiness as positive or negative and sends the evaluation to the file reputation manager. The evaluated value is also sent to the peer reputation manager of the provider. If the file gets positive reputation, the peer provided the file also gets the same value.

3.4   Update Repository

In this phase, the evaluations of previous phase are applied in the system. The file reputation manager and the peer reputation manager received the evaluation data update their file and peer repositories, respectively. Malicious evaluators, however, can forge the reputation value by giving positive evaluation to an untrustworthy file or giving a negative evaluation to a trustworthy file. To prevent this, every reputation manager confirms whether the evaluator is trustworthy or not before updating the value.

When a reputation manager receives an evaluation data from evaluator, it hashes the evaluator's ID_{peer} and queries the peer reputation manager of the evaluator by sending *QueryPeer* message: *QueryPeer (Hash(ID_{peer}))*. The peer reputation manager received the *QueryPeer* message searches its peer repository, calculates the level of peer reputation like file reputation and sends the

ResponsePeer (Hash(ID_{peer}), level) to the requester. The opinion of the evaluator is treated differently depending on the evaluator's reputation. If the level of evaluator's reputation is *trustworthy*, the manager updates the reputation value of the corresponding file and peer. And if the level is *untrustworthy*, the value is not reflected in the repository. If the level is *unknown*, only a partial value, e.g. a half of its trustworthiness is reflected. Through reflecting the opinion of the *unknown* peer relatively less than that of the *trustworthy* peer, we can reduce the probability of polluting the repositories.

4   Replication

The proposed scheme prevents malicious peers from fabricating their own reputation by choosing reputation manager other than themselves. But, the possibility of forging the reputation of others in order to subvert the system still exists. As we mentioned earlier, this is an important problem that harms the integrity and usefulness of the reputation system. In addition, since joining and leaving of peers occur frequently in P2P systems, it is possible that peers could leave the system without handing over their repositories to other proper peers. If a peer leaves the system silently, the information that it has managed is lost. To prevent these two problems – information loss caused by a silently disappearing peer and information pollution caused by a malicious peer, we replicate the reputation information to multiple peers. There are some works reported previously on replication schemes [11, 9, 15]. The difference among them is how to select multiple replication peers. Ratnasamy *et al.* [11] used k different hash functions to select peers and other works [9, 15] used neighbors of the responsible peer in the identifier space. Unlike the previous works, we use replicated data for load balancing as well as backup. If identical data exists in multiple positions of the identifier space, it is more efficient to use the nearest one. We explain the replication scheme based on Chord. As shown in Figure 2, two replication sets exist. Each set consists of a replication root, which is shown as a black oval, and its k successors in the identifier space. k is a tolerance parameter and at least $k/2$ peers must work correctly.

The first replication root is the original responsible peer that is determined by the hash function. Assume that the system has m-bit identifier space. The second replication root is determined by adding 2^{m-1} to the binary value of first replication root's identifier. Since Chord is based on ring topology, the second replication root becomes the symmetric position of the first. A peer that wants to retrieve data computes the identifiers of two replication roots and chooses the nearest one. If the first replication root is near the requesting peer, it sends queries to the first replication root and its k neighbors independently and receives k responses. Among k responses, the peer takes the majority value as the result. Updating data is similar to the retrieve case. So a peer sends update messages independently to k peers. Since peers send messages to one of the nearest replication sets, two replication sets must synchronize themselves. Whenever peers receive an update message, they send it to the k other replicated

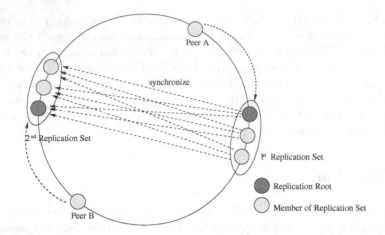

Fig. 2. Replication

peers independently. Since we assume more than $k/2$ peers work properly, the other replicated peers receive more than $k/2$ update messages. If peers receive more than $k/2$ identical update messages from the other set, they update their repositories.

By using peers in the symmetric position as the replication set, we can divide the Chord-ring into two. Therefore, it reduces the distance over which the messages are delivered by half. In Chord, the symmetric position is the last entry of the finger table (routing table) [14]. Since each peer periodically exchanges message with the entries of the routing table to maintain correct routing information, the synchronization process does not create much load.

5   Performance Evaluation

We have performed two experiments to show that our proposed scheme effectively reduces the untrustworthy downloading rate with low message overhead. The first experiment evaluates the effect of the reputation system in trust management and the overall message overhead caused by managing the additional reputation data. In first experiment, we have assumed that malicious peers continuously conduct bad behavior without changing their identifier. But in the second experiment, malicious peers change their identities periodically to hide their malicious behavior. The second one shows the effect of using peer and file reputation together compared to only using peer reputation.

5.1   Simulation Environments

For the simulation, we have implemented three types of P2P file sharing system on Chord : *Normal-System, PeerRep-System, PFRep-System.*

- *Normal-System* means a normal DHT-based P2P file sharing system which does not use any reputation scheme. In this system, a peer sends a query using the Chord algorithm and receives the list of providers for the requested file. Then, the provider is chosen randomly.
- *PeerRep-System* means a DHT-based p2p system which adopts only the peer reputation scheme. Only the reputation informations of peers are managed by other peers. A peer sends a query using the Chord algorithm like *Normal-System* and also receives the list of providers of the requested file. But, in this system, a peer selects a file and a provider by the reputation of the provider. If the reputation of provider is high, its file is selected.
- *PFRep-System* means a DHT-based p2p system which uses our proposed reputation scheme. The reputation informations of peers and files are managed by peer reputation manager and file reputation manager, respectively. A peer also sends a query like others and receives file reputation information and file index information together. Using file reputation information, peers select a trustworthy file. If file reputation information is insufficient, they reference the peer reputation information.

The experiments are performed under a static P2P network with 1,000 peers. The percentile of malicious peers and files are from 5% to 20%. Initially, every peer has 5 different kinds of files. Each peer shares the downloaded file again when the file and the peer are both untrustworthy or both trustworthy. We have presumed that malicious peers only have untrustworthy files and give a negative reputation to the trustworthy file to subvert the system and trustworthy peers only have the trustworthy files and act correctly. We used the rate of downloading untrustworthy files among total downloading as a metric.

5.2   Simulation Results

Based on the above environment, we have performed two experiments and compared three systems. In the first experiment, we measured the rate of untrustworthy file downloads and the message overhead in case that malicious peers do not change their identities. Figure 3 and Figure 4 show the results of the first experiment.

Figure 3 shows the rate of untrustworthy downloads when the rate of malicious peers is 10%. The x-axis represents the total number of downloads performed by peers and the y-axis represents the rate of malicious downloads among the total downloads. We can see that the rate of untrustworthy downloads decreases gradually as the total number of downloads increases. Although all peers and files are started with unknown reputation state, the system learns the reputation of peers and files as the number of downloads increases. The result shows that two systems adopted reputation scheme, *PFRep-System* and *PeerRep-System*, effectively restrain the untrustworthy downloads and the *PFRep-System* is slightly better than the *PeerRep-System*. Whereas, the *Normal-System* continuously suffered from untrustworthy downloads.

Figure 4 shows the number of generated messages in the first experiment. The number of messages which is generated in the same interval is represented

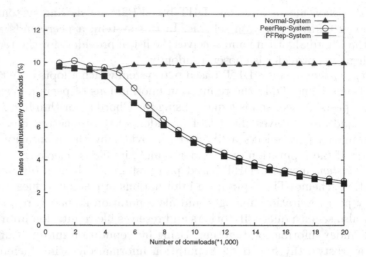

Fig. 3. Rate of untrustworthy downloads

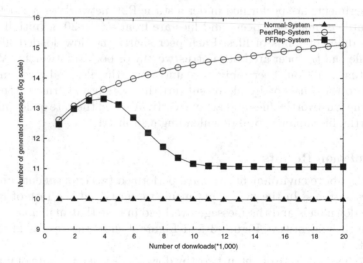

Fig. 4. Number of generated messages

in log scale. Only the messages used in searching file and managing reputation informations are reflected. *PFRep-System* initially generates many messages like *PeerRep-System* since the file reputation data is not enough to decide the trustworthiness of file. However, after the system gathers enough reputations *PFRep-System* does not create many messages since the reputation information is carried with a search query. Additional generated messages are used to update the reputation data and query peer reputation for unknown files.

The second experiment is similar to the previous one except that malicious peers change their identifiers periodically. After every 2,000 downloads are performed, all malicious peers change their identity and pretend to be new-comers.

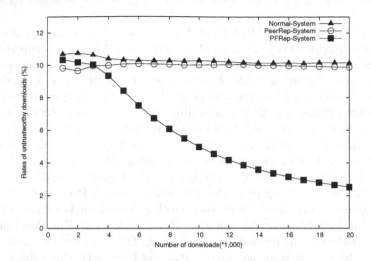

Fig. 5. Rate of untrustworthy downloads when allowing malicious peers to change their identity at every 2,000 downloads

Figure 5 shows the result of the second simulation. We can see that the rate of untrustworthy downloads are only decreased in *PFRep-System*. In the *PeerRep-System*, since the reputation information is only referenced by the ID_{peer}, changing identities by malicious peers makes the reputation system useless. But, since PFRep-System still keeps the reputation information based on the files, changing identities does not influence the system. That is, the proposed scheme works better in preventing untrustworthy files from spreading than existing systems even in cases where malicious peers change their identities.

6   Related Works

There have been several studies addressing managing reputation on P2P networks. These studies can be classified into *unstructured or structured* according to the base architecture of P2P networks.

Because many famous P2P file sharing applications [3, 2] are implemented on unstructured P2P networks for practical reason, most previous works [7, 8, 13] about reputation management systems are based on unstructured P2P networks. Among them, Xrep [7] is similar to ours in terms of using combined reputations of peers and resources to recognize untrustworthy resources regardless of its provider. But, it has several weak points. First, it creates too many messages and is not scalable since it gathers opinions about resources and peers using a distributed polling algorithm. Second, it does not use the reputation information effectively since it does not use the reputation information on selection but only use it for verifying the selection. Third, it lacks a reliable method to verify the trustworthiness of voters.

Recently, several reputation systems in structured P2P networks have been proposed. EigenTrust [8] and PeerTrust [16] are reputation management systems in structured P2P networks such as CAN [11] and P-Grid [6], respectively. In EigenTrust, each peer has multiple score (reputation) managers that are determined effectively by using CAN characteristics. However, since a peer's trust value is computed using the trust value of the neighbors of the requester, the computed trust value is different according to the requester. To get a unique global value from any starting position in the system it must contact lots of neighbors. Also, the normalizing technique used in EigenTrust makes it impossible to distinguish between malicious peers and newly joined peers. But, the notion of transitive trust and giving weights to trust peers according to its own experience raises the integrity of the reputation system. PeerTrust also stores the trust data in a distributed way using DHT and uses the trust manager that is responsible for feedback submission and trust evaluation. But PeerTrust just suggests an independent reputation system using DHT, we present more adaptable system by adding some columns to existing DHT structure. Since both of them consider only the peer reputation, they can not prevent malicious peers from changing their identities.

Our work differs from others in two aspects. First, we present detailed data structures and algorithms to manage reputation information in DHT-based structured P2P networks. Our proposed scheme can be easily implemented to use index tables and routing protocols of DHTs. Second, we use file reputation and peer reputation together unlike EigenTrust [8] and PeerTrust [16]. Therefore, we can prevent untrustworthy files from spreading even in the case where malicious peers change their identities.

7   Conclusion

We have presented an effective trust management scheme using file reputation and peer reputation together in DHT-based structured P2P networks. The proposed scheme can prevent untrustworthy files from spreading by checking file reputation in addition to peer reputation. The proposed scheme could also prevent them in cases where malicious peers change their identities. The scheme used DHTs in order to store and retrieve reputation information in a scalable and distributed way. Also, the scheme used replication of reputation information for integrity and availability. Using simulation, we showed that the proposed scheme works better in preventing untrustworthy files from spreading than existing systems even in cases where malicious peers change their identities.

Acknowledgments

This research was supported by the MIC(Ministry of Information and Communication), Korea, under the Chung-Ang University HNRC-ITRC(Home Network Research Center) support program supervised by the IITA(Institute of Information Technology Assessment).

References

1. eBay homepage Http://www.ebay.com
2. Gnutella homepage Http://www.gnutella.com
3. Kazza homepage Http://www.kazaa.com
4. Vbs.gnutella worm Http://securityresponse.symantec.com/avcenter/venc/data/vbs.gnutella.html
5. W32.supova worm Http://securityresponse.symantec.com/avcenter/venc/data/w32.supova.worm.html
6. Aberer, K.: P-grid: A self-organizing access structure for p2p information systems. Proceedings of ACM Conference on Information and Knowledge Management (CIKM) (2001)
7. Damiani, E., di Vimercati, D.C., Paraboschi, S., Samarati, P., Violante, F.: Reputation-based approach for choosing reliable resources in peer-to-peer networks. Proceedings of the 9th ACM Conference on Computer and Communications Security (2002)
8. Kamvar, S.D., Schlosser, M.T., Garcia-Molina, H.: The eigentrust algorithm for reputation management in p2p networks. Proceedings of the 12th International World Wide Web Conference (2003)
9. Maymounkov, P., Mazieres, D.: Kademlia: A peer-to-peer information system based on the xor metric. Proceedings of the 1st International Workshop on Peer-to-Peer Systems (IPTPS'02) (2002)
10. Ooi, B.C., Liau, C.Y., Tan, K.L.: Managing trust in peer-to-peer systems using reputation-based techniques. Proceedings of the International Conference on Web Age Information Management (2003)
11. Ratnasamy, S., Francis, P., Handley, M., Karp, R., Shenker, S.: A scalable content addressable network. Proceedings of the ACM 2001 SIGCOMM Conference (2001)
12. Resnick, P., Zeckhauser, R., Friedman, E., Kuwabara, K.: Reputation systems. Communications of the ACM, 43(12):45-48 (2000)
13. Selcuk, A., Uzun, E., Pariente, M.: A reputation-based trust management system for p2p networks. Proceedings of the International Workshop on Global and Peer-to-Peer Computing, IEEE/ACM CCGRID (2004)
14. Stoica, I., Morris, R., Karger, D., Kaashoek, F., Balakrishnan, H.: Chord: A scalable Peer-To-Peer lookup service for internet applications. Proceedings of the 2001 ACM SIGCOMM Conference (2001)
15. Vishnumurthy, V., Chandrakumar, S., Sirer, E.: Karma: A secure economic framework for peer-to-peer resource sharing. Proceedings of the Workshop on Economics of Peer-to-Peer Systems (2003)
16. Xiong, L., Liu, L.: Peertrust: Supporting reputation-based trust for peer-to-peer electronic communities. IEEE Transactions on Knowledge and Data Engineering 16(7), 843–857 (2004)

Incentive-Compatibility in a Distributed Autonomous Currency System

Kenji Saito[1], Eiichi Morino[2], and Jun Murai[3]

[1] Graduate School of Media and Governance, Keio University
5322 Endo, Fujisawa
Kanagawa, 252-8520 Japan
ks91@sfc.wide.ad.jp
[2] Gesell Research Society Japan
[3] Faculty of Environmental Information, Keio University

Abstract. *Peer-to-peer complementary currencies* can be powerful tools for promoting exchanges and building sustainable relationships among selfish peers on the Internet.

i-WAT[1] is a proposed such currency based on the WAT System, a polycentric complementary currency using *WAT tickets* as its media of exchange. Participants spontaneously issue and circulate the tickets as needed, whose values are backed up by chains of trust. *i*-WAT implements the tickets electronically by exchanging messages signed in OpenPGP.

This paper claims that the design of *i*-WAT is incentive-compatible as to protection against moral hazards, or threats caused by selfish peers because they may take advantage of the rules; such hazards are defused in *i*-WAT if the participants react against misbehaviors of others by pursuing their own benefits.

A reference implementation of *i*-WAT has been developed in the form of an XMPP instant messaging client. We have been putting the currency system into practical use since June 2004.

1 Introduction

Exchanging is a necessary building block of peer-to-peer (P2P) systems, which can potentially harness the under-utilized power of the network of computers connected one another via the Internet. Since the resources are distributed over autonomous entities, such exchanging needs to be performed in an *incentive-compatible*[2] way: the coordination must be accomplished by collection of selfish behaviors. A medium of exchange which represents a guaranteed value should take an important role in the design of P2P systems.

Money is a well-known medium of exchange, but its scarcity has caused a lot of problems. *Complementary currencies*, or alternative forms of monetary media, have been proposed and tested in real life to achieve an autonomous, sustainable local economy even in short of money. There have been successful cases, such as experiments in Wörgl in 1932 (stamp money[3]), in Comox Valley in 1983 (LETS[4]) and in Ithaca since 1991 (Ithaca HOURs[5]).

Z. Despotovic, S. Joseph, and C. Sartori (Eds.): AP2PC 2005, LNAI 4118, pp. 44–57, 2006.

Those complementary currencies are used to support values which are not readily circulated in today's economy, such as volunteer works or skills that are not regularly utilized. Translating them onto the Internet would benefit the design of P2P systems, which are also intended to make use of under-utilized resources. But then, those currencies also need to be peer-to-peer.

We proposed *i*-WAT[1] in year 2003 as such a currency usable on the Internet, based on the WAT System[6]. The WAT System is a system of polycentric complementary currencies using *WAT tickets* as its media of exchange. A WAT ticket is like a bill of exchange, but without a specified redemption date or place. *i*-WAT implements the tickets electronically by exchanging messages signed in OpenPGP. It has been put into practical use since June 2004.

This paper begins by describing the core design and the trust/incentive models of *i*-WAT. It then shows, by a game-theoretical analysis, that the design of *i*-WAT is incentive-compatible as to protection against moral hazards: taking advantage of the rules will result in the subject's confrontation to an uncontrollable risk. Since *i*-WAT has no fixed authority, such risks are imposed by rational behaviors of other participants. The hazards in concern will include impostors, unintentional breach of trust and collusions.

2   WAT/*i*-WAT Currency System

2.1   The WAT System

Overview. The WAT System[6] is a complementary currency designed by Eiichi Morino, a coauthor of this paper. It has been used broadly, especially in Japan, since its introduction in August 2000.

A *WAT ticket*, a physical sheet of paper resembling a bill of exchange, is used as the medium of exchange in the system. A lifecycle of a WAT ticket involves three stages of trading as illustrated in Fig. 1:

1. Issuing – the birth of a WAT ticket
   A *drawer* issues a WAT ticket by writing on an empty form the name of the provider (*lender*) of the goods or service, the amount of debt[1], the present date, and the drawer's signature. The drawer gives the ticket to the lender, and in return obtains some goods or service.
2. Circulation – ordinary exchange
   The person to whom the WAT ticket was given can become a *user*, and use it for another trading. To do so, the user writes the name of the recipient, as well as their own, on the reverse side of the ticket. The recipient will become a new user, repeating which the WAT ticket circulates among people.
3. Redemption – the return of the WAT ticket
   The WAT ticket is invalidated when it returns, as a result of a trade, to the drawer.

---

[1] Typically in the unit kWh, which represents cost of producing electricity from natural energy sources.

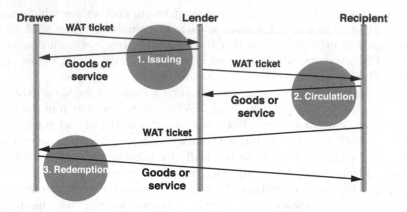

Fig. 1. Three stages of trading with a WAT ticket

Distinctive Features of the WAT System

Autonomy. Anyone can spontaneously become a member of the WAT System with a sheet of paper if they follow the above protocol.

Compatibility. A WAT ticket is compatible with any other WAT tickets in the world, so that the currency system is operable globally, as long as the drawer can be credited.

Extensibility. The protocol illustrated in Fig. 1 defines *the WAT Core*, the essence of the WAT System. An *extended part* can be defined for a new currency based on the WAT System, stating, for example, the region, group and duration in which the tickets are usable, as well as the unit in which the debt is quantified.

Security. In case the drawer fails to meet their promise on the ticket, the lender assumes the responsibility for the debt. If the lender fails, the next user takes over. The responsibility follows the chain of endorsements. The longer the chain is, the more firmly backed up the ticket is. Therefore the length of the chain of endorsements represents the extent of trust the ticket has gained.

2.2   *i*-WAT: The Internet WAT System

Overview. *i*-WAT is a translation of the WAT Core onto the Internet. We have made a reference implementation available, which has been used mainly by the members of the WAT System.

In *i*-WAT, messages signed in OpenPGP (*i-WAT messages*) are used to implement transfers of an electronically represented WAT ticket (*i-WAT ticket*).

An *i*-WAT ticket contains the identification number, amount of debt and public key user IDs of the drawer, users and recipients. Endorsements are realized by

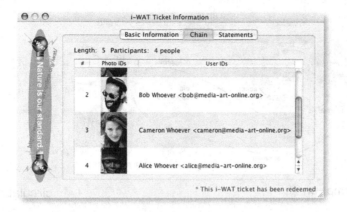

Fig. 2. Visual representation of an *i*-WAT ticket

Table 1. *i*-WAT messages

Message	Sender	Receiver	Function
<draw/>	drawer	recipient (lender)	draws an *i*-WAT ticket.
<use/>	user	recipient	uses an *i*-WAT ticket.
<accept/>	recipient	drawer and user	confirms readiness to accept the *i*-WAT ticket once it is validated.
<reject/>	recipient	drawer or user*	rejects an *i*-WAT ticket.
<approve/>	drawer	user and recipient	validates an *i*-WAT ticket, and approves the transaction.
<disapprove/>	drawer	user and recipient	denies an *i*-WAT transaction.

* depending on whether the ticket has just been issued or in circulation, respectively.

nesting PGP signatures. In our reference implementation, the chain of signatures is visualized as illustrated in Fig. 2, using the PGP photo IDs.

Table 1 shows the types of *i*-WAT messages. All *i*-WAT messages are signed by the senders, and are formatted in the canonical form of XML with nested signatures. The messages cause state transfers of a ticket as illustrated in Fig. 3.

Upon translating the WAT Core onto the digital communication domain, we have made the following changes from the state machine of a WAT ticket:

1. Trades need to be asynchronously performed. Intermediate states, such as waiting for acceptance or approval, are introduced.
2. Double-spending needs to be prohibited. The drawer is made responsible for guaranteeing that the circulating ticket is not a fraud. This means that every trade has to be approved by the drawer of the involved ticket.

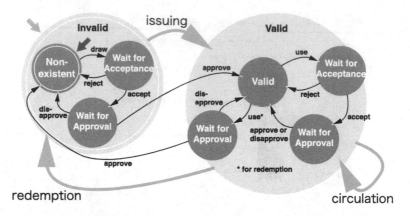

* Gray arrows represent WAT state-transfer.
* Black arrows represent *i*-WAT state-transfer.

Fig. 3. State machine of a WAT/*i*-WAT ticket

Protocol

Issuing – the birth of an i-WAT ticket

1. The drawer sends a <draw/> message which contains the public key user IDs of the drawer and lender, identification number and amount of debt. This message becomes the original *i*-WAT ticket after the protocol is completed.
2. The lender sends back the content of the message as an <accept/> message.
3. The drawer sends an <approve/> message to the lender.

Circulation – ordinary exchange

1. The user adds to the *i*-WAT ticket the public key user ID of the recipient, and sends it to the recipient as a <use/> message. This message becomes a valid *i*-WAT ticket after the protocol is completed.
2. The recipient forwards the content of the message to the drawer and user as an <accept/> message.
3. The drawer verifies the ticket, and sends an <approve/> message to the user and recipient.

Redemption – the return of the i-WAT ticket

1. The user sends a <use/> message to the recipient, who equals the drawer.
2. The drawer verifies the ticket, and invalidates it as the debt is now redeemed. The drawer sends an <approve/> message to the user.

Generalized Ticket Value. We have recently made a generalization to the value of an *i*-WAT ticket such that it is expressed as a tetrad $\langle V_0, V_m, V_x, f \rangle$

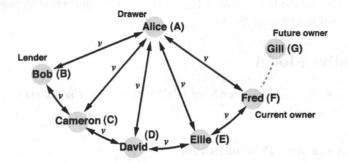

Fig. 4. *i*-WAT trust model

presented by the drawer, where V_0 is the face value (initial value) of the ticket, V_m is the minimum value, V_x is the maximum value, and $f(t)$ is the differentiation (derivative) of a function of time $F(t)$. V_m/V_x are set to be $\perp/\top$ respectively if those values are not applicable.

The effective value V_t of a ticket at time t is given by the following equation:

$$V_t = \min(\max(\int_0^t f(t)dt + V_0, V_m), V_x)$$

This is a generalization to allow the value of a ticket to vary over time, limited by some minimum/maximum values. Typically, it holds that either $f(t) = 0$ for all t (*regular ticket*), $f(t) < 0$ for all t (*reduction* ticket) or $f(t) > 0$ for all t (*multiplication* ticket).

The incentive mechanism for reduction and multiplication tickets have been discussed in [7] and [8], respectively.

3   Trust Model

Fig. 4 shows the *trust model* of *i*-WAT, which is a definition of mutually validating relation $\overset{v}{\leftrightarrow}$, where A $\overset{v}{\leftrightarrow}$ B means that A and B validate the public keys of each other.

To implement the model by dynamically building an appropriate web of trust, [9] showed that it would suffice if the behaviors of participants satisfy the following three properties:

1. *mutual signing by knowing*, or any two mutual acquaintances sign the public keys of each other,
2. *mutual signing by participation*, or the drawer and a user of an *i*-WAT ticket sign the public keys of each other, and
3. *mutual full trust by participation*, or the drawer and a user of an *i*-WAT ticket fully trust each other, and a recipient fully trusts the corresponding user of a ticket, in the context of PGP public key signing.

Software features to help automating *mutual signing/full trust by participation* will be released in the near future.

4   Incentive Model

We model a series of trades with an *i*-WAT ticket as a sequential game with incomplete information.

4.1   Notations and Preconditions

Participants. Users are denoted as W (for WAT friends) indexed by the order of their appearance: drawer $= W_0$, lender $= W_1$, ..., current recipient $= W_n$. For the sake of argument, there assumed to be $n + 1$ unique participants, and the webs of trust around them are built from scratch as transactions proceed.

Probability of Default. Probability p_i devides W_i into two types: *successful* (appears by probability $1 - p_i$) or *failing* (appears by probability p_i) to redeem the ticket in concern.

Timing of Usage. The time at which W_i uses the ticket is regarded i to simplify reasoning. This means that the time is not evenly distributed in the model. Still, for any *reduction* tickets, it holds that $V_i < V_{i-1}$, and for any *multiplication* tickets, it holds that $V_i > V_{i-1}$, where $i > 0$.
   Redemption takes place at time r.

Utility of Exchange. There assumed to be some utility of having an exchange medium instead of having specific goods or unutilized services. This utility for W_i is denoted as UX_i.
   UX_0 is a special case, where the value is divided into utility of spending UX_0^S and utility of earning (redeeming) UX_0^E, to reflect the fact that these events are not adjacent in the time line.

Cost of Trust. Cost to rebuild trust relationships for W_i is CT_i. The cost includes that of *whitewashing*, or that one disappears and assumes a new identity. It is assumed that this cost does not vary in a large extent among participants, and is generally worth more than a value of a ticket. These assumptions should be justified by the fact that the *i*-WAT trust model requires construction of a *web of trust*[9], which requires that a new participant must know someone in person in the circle of friends around the *i*-WAT ticket.

Cost of Lazy Approval. Cost of lazy approval by W_0 for a recipient W_i is denoted as CL_i. It is apparent that this cost exists for a *reduction* ticket, whose value is reduced over time. The cost exists for other types of tickets too, because it affects the usability of the ticket in concern; the ticket will not be usable by W_i until W_0 approves the transaction in which W_i received the ticket.

Laziness of W_0 is assumed to be observable from others. This assumption is justifiable by a software design; participants can observe how often W_0 becomes online in an i-WAT-enabled presence-sharing system.

Cost of Premature Redemption. Cost of unexpectedly early redemption for W_0 is denoted as CP_0. Note that W_0 is incentivized to delay redemption even for *multiplication* tickets, which will often be used to control the timing of redemption by giving users incentives to wait.

Cost of Communication. Communication cost is negligible for i-WAT, which is the reason why the WAT System was electronized and made usable on the Internet.

Accounting. The sum of effective values of all tickets issued by W_0 in circulation is denoted as $\sum V$. This information is assumed to be made available to all prospective participants. Feasibility of this is discussed in section 6.

Since the cost of trust CT_0 is to be applied just once when W_0 whitewashes their identities, W_0 can minimize the effectiveness of the cost by issuing as many tickets as they can and then go on to default (see section 5.5). Therefore prospective lenders are interested in this information.

4.2 Game Trees

A *game tree* is a graph consisting of players' decision points as nodes, which are connected in the order of their occurrences. Each player has an *information set*, or a set of decision points from which they can choose an action. In the end of the graph, the gains of all players are drawn as leaves.

In the figures to follow, types of participants are not made explicit in the trees except for those of W_0, which are distinguished by probability p_0.

Payoffs for Issuing. Fig. 5 shows a game tree for issuing an i-WAT ticket.

The first player is the nature who chooses between two types of W_0 as the drawer: *successful* or *failing* to redeem the ticket. These types appear by probabilities of $(1 - p_0)$ and p_0, respectively, for reasons either situational of strategic which are not distinguishable by other participants.

The lender W_1 has an information set in which the player is uncertain about W_0's type. Depending on the player's belief, W_1 chooses to either accept or refuse the ticket presented by W_0.

Inside parentheses are the gains of W_1 and W_0 in each combination of W_0's type and W_1's action.

1. If W_1 chooses to accept the ticket
   - W_1's expectation is $U_1 - C_1 p_0$
   - W_0's expectation is $U_0 - C_0'(1 - p_0) - C_0 p_0$

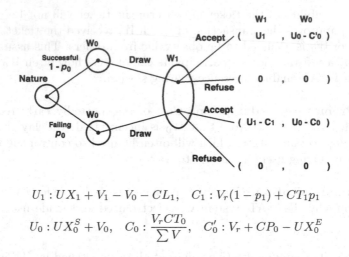

$$U_1 : UX_1 + V_1 - V_0 - CL_1, \quad C_1 : V_r(1 - p_1) + CT_1 p_1$$

$$U_0 : UX_0^S + V_0, \quad C_0 : \frac{V_r CT_0}{\sum V}, \quad C_0' : V_r + CP_0 - UX_0^E$$

Fig. 5. Game tree for issuing. $V_r = V_1$ and $p_1 = 0$ if W_1 is the last user.

2. If W_1 chooses to refuse the ticket
    – Both W_0 and W_1 gain or lose nothing.

The utility UX_1 depends in large part on whether the ticket will be accepted by W_2 or not. It is also an important factor for minimizing $|V_1 - V_0|$ for a *reduction* ticket, in which case both W_0 and W_1 wish V_r to be zero. In case of a *multiplication* ticket, W_1 will typically wait until the effective value reaches V_x, and then use the ticket against W_0 for both maximizing their gain $V_1 - V_0$ (in case of successful W_0) and minimizing their loss to V_0 (in case of failing W_0).

In any case, p_0 is an important factor for W_1 to make a decision.

Payoffs for Circulation. Fig. 6 shows a game tree for circulating an *i*-WAT ticket. The tree is an extension to Fig. 5.

1. If W_n chooses to accept the ticket
    – W_n's expectation is $U_n - C_n p_0$
2. If W_n chooses to refuse the ticket
    – W_n gains or loses nothing.

If n is small, W_n is interested in the trustworthiness of all participants W_i where $0 \le i < n$. Since $\prod_{i=1}^{n-1} p_i$ approaches zero as n increases, W_n will be indifferent of the type of W_0 if n is sufficiently large; they will tend to accept the ticket.

This may lead to a moral hazard, but still W_n will be interested in maintaining the trust model of *i*-WAT as described in the following section.

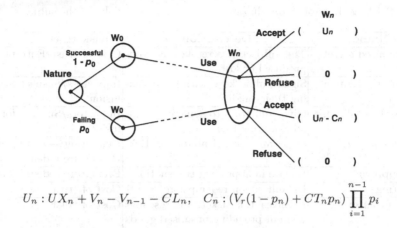

$$U_n : UX_n + V_n - V_{n-1} - CL_n, \quad C_n : (V_r(1 - p_n) + CT_n p_n) \prod_{i=1}^{n-1} p_i$$

Fig. 6. Game tree for circulation. $V_r = V_n$ and $p_n = 0$ if W_n is the last user.

5   Protections Against Moral Hazards

5.1   Overview

Table 2 shows the list of hazards in concern.

A case of someone receiving goods or service and escaping without providing a ticket is not discussed because it does not involve a successful i-WAT transaction, and there can be no proof of the incident within the context of the WAT Core (operational solutions need to be pursued).

Double-spending is also excluded from the list because its detection can be automated (it is in our reference implementation), and W_0 has no incentive to turn off such a software feature.

5.2   Sloppy Key Management

i-WAT uses public key cryptography as a protection against impostors. Failing to follow the good practice is considered a moral hazard. Keeping the good practice, on the other hand, maintains the trust model, and prevents offenders from getting away with unpaying the cost of trust.

This section describes how failing to follow the good practice in key management is against the subject's own interest. Discussions at later sections assume that the trust model is maintained.

Compromised Secret. If a secret key is compromised or lost, the key needs to be declared invalid, and replaced with a new one. Since an i-WAT ticket records the public key user IDs[2] instead of the identifiers of the keys themselves, replacing

---

[2] A public key user ID is a character string. Under the current operation of PGP, it is typically an e-mail address.

Table 2. Possible moral hazards and the imposed risks to the subjects

Name	Description	Risk to the Subject
Compromised secret	The subject's secret key is compromised or lost.	Cost of trust/Entrapment
Evidenceless signing	Signs public keys without checking their validity.	Impostors/Suspect for collusion
Evidenceless full trust	Gives full trust to someone without knowing them.	Impostors/Suspect for collusion
Excessive issuing	Issues an excessive amount of tickets.	Defaulting $\rightarrow$ cost of trust/ Premature redemptions
Lazy approval	Be late in approving transactions.	Premature redemptions
Defaulting	Defaults upon redemption.	Cost of trust
Empty promise	Receives the ticket and escapes without providing promised goods or service	Cost of trust

the key does not affect the correctness of the data. However, this replacement costs equivalent to CT_i for W_i with the secret key in question because it involves reconstruction of the web of trust. Besides, the compromised key may be used for an entrapment (section 5.7).

Evidenceless Signing/Full Trust. If participants sign public keys of others without personally validating them, or if they fully trust other participants without knowing their trustworthiness, there is a risk of allowing impostors of real or imaginary persons in the circle of friends around the i-WAT ticket.

Such impostors may perform misbehaviors like an empty promise, by which the signer/truster may be victimized. Or worse, they may be suspected as collaborators of such misbehaviors.

5.3   Excessive Issuing

Excessive issuing can mean more debt than W_0 can handle, so that there is a risk of defaulting (increased p_0), which discourages both W_0 and W_1 to give birth to a ticket.

Furthermore, since excessive issuing is assumed to be observable from current ticket owners, they would want W_0 to redeem the tickets quickly, in order to avoid W_0's defaulting with the tickets they have. This should be especially true for those tickets whose chains of endorsements are still short. Which means that excessive and intensive issuing attracts premature redemptions.

5.4   Lazy Approval

There is a risk that circulation may be stalled by negligence of W_0 in their role of approving transactions.

Let us stand upon W_{n-1}'s view point. If W_0 is late to respond to the request for approval, the prospective transaction is delayed, costing CL_n to W_n which W_{n-1}

knows that W_n can predict. Meanwhile, W_0 is not affected by their own laziness because acceptance and approval happen at the same time. When likelihood of acceptance is in question, W_{n-1}'s natural choise is to ask W_0 for redemption.

Therefore, being lazy is to risk premature redemptions, and W_0 is incentivized to respond quickly.

5.5 Defaulting

W_0 would want to minimize C_0 upon defaulting. If V_r can be reduced (as in the case of a *reduction* ticket), there may be no reason to default to begin with. Therefore, the only option for W_0 is to increase $\sum V$ to minimize the effect of CT_0. However, the value is monitored by all prospective lenders, so that W_0 cannot increase it over a reasonable amount.

5.6 Empty Promise

If there is a proof of an empty promise, W_0 can disapprove further transactions with the ticket. If the ticket has not been used further, W_{n-1} can safely become the valid owner of the ticket by a roll back.

The proof of the incident becomes a source of bad reputation for W_n, which can only be whitewashed by paying the cost of trust.

5.7 Collusions

There may be a colluded defaulting by every W_i where $0 \leq i < n$, so that W_n is victimized. However, the trust model implies that W_n must have needed to know someone in person in the chain of endorsement. At least that someone can be made to pay the cost of trust, which makes such collusion difficult.

There may be a colluded empty promise by W_0 and W_n so that W_{n-1} is victimized. This means that W_0 escapes too, in which case W_1 can take over the responsibility of the drawer. If it fails and the responsibility is forwarded upto W_{n-1}, it is indistinguishable from the state in which every W_i where $0 \leq i < n-1$ is colluding. The rest is the same as the case of a colluded defaulting.

Another form of colluding may be to entrap W_i so that it looks as if W_i committed a misbehavior such as an empty promise. This is only possible with a compromised secret key or a forged key pair, because there needs to be a verifiable signed message to prove that W_i did it. This requires a breach of the trust model.

6 Future Work

We have been implementing *i*-WAT as a plug-in for a messaging client called *wija*, which we are also developing. *wija* conforms to XMPP (Extensible Messaging and Presence Protocol) , and is available at the following URL:

– http://www.media-art-online.org/wija/

We intend to implement features to our software for monitoring excessive issuing: sharing information about tickets issued by others in circulation. We believe this can be done in a decentralized and trusted way. [10] briefly discusses a technique for doing this, which is an application of the protocol for *fair sharing* described in [11].

7   Related Work

Geek Credit[12] is an example of exchange medium usable on the Internet, which is close to *i*-WAT. It defines *Geek Credit policy*, which is similar to the *i*-WAT state machine, but the problem of double-spending is handled differently. Geek Credit detects double-spending at redemption, so that each trading does not need to be consulted with the drawer.

While this simplifies the protocol, the risk of attacks is higher for Geek Credit than for *i*-WAT. Recovery is also more difficult because the incident is only revealed at a later stage.

PPay[13] is another example of exchange medium which is similar to *i*-WAT. PPay handles the problem of double-spending in almost the same way as *i*-WAT does; it requires approval (process of *reassignment*) by the issuer of the coins when they are transferred to other parties. The difference is that this authority is duplicated in PPay. It assumes that an external banking facility exists, which exchanges the governments' fiat money with digital coins. Such facility may be given authority to reassign coins.

This makes the currency more available, but it also makes the protocol more complicated that that of *i*-WAT. We believe that availability of the issuers can be increased by applying existing fault-tolerance techniques, independently from the currency design. Since it can avoid premature redemptions and increase the utility of their freedom of creating exchange media, some issuers may find it beneficial to pay the cost of applying such techniques.

8   Conclusions

A medium of exchange which represents a guaranteed value should take an important role in the design of peer-to-peer systems, in which under-utilized resources are shared among selfish participants.

This paper showed that the design of i-WAT is incentive-compatible as to protection against moral hazards: taking advantage of the rules will result in the subject's confrontation to an uncontrollable risk, which is imposed by rational behaviors of other participants.

References

1. Saito, K.: Peer-to-peer money: Free currency over the Internet. In: Proceedings of the Second International Conference on Human.Society@Internet (HSI 2003), Lecture Notes in Computer Science 2713, Springer-Verlag (2003)

2. Feigenbaum, J., Shenker, S.: Distributed algorithmic mechanism design: Recent results and future directions. In: Proceedings of the 6th International Workshop on Discrete Algorithms and Methods for Mobile Computing and Communication (DIALM '02). (2002)
3. Schwarz, F.: Das experiment von Wörgl (1951) Hypertext document. Available electronically at http://userpage.fu-berlin.de/~rochrigw/woergl/
4. Seron, S.: (Local Exchange Trading Systems 1 - CREATION AND GROWTH OF LETS) Hypertext document. Available electronically at http://www.gmlets.u-net.com/resources/sidonie/home.html.
5. Glover, P.: (Ithaca HOURs Online) Hypertext document. Available electronically at http://www.ithacahours.com/.
6. watsystems.net: (WATSystems home page) Hypertext document. Available electronically at http://www.watsystems.net/.
7. Saito, K., Morino, E., Murai, J.: Reduction over time: Easing the burden of peer-to-peer barter relationships to facilitate mutual help. In: Proceedings of the Second International Workshop on Computer Supported Activity Coordination (CSAC 2005). (2005)
8. Saito, K., Morino, E., Murai, J.: Multiplication over time to facilitate peer-to-peer barter relationships. In: Proceedings of the 2nd International Workshop on P2P Data Management, Security and Trust (PDMST '05). (2005)
9. Saito, K.: WOT for WAT: Spinning the web of trust for peer-to-peer barter relationships. In: IEICE TRANSACTIONS on Communication, The Institute of Electronics, Information and Communication Engineers (2005)
10. Saito, K.: Maintaining trust in peer-to-peer barter relationships. In: Proceedings of 2004 Symposium on Applications and the Internet (SAINT 2004 Workshops), IEEE Computer Society Press (2004)
11. Ngan, T.W.J., Wallach, D.S., Druschel, P.: Enforcing fair sharing of peer-to-peer resources. In: 2nd International Workshop on Peer-to-Peer Systems (IPTPS), Berkeley, California (2003)
12. Komarov, A.: (Geek Credit homepage) Hypertext document. Available electronically at http://home.gna.org/geekcredit/.
13. Yang, B., Garcia-Molina, H.: PPay: micropayments for peer-to-peer systems. In: Proceedings of the 10th ACM conference on Computer and communications security (CCS '03). (2003)

Handling Free Riders in Peer-to-Peer Systems

Loubna Mekouar, Youssef Iraqi, and Raouf Boutaba

University of Waterloo, Waterloo, Canada
{lmekouar, iraqi, rboutaba}@bbcr.uwaterloo.ca

Abstract. In reputation-based peer-to-peer systems, reputation is used to build trust between peers and help selecting the right peers to download from. In this paper, we argue that reputation should not be used for service differentiation among the peers. To provide the right incentives for peers to share files and contribute to the system, the new concept of *Contribution Behavior* is introduced for partially decentralized peer-to-peer systems. Service differentiation is achieved based on the *Contribution Behavior* of the peers rather than their reputations. Simulation results assess the ability of the proposed algorithm to effectively identify free riders and malicious peers that upload malicious content, hence reducing the level of service provided to these peers and preserving network resources. On the other hand, good peers that contribute to the system receive better services which increases their satisfaction significantly.

1   Introduction

In a Peer-to-Peer (P2P) file sharing system, peers communicate directly with each other to exchange information and share files. In an open P2P system, peers often have to interact with unknown peers (i.e. strangers) and need to manage the risks involved with the interactions. For example, if a user wants to download a file, the user is given a list of peers that can provide the requested file. The user has then to choose one peer from which the download will be performed. Since the open and anonymous nature of Peer-to-Peer systems open the door to misuses (by malicious peers) and abuses (by free riders), peers need to be able to reason about trust in order to avoid untrustworthy peers.

Trust management is any mechanism that allows to establish mutual trust which will motivate peers to cooperate. Building trust is difficult especially when we are dealing with strangers in virtual communities. In such interactions, risk is involved and in order to minimize this risk and get advantage from these interactions, trust is needed. Several reputation-based P2P systems [1, 2, 3, 4, 5] were introduced to build trust among peers. These systems are used to attribute a value to a peer based on its past transactions. The higher the reputation score, the more confident we are that this peer will upload an authentic file. When people interact with each other over time, the history of past transactions will help inform them about their real behavior. In addition, peers are motivated to display good behavior as it will have an impact on their future interactions. Political scientist Robert Axelrod refers to this phenomenon as the *shadow of future* [6].

Z. Despotovic, S. Joseph, and C. Sartori (Eds.): AP2PC 2005, LNAI 4118, pp. 58–69, 2006.
© Springer-Verlag Berlin Heidelberg 2006

1.1   Motivation and Contribution

Almost all of the proposed reputation management schemes try to achieve one
or more of the following goals:

1. Isolate malicious peers from the network by downloading files from the reputable peers, hence reducing malicious uploads
2. Increase the users satisfaction
3. Use the network resources more efficiently
4. Motivate peers to share files and contribute to the system
5. Reward the reputable peers by providing better services to them

Goals 1, 2 and 3 have been more or less addressed by most reputation management schemes. Goals 4 and 5 are mostly related to providing incentives and
service differentiation. Few works have addressed service differentiation. Section
6 presents the most important works.

Most proposed reputation management schemes help reduce malicious uploads
by choosing the high reputable peers for downloads. They also help increase the
peers satisfaction. However, they do not provide incentives for peers to have a
high reputation value and hence share. Indeed, the reputation considered in the
proposed schemes is for trust (i.e. maliciousness of peers), based on the accuracy
and quality of the files uploaded.

In eBay, members have interest in building trust and get a high reputation
value in case they want to become "sellers". The higher is the reputation of a
member, the higher is the chance that buyers will trust to deal with him.

In a P2P file sharing system, the situation is different. What is the interest
that a peer can gain from having a high reputation value? This peer will be more
and more requested for uploads which is not a gain for this peer, but more for
the peers that download from it. This is why service differentiation is needed.

Few reputation schemes proposed service differentiation among the peers (cf.
Section 6). However, these schemes considered peers' reputation as a guideline
for service differentiation. This means that a peer with a high reputation, will
receive better service than a peer with a lower reputation.

This however does not address the problem of free riders. Free riders are
peers that take advantage of the system without contributing to it[1]. Providing
a mechanism to detect free riders is an important issue since in [7], it has been
found that most of the shared content in Gnutella is provided by only 30% of
the peers. This means that 70% of the peers are free riders. There should be a
mechanism to reward the contributing peers and encourage other peers to share
their content.

However, free riders can have a high reputation[2], but this only means that
the files that they are providing are authentic. If the reputation is used as a
guideline for service differentiation, then free riders will also receive the same

---

[1] Or with a very small contribution.

[2] E.g. a free rider may upload few authentic files and get a high reputation. Then, the
free rider starts taking advantage of the system thanks to its high reputation. In the
literature, this phenomenon is called "milking".

service as the participating peers. Using reputation for service differentiation, will not allow detecting free riders. It will however provide better service to high reputable peers and low or no service to low reputable peers.

In this paper, we argue that a good scheme for service differentiation should be able to detect free riders and malicious peers and lower the service provided to them. This will have a double effect. On one hand, this will encourage free riders and malicious peers to change their behavior. And, on the other hand, good peers will receive a better service and will be motivated to continue providing good service. In this paper, we propose such a scheme and show that it is able to detect free riders and malicious peers and reduce the services provided to them while providing good peers with a better service.

The paper is organized as follows. Section 2, describes briefly the reputation management scheme considered in this work. Section 3 presents the proposed new contribution management scheme while, section 4 discusses service differentiation issues for partially decentralized P2P systems. Section 5 presents the performance evaluation of the new scheme and Section 6 describes the related works. Finally, section 7 concludes the paper.

2   Reputation Management

In this section, we describe briefly the reputation management scheme considered in this paper. For more details, please refer to [8].

2.1   Notations and Assumptions

In this paper, we consider partially decentralized P2P systems. In these systems, supernodes index the files shared by peers connected to them, and proxy search requests on behalf of these peers. Queries are therefore sent to supernodes, not to other peers. In the remaining of the paper, the following notations are used:

- Let P_i denotes peer i
- Let $D_{i,j}$ denotes the size of downloads performed by peer P_i from peer P_j
- Let $D_{i,*}$ denotes the size of downloads performed by peer P_i
- Let $D_{*,j}$ denotes the size of uploads by peer P_j
- Let $A_{i,j}^F$ be the appreciation of peer P_i of downloading the file F from P_j
- Let $Sup(i)$ denotes the supernode of peer i

2.2   The Reputation Management Scheme

After downloading a file F from peer P_j, peer P_i will evaluate this download. If the file received corresponds to the requested file, then we set $A_{i,j}^F = 1$. If not, we set $A_{i,j}^F = -1$. In the latter case, either the file has the same title as the requested file but different content, or that its quality is not acceptable. Each peer P_i in the system has four values, called *reputation data* (REP_{P_i}), stored by its supernode:

1. $D_{i,*}^+$: Satisfied downloads of peer P_i from other peers,
2. $D_{i,*}^-$: Unsatisfied downloads of peer P_i from other peers,
3. $D_{*,i}^+$: Satisfied uploads from peer P_i to other peers,
4. $D_{*,i}^-$: Unsatisfied uploads from peer P_i to other peers

Note that we have: $D_{i,*}^+ + D_{i,*}^- = D_{i,*}$ and $D_{*,i}^+ + D_{*,i}^- = D_{*,i} \forall i$.

When a peer P_i joins the system for the first time, all values of its *reputation data* REP_{P_i} are initialized to zero[3].

When receiving the appreciation (i.e. $A_{i,j}^F$) of peer P_i, its supernode $Sup(i)$ will perform the following operation:

If $A_{i,j}^F = 1$ then $D_{i,*}^+ = D_{i,*}^+ + Size(F)$,

else $D_{i,*}^- = D_{i,*}^- + Size(F)$.

Then, the appreciation is sent to $Sup(j)$ that will perform the following operation:

If $A_{i,j}^F = 1$ then $D_{*,j}^+ = D_{*,j}^+ + Size(F)$,

else $D_{*,j}^- = D_{*,j}^- + Size(F)$.

We compute the *Authentic Behavior* of a peer P_j as:

$$AB_j = \frac{D_{*,j}^+ - D_{*,j}^-}{D_{*,j}^+ + D_{*,j}^-} = \frac{D_{*,j}^+ - D_{*,j}^-}{D_{*,j}} \quad \text{if } D_{*,j} \neq 0$$
$$AB_j = 0 \qquad\qquad\qquad\qquad\qquad \text{otherwise}$$
(1)

Note that AB_i is a real number between -1 (if $D_{*,j}^+ = 0$) and 1 (if $D_{*,j}^- = 0$).

3   Contribution Management

We believe that trust in a peer-to-peer system should be addressed according to the following dimensions: 1) *Authentic Behavior*, 2) *Credibility Behavior*, and 3) *Contribution Behavior*

Authentic Behavior (AB): this is the reliability of a peer in providing accurate and good quality files. Good peers have usually a high *authentic behavior* value, while malicious peers usually get lower values since they are providing malicious content. This value represents the reputation of a peer. It allows to differentiate between good and malicious peers.

Credibility Behavior (CB): this represents the sincerity of a peer in providing a honest feedback. The *credibility behavior* is an important indicator that allows to identify liar peers and reduce their effect on the reputation system. In [5], the concept of *Suspicious Transaction* was introduced to compute the *credibility behavior*.

Contribution Behavior (CTB): in this paper, we introduce the new concept of *Contribution Behavior* that allows to distinguish between peers that contribute positively[4] to the system (i.e. altruistic) and the free riders (i.e. egoistic).

---

[3] This is a neutral reputation value.
[4] We do not consider uploading malicious content as a contribution. Only authentic uploads are taken into consideration.

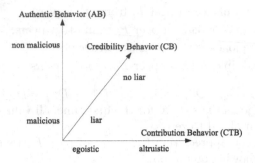

Fig. 1. Peer Behavior Dimensions

The behavior of a peer P_i is characterized by the triplet (AB_i, CB_i, CTB_i) (cf. Figure 1) which characterizes the behavior of the peer in terms of *Authentic Behavior* (sending authentic or inauthentic files), *Credibility Behavior* (lying or not in the feedback) and *Contribution Behavior* (contributing positively or not to the system). Good peers will have high values along the three defined dimensions.

We compute the *Contribution Behavior (CTB)* of a peer P_j as follows:

$$
\begin{aligned}
CTB_j &= \frac{D^+_{*,j} - D^-_{*,j}}{D^+_{j,*} + D^-_{j,*}} = \frac{D^+_{*,j} - D^-_{*,j}}{D_{j,*}} && \text{if } D_{j,*} \neq 0 \\
CTB_j &= D^+_{*,j} - D^-_{*,j} && \text{otherwise}
\end{aligned}
\tag{2}
$$

The intuition behind equation 2 is as follows. While the reputation value is based only on the uploads of a peer to reflect its authentic behavior (cf. equation 1), the contribution behavior should be based on both the uploads and the downloads of the peer.

The contribution of a peer is the ratio between what the peer has provided to the system and what it has consumed from it. The term $D^+_{*,j} - D^-_{*,j}$ means that the contribution value is sensitive to the maliciousness of the peer. This term allows to affect both free riders and malicious peers.

Ideally, a peer should be charged only for its authentic downloads since it is not responsible for the malicious content that it received from other peers. However, some malicious peers may rate all their downloads as inauthentic so that these downloads will not be counted in the contribution value. To avoid this situation, the total downloads is used for computing the contribution value. This will motivate the peers to deal only with the high reputable peers.

4   Service Differentiation

We divide service differentiation into two categories: *implicit* and *explicit*.

Implicit service differentiation, is the service differentiation that results from the normal evolution of the system. For example, when a peer has a low reputation, this peer will have a low probability of being selected for uploads, which will not allow it to increase its contribution value nor its reputation.

Explicit service differentiation, is the one that results from the explicit decision of system entities. For example, a supernode may decide to enforce service differentiation policies on the peers it manages. *Explicit* service differentiation can also be enforced at the level of the peer. For example, a peer may decide not to upload a file to a peer with a low credibility value (along the *Credibility Behavior* dimension), since the later peer may wrongfully send negative feedback and affect badly the reputation of the peer performing the upload. A peer may also decide not to upload a file to a peer with a low contribution value (along the *Contribution Behavior* dimension), since the peer requesting the upload may be a free rider.

The new concept of *Contribution Behavior* can be used to enforce service differentiation at any level (i.e. supernode or peer). To show its effectiveness, in this paper we enforce service differentiation policies at the supernode level. When a peer P_i sends a request to its supernode $Sup(i)$, this later will associate to the request a probability $prob_i$ according to the contribution level of peer P_i. This is the probability of performing the requested service by $Sup(i)$. The higher the contribution value is, the more chances the supernode will execute the requests for this peer[5]. This probability is computed as follows:

if $D_{i,*} \leq MinDownload$ $prob_i = 1$
else
    if $CBT_i \leq 0$ $prob_i = 0$
    else $prob_i = Min\{CBT_i, 1\}$

Since a new peer that joins the system will have its contribution value set to 0, we allow these new peers to download a minimum amount set to a parameter $MinDownload$. In this case, the probability used by the supernode is 1. After exceeding this minimum amount of download, the probability used by the supernode will be computed according to the contribution value of the peer. The value of $MinDownload$ should be carefully chosen not to encourage peers to change identities and benefit from free downloads. Note that in case that $CBT_i \geq 1$, $prob_i$ is set to 1. This means that the peer is contributing to the system more than what it is consuming from it.

5   Performance Evaluation

In the performance evaluation section, we will compare the following schemes:

1. The reputation management scheme with no service differentiation ($NOSD$). This is the same scheme presented in [8]. This is to show the importance of service differentiation among the peers.

---

[5] To prevent peers from repeatedly sending the same request to the supernode over and over until the request is handled, a time period can be associated with each request. This will motivate peers to contribute if they want their requests to be processed by the system.

2. The reputation management scheme with the reputation value as a guideline for service differentiation. We will call this scheme the Reputation-Based Service Differentiation ($RBSD$). Since the reputation values (i.e. AB_i) are between -1 and 1, in this scheme, the probability $prob_i$ is computed as follows: $prob_i = (1 + AB_i)/2$, where AB_i is computed as in Eq. 1.
3. The reputation management scheme with the *Contribution Behavior* as a guideline for service differentiation. We will call this scheme the Contribution-Based Service Differentiation ($CBSD$).

To assess the effectiveness of the considered schemes in identifying free riders, a high percentage of free riders is assumed. In this section, we do not consider peers that lie in their feedbacks. This issue has been addressed in [8].

5.1   Simulation Parameters

We use the following simulation parameters:

- We simulate a system with 1000 peers and 1000 files.
- File sizes are uniformly distributed between 10MB and 150MB.
- At the beginning of the simulation, each peer has at most 45 randomly chosen files and each file has at least one owner.
- As observed by [9], KaZaA files' requests do not follow the Zipf's law distribution. In our simulations, file requests follow the real life distribution observed in [9]. This means that each peer can ask for a file with a Zipf distribution over all the files that the peer does not already have. The Zipf distribution parameter is chosen close to 1
- Peers are divided into two categories: Contributors and Free riders. Free riders constitute 70% of the peers. From each category, 30% of the peers are malicious peers that send inauthentic content. Peers behavior and distribution are summarized in table 1.
- To assess the performance of the considered schemes in a highly dynamic environment, only 40% of all peers with the requested file are found in each search request. This is due to the partial search results obtained in partially decentralized P2P systems with supernodes.
- Free riders share files with a probability of 5%. In addition, 250 of the non malicious free rider peers will accept uploading the first file to get a high reputation.
- *MinDownload* is set to the average file size (i.e. 70MB).
- We simulate 90000 requests.

According to table 1, peers with indices from 1 to 700 belong to the category of free riders, peers with indices from 701 to 1000 belong to the category of contributor peers. Accordingly, peers with indices from 491 to 700 are malicious peers that provide malicious content in addition of being free riders. Peers with indices from 701 to 790 provide malicious content but still participate in uploading files to other peers. We have considered a situation where we have a high percentage of free riders as observed by [7] to show the effectiveness of our proposed scheme in identifying and isolating free riders and malicious peers.

Table 1. Peer Behavior and Distribution

Category of peers	Percentage	Probability of sending inauthentic files	
		Malicious (30%)	Non malicious (70%)
Contributors	30%	0.9	0.01
Free Riders	70%	0.9	0.01

5.2   Performance Parameters

In these simulations, we will focus on the following performance parameters:

- Percentage of successful requests: computed as the total number of requests that have been performed for the peer during the simulation over the total number of all submitted requests by this peer.
- Peer contribution level: shows the contribution behavior of each peer which is computed using equation 2.
- Peer load share: this parameter is computed as the normalized load supported by the peer. This is computed as the sum of the uploads performed by the peer over the total uploads in the system.

5.3   Simulation Results

No Service Differentiation Case:

Figure 2 depicts the peer load share in the case of the $NOSD$ scheme. The X axis represents the number of requests while the Y axis represents the peer load share. From the figure, it is clear that the reputation management scheme is able to isolate malicious peers (i.e. peer id 491 to 790), as they are not requested for uploads. It is also clear that the free riders do not contribute significantly

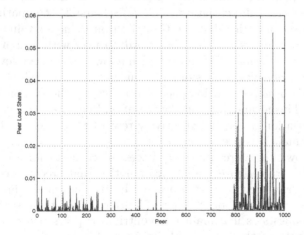

Fig. 2. Peer Load Share for $NOSD$

to the system. All the load is almost supported exclusively by non malicious contributor peers (i.e. peer id 791 to 1000).

Since there is no service differentiation, all the requests sent to the supernode will be performed regardless of the contribution of the peers. This is obviously unfair to the peers that contribute to the system.

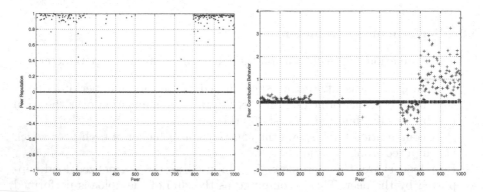

Fig. 3. (a) Peers Reputation in $RBSD$, (b) Peers Contribution Behavior in $CBSD$

Service Differentiation Case:

Figure 3.a depicts the reputation values of the peers in the case of the Reputation Based Service Differentiation ($RBSD$) scheme. It is clear that the scheme is able to identify malicious peers. However, the scheme is not able to differentiate between free riders and contributor peers. Reputation is not a good indicator of the contribution of the peer as we can see from comparing figure 2 and figure 3.a.

Figure 3.b depicts the *Contribution Behavior* value in the case of the Contribution Based Service Differentiation ($CBSD$) scheme. By comparing this figure with figure 2, we can notice that the Contribution Behavior value is a good indicator of the peer load share. In other words, a peer with a high contribution level will support more load than a peer with a low contribution level. Note that the Contribution Behavior values of malicious peers (i.e. peer id 491 to 790) are negative. This is because malicious peers are harming the system by uploading malicious files. This means that the Contribution Behavior value can be used for service differentiation which will effectively reward good peers and punish both free riders and malicious peers.

Figure 4 shows the percentage of successful requests for (a) $RBSD$ and for (b) $CBSD$. From figure 4.a, we can notice that free riders have about 50% chance to have their request processed by the supernode. Free riders with high reputation values (i.e. peer id 1 to 250) have almost the same percentage of successful requests as non malicious contributor peers. However, free riders did not contribute at the same level. In figure 4.b, free riders with IDs from 1 to 250, have a lower percentage of successful requests since they uploaded

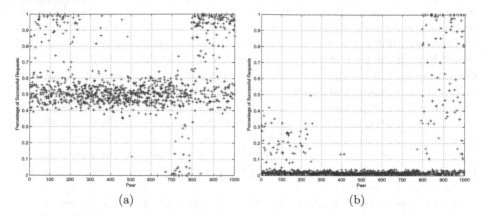

(a)   (b)

Fig. 4. Percentage of Successful Requests (a) $RBSD$, (b) $CBSD$

only few files compared to non malicious contributor peers. The later peers receive a high percentage of successful requests since they have supported almost all the load. They contributed significantly and positively to the system. The supernode processed their requests with a high probability. Some of the malicious peers uploaded more malicious content than good one, hence their percentage of successful requests is very low. This is because their contribution is negative as shown in figure 3.b.

Note that in these simulations, we assumed a static peer behavior. This means that peers do not change their behavior over time. This is to assess the capability of the proposed scheme in detecting malicious and free rider peers and preventing them from obtaining good service. In a real life system, however, peers will tend to change their behavior and we expect free rider peers with rational behavior to change from free riding to contributing to the system.

6   Related Work

The authors in [10] proposed a service differentiation protocol (SDP) for completely decentralized unstructured P2P networks. This protocol works by sending the *reputation score* of the requesting peer to other peers. These peers will map the reputation score to a Level of Service. These peers will provide service to the requesting peer according to this level. In addition of being proposed for completely decentralized P2P systems, this scheme does not take into account the maliciousness of the peers.

In [11], the authors introduce a reputation-based mechanism that assigns a better service to higher performing peers. The proposed scheme provides incentives for peers to improve their performance. The reputation is classified into two categories: provider selection and contention resolution. In provider selection, a peer among the peers offering a service is chosen to provide the service. In contention resolution, a peer among the peers requesting a service is selected by the provider peer. This scheme uses the reputation value as a guideline for service differentiation. In this paper, we have shown that this does not lead to a useful service differentiation. In addition, it proposes providing the peer requesting a file from the peers with a similar reputation value (i.e. concept of "Layered Communities"). This approach will most probably incur an important increase of malicious uploads. Indeed, if a peer receives a service from a low reputation peer, it will most probably receive bad service (e.g. malicious file) and hence does not help the peer in providing good service to others. In this paper, we propose to provide only eligible peers with the requested service. Once the request is approved, peers will receive the service from the most reputable providers. Receiving malicious content will just pollute the P2P file sharing system and waste network's resources.

In [12], the authors analyze the effectiveness of different incentives mechanisms to motivate peers to share files. The paper proposes the *reputation-based peer-approved* that uses a reputation mechanism based on rating peers according to the number of files they are advertising. Peers are allowed to download files only from peers with lower or equal rating. However, rating peers according to the number of files they are advertising is not efficient. Malicious peers can advertise a high number of malicious files. These peers will still receive good services since they will be able to upload from other peers that have a high rating value. Even non malicious peers may advertise a large number of useless files and still benefit from the system.

KaZaA, a proprietary partially-decentralized P2P system, has introduced the *participation level* for rating peers. In KaZaA, the participation level is computed as follows: (Uploads in MB/Downloads in MB)*100. Priority is given to peers with high participation level, however the exact process of how this priority is given is not known. In KaZaA, malicious peers that upload malicious content will still have a high value of participation level. As shown in [8], KaZaA is not able to detect malicious peers.

7   Conclusion

In this paper, we propose a contribution management scheme for partially decentralized peer-to-peer systems. We introduce the new concept of "*Contribution Behavior*" which is used for service differentiation rather than the use of reputation. The use of contribution behavior as the basis for service differentiation, provides the right incentives for peers to share files and contribute positively to the system. Simulation results have shown the ability of the proposed scheme to effectively identify free riders and malicious peers and prevent them from using fully the system. The use of *Contribution Behavior* for service differentiation along with the use of the *Authentic Behavior* for reputation management solve the main problems of peer-to-peer systems; free riders and malicious peers. This will provide good peers with higher satisfaction and will achieve better network resource utilization.

References

1. Aberer, K., Despotovic, Z.: Managing Trust in a Peer-2-Peer Information System. In: The 9th International Conference on Information and Knowledge Management, Atlanta, USA (2001) 310–317
2. Cornelli, F., Damiani, E., di Vimercati, S.D.C., Paraboschi, S., Samarati, P.: Choosing Reputable Servents in a P2P Network. In: The 11th International World Wide Web Conference, Honolulu, USA (2002) 376–386
3. Kamvar, S.D., Schlosser, M.T., Garcia-Molina, H.: The EigenTrust Algorithm for Reputation Management in P2P Networks. In: The 12th International World Wide Web Conference, Budapest, Hungary (2003) 640–651
4. Gupta, M., Judge, P., Ammar, M.: A Reputation System for Peer-to-Peer Networks. In: ACM 13th International Workshop on Network and Operating Systems Support for Digital Audio and Video, Monterey, USA (2003) 144–152
5. Mekouar, L., Iraqi, Y., Boutaba, R.: Peer-to-peer most wanted: Malicious peers. to appear in the Computer Networks Journal (2005)
6. Axelrod, R. In: The Evolution of Cooperation. Basic Books, New York (1984)
7. Adar, E., Huberman, B.A.: Free Riding on Gnutella. Technical report, HP (2000) http://www.hpl.hp.com/research/idl/papers/gnutella/.
8. Mekouar, L., Iraqi, Y., Boutaba, R.: Detecting Malicious Peers in A Reputation-Based Peer-to-Peer System. In: The IEEE Consumer Communications and Networking Conference (CCNC), Las Vegas, USA (2005)
9. Gummadi, K., Dunn, R.J., Saroiu, S., Gribble, S.D., Levy, H.M., Zahorjan, J.: Measurement, Modeling, and analysis of a Peer-to-Peer File Sharing Workload. In: The 19th ACM Symposium on Operating Systems Principles, New York, USA (2003) 314–329
10. Gupta, M., Ammar, M.: Service Differentiation in Peer-to-Peer Networks Utilizing Reputations. In: ACM Fifth International Workshop on Networked Group Communications, Munich, Germany (2003)
11. Papaioannou, T.G., Stamoulis, G.D.: Effective use of reputation in peer-to-peer environments. In: Proceedings of IEEE/ACM CCGrid: International Symposium on Cluster Computing and the Grid. (2004)
12. Ranganathan, K., Ripeanu, M., Sarin, A., Foster, I.: Incentive mechanisms for large collaborative resource sharing. In: Proceedings of IEEE/ACM CCGrid: International Symposium on Cluster Computing and the Grid. (2004)

Highly Available DHTs: Keeping Data Consistency After Updates[*]

Predrag Knežević[1], Andreas Wombacher[2], and Thomas Risse[1]

[1] Fraunhofer IPSI
Integrated Publication and Information Systems Institute
Dolivostrasse 15, 64293 Darmstadt, Germany
{knezevic, risse}@ipsi.fraunhofer.de
[2] University of Twente
Department of Computer Science
Enschede, The Netherlands
a.wombacher@cs.utwente.nl

Abstract. The research in the paper is motivated by building a decentralized/P2P XML storage on top of a DHT (Distributed Hash Table). The storage must provide high data availability and support updates. High data availability in a DHT can be guaranteed by data replication. However, DHTs can not provide a centralized coordination guaranteeing data consistency upon updates. In particular, replicas may have different values due to concurrent updates or partitioning of the P2P network. An approach based on versioning of replica values is presented proposing a decentralized concurrency control system, where probabilistic guarantees can be provided for retrieving a correct replica value. This paper presents the protocol as well as a statistical analysis of the lower bound of the probabilistic guarantees.

Keywords: Peer-to-Peer Computing, Decentralized Data Management, DHT.

1 Introduction

The research presented in this paper is motivated by the BRICKS[1] project, which aims to design, develop and maintain a user and service-oriented space of digital libraries that share knowledge and resources in the Cultural Heritage domain. The project defines a decentralized, service-oriented infrastructure that uses the Internet as a backbone and fulfills the requirements of expandability, scalability and interoperability. At the same time, the membership in the BRICKS community is very flexible; parties can join or leave the system at any time.

BRICKS community needs to have service descriptions, administrative information about collections, ontologies and some annotations globally available all

---

[*] This work is partly funded by the European Commission under BRICKS (IST 507457).

[1] BRICKS - Building Resources for Integrated Cultural Knowledge Services, http://www.brickscommunity.org

Z. Despotovic, S. Joseph, and C. Sartori (Eds.): AP2PC 2005, LNAI 4118, pp. 70–80, 2006.
© Springer-Verlag Berlin Heidelberg 2006

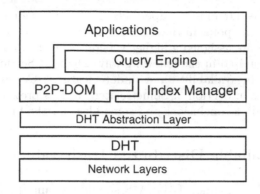

Fig. 1. Decentralized XML Storage Architecture

the time [1]. An important aspect is that data are changeable during the runtime, i.e. updates must be allowed. Therefore, the data management is based on our recently proposed decentralized XML data store [2]. The store is based on top of a DHT (Distributed Hash Table) overlay, i.e. large XML documents are split into sets of XML nodes stored then as DHT values. DHTs are low-level structured P2P systems that provide a consistent way of routing information to the final destination, can handle the changes in topologies and have an API similar to the hash table data structure.

Figure 1 presents the proposed system architecture. All layers exist on every peer in the system. The datastore is accessed through the P2P-DOM component or by using the query engine (e.g. XPath or XQuery). The query engine could be supported by an optional index manager that would maintain indices. The P2P-DOM exports a large portion of the DOM [3] interface to the upper layers, and maintains parts of a XML tree in a DHT. More details about the storage and selected research issues can be found in [2].

Unfortunately, a DHT layer does not guarantee the availability of data it manages. Whenever a peer goes offline, locally stored (**key, value**) pairs become inaccessible. The research done in [4] proposed a wrapper around the DHT that is able to self-manage data availability by using replication within the requested probabilistic guarantees.

The research presented here investigates in detail data consistency, i.e. ensuring it after an update is preformed. When a peer is offline, locally stored replicas are inaccessible. Therefore, an update might not address all replicas, leaving some of them unmodified. Further, uncoordinated concurrent updates of an object result in unpredictable values of object replicas. As a consequence, different object replicas may have different values. Thus, the main issues are how to:

- Ensure that the correct value is read
- Synchronize offline replicas after going online again
- Handle concurrent updates on the same data

The approach presented in the paper gives probabilistic guarantees on accessing correct data at any point in time. Also, replicas are updated in a predefined sequence, and they are assigned a higher version number.

The paper is organized in the following way. The next Section introduces the DHT with high data availability and update features. Consistency issues are analyzed afterwards in Section 3. Some related work is presented in Section 4. Finally, Section 5 gives conclusions and some ideas for the future work.

2   Highly Available Distributed Hash Table

As suggested in [5], a common DHT API should contain at least the following methods: **route(Key, Message)** (deterministic routing of a message according to the given key to the final destination), **store(Key, Value)** (store a value with the given key in DHT), and **lookup(Key)** (returns the value associated with the key).

Every peer is responsible for a portion of the key space, so whenever a peer issues a **store** or **lookup** request, it will end up on the peer responsible for that key. When the system topology is changed, i.e. peers go offline, some peers will be now responsible for the key space that has belonged to the offline peers. Also, peers joining the system will take responsibility for a part of the key space that has been under control of other peers until that moment. All **(key, value)** pairs stored on an offline peer are not available until the peer comes back again.

Every value and its replicas are associated with a key that is used for **store** and **lookup** operation. The first replica key is generated using a random number generator. All other replica keys are correlated with the first one, i.e. they are derived from it by using the following rule:

$$replicaKey(i) = \begin{cases} c & : \quad i = 1 \\ hash(replicaKey(1) + i) & : \quad i \geq 2 \end{cases} \quad (1)$$

where c is a random byte array, $hash$ is a hash function with a low collision probability. $replicaKey$ and i are observed as byte arrays, and $+$ is an array concatenation function. Thus, the key of the original is determiend to be a random value c, while the key of the ith replica is calculated by combining the randoam value c with the order number of the replica i and using the resulting value as a basis for a hash function delivering the key. The above rule enables uniqueness of all replica keys in system, and since distance between keys is high, it increases a probability that keys are placed on different peers in system. At the same time by knowing the first replica key, all other replica keys can be generated with no communication costs.

2.1   Operations

In order to add data availability feature to the existing DHT, every stored value must be replicated R number of times. Every peer calculates it from measured average peer online probability and the requested data availability. During joining phase, a peer can get an initial value for R from other peers in the system, or it can assume some default one.

High data availability in a DHT is achieved by self-adaptive replication protocol, i.e. missing replicas of locally stored values are recreated within refreshment rounds. The approach is proactive; a peer wants to secure that values from its storage which will be available even if the peer goes offline at any point in time. Remembering the key generation schema in Formula 1, recreation of replicas would require access to the first replica key. Therefore, it must be attached to the stored value.

Another important aspect of the protocol are updates. As it has already been mentioned, ensuring consistency is the main issue. Basically, there are two possible groups of approaches [6]:

- **Pessimistic**
  Pessimistic approaches are based on locking and a centralized lock management. When a peer in decentralized/P2P environment goes offline, it and its data are not reachable. In addition, this may cause network partition, thus not even all online peers are reachable. All this unreachable peers cannot receive a lock, thus the locking-based approach is not applicable.
  Quorum-based replica protocols require presence of quorums both for a read or write operation. In environments with low online probability, such quorums are hard to get and this makes the quorum-based protocols not a very good candidate [7].
- **Optimistic**
  In an optimistic approach, objects are not locked, but when a conflict occurs, the system tries to resolve it, or they are resolved manually. Optimistic approaches are simpler to implement and they are good if the probability for updating the same object with different values at the same time is low.

In order to determine the latest value version, we need to track it. To summarize, a DHT value will be wrapped in an instance of the following class:

```
class Entry {
  Key first;
  long version;
  Object value;
}
```

Since the wrapper around DHT implements common DHT API introduced in Section 2, **store** and **lookup** operations must be re-implemented. Further, the mechanism for self-managing, i.e. refreshment rounds and rejoins of peers are introduced.

lookup(Key) When a peer wants to get a value, it is not sufficient to return any available replica. Instead of that, we must return the replica with the highest version number to ensure that the peer gets the most up-to-date available version. However, if two or more replicas with the same version (e.g. as a result of network partitioning, but with different values are found), it is a conflict that could be resolved by applying heuristics, data semantics, or has to be resolved manually. Currently, we do not assume any heuristics, i.e. a failure is returned, which has to be compensated by the requester.

It is important to notice that during a **lookup** operation, all online replicas must be checked in order to find the latest available. Doing this by broadcasting the request would be fully inefficient: the whole network would be flooded. Using DHT overlay makes communication more efficient: the request is routed only to peers that could potentially have a replica. Although, obviously the required communication for deriving the value is higher then in DHTs without high data availability.

store(Key, Value) When a value is created, it is wrapped in R instances of `Entry` class, appropriate keys are generated and the version number is assigned to 1. With every update, the version number is incremented by 1. During an update, replicas are modified in sequence, i.e. first the 1st replica, then 2nd replica until R^{th} replica. If the update of any replica fails, the update stops and the rest of the replicas are not touched. The update fails if a peer that receives the update request already has a replica with a higher version or the same version containing different value. The proposed write operation ensures that in case of concurrent updates only one peer completes the operation. The rest of them must compensate the request.

In order to know what should be the next version number, the replication layer must keep a log of (key, version) pairs of successful lookups. The log size and its organization are part of our future work.

During a **refreshment round**, a peer iterates over locally stored data, checks for missing replicas and recreates them. Every peer proceeds independently, there are no global synchronization points in time. Another important aspect of refreshment is that peers get more recent data versions from other peers and if there are no topology changes, the system will eventually stabilize. Also, at the beginning of a refreshment round, a peer can measure the average online probability of replicas, and compute the average data availability. If the obtained value is above a specified threshold, refreshment rounds can be made longer, so bandwidth utilization is saved, and/or number of replicas can decrease saving storage space. If the data availability is below the threshold, a peer should recreate replicas often, and/or create more replicas, trying to catch up requested data availability.

Measuring the average replica online probability could be done by checking all replicas in the system. Unfortunately, this is not feasible, because we simply do not know how many replicas are out there. Even if we knew that, measuring would be very inefficient and unscalable. Therefore, we use the confidence interval theory [8] to find out what is the minimal number of replicas that has to be checked, so the computed average replica online probability is accurate with some degree of confidence. For example, to achieve an accuracy with an error of 15% in a community of 1000 peers, we have to check only 12 randomly chosen replicas. It can also be shown that in large communities the approach is scalable.

In practice, a peer selects on random basis a few locally stored replicas, generates needed number of replica keys, checks if they are available, and computes the average replica online availability.

When a peer **rejoins** the community, it does not change its ID, so the peer will be now responsible for a part of the key space that intersects with the previously managed. Therefore, the peer keeps previously stored data, but no explicit data synchronization with other peers is required. Upcoming requests are answered using the latest locally available versions. With a new refreshment round or update, old replicas will be eventually overwritten. Replicas, whose keys are not anymore in the part of key space managed at the rejoined peer, can be removed or sent to peers that should manage them.

3 Data Consistency

The **store** operation from the previous section has been defined so that it is able to update data, even if not all replicas are online. Namely, a **store** will update all online replicas and recreate a higher version of replicas that are at that moment offline. From then, some replicas will be represented in the system with multiple versions, some of them will be online, some of them offline; some replicas will be up-to-date (i.e. correct), some odd (incorrect). This Section analyzes the probability that the correct data are found with every **lookup** operation.

Obviously, a correct data version will be read by a peer only if at least one correct replica is available. In order to compute the probability of this case, we need to model the life cycle of a replica, after it is initially created: the replica can be online or offline, and correct (up-to-date) or wrong (containing an older version). Therefore, during its life cycle, the replica can be in the following states: online and correct, online and wrong, offline and correct, and offline and wrong.

3.1 Settings

Before doing the analysis, we define the environment in which the proposed update protocol will be analyzed:

- Peers are independent
- Measured peer average online probability is p
- Because of the DHT properties, at any point in time, every object can have at most R accessible replicas.
- Success of an update is represented by a random variable U, i.e. successful update ($U = 1$) and unsuccessful update ($U = 0$). An unsuccessful update could change some replicas, but not all of them. At least one replica is correct.
- Reading of a correct object version is represented by a random variable C, i.e. correct read ($C = 1$) and incorrect read ($C = 0$)
- Random variable S represents the replica state, i.e. online-correct ($S = S1$), offline-correct ($S = S2$), online-wrong ($S = S3$), and offline-wrong ($S = S4$). Therefore, $p = P(S = S1) + P(S = S3)$.

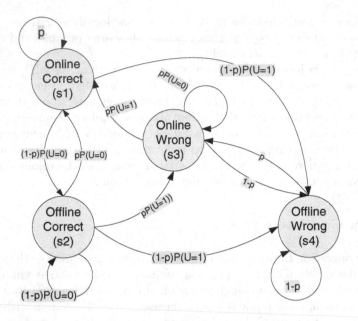

Fig. 2. The life cycle of replica after creation

- No partitions are assumed
- There is no need for recovery, i.e. going offline does not destroy locally stored data

The correct object version is going to be read, if at least one correct replica is online. In other words, it is the counter probability that none of online-correct replicas ($P(S = S1)$) is available. Therefore, the probability of reading the correct object ($P(C = 1)$) can be expressed as

$$P(C = 1) \geq 1 - (1 - P(S = S1))^R \qquad (2)$$

After an update R replicas are online, but there might be some other offline replicas in the system. Therefore, Formula 2 is the lower-bound of the correct read probability.

3.2 Life Cycle of Replica

In order to describe the life cycle of a single replica we define a discrete-time Markov chain, represented by the state diagram on Figure 2. Transition probabilities are displayed next to each arc.

An online-correct replica stays in this state as long as it is online. Also, a replica can come to this state, if it has been offline-correct and comes online again while no update has happened in the meantime. An online-wrong replica becomes correct after a successful update is performed.

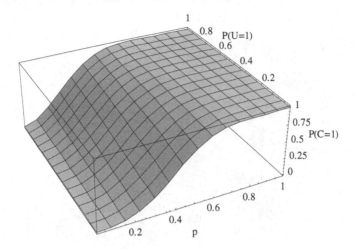

Fig. 3. The probability that correct value is read after update

A replica stays offline-correct if there are no successful updates. If they are successful, the replica is not up-to-date anymore and the state is changed to offline-wrong. Also, a replica comes into offline-correct state if it has been online-correct before and no updates happen when it goes offline.

A replica remains in offline-wrong state until it goes online. Then, when it is back online again, it goes to online-wrong state.

The probability of every described state ($P(S = S1, S2, S3, S4)$) can be calculated by applying long-run analysis of discrete-time Markov chains (i.e. equilibrium analysis) [9]. To compute the probability of correct read $P(C = 1)$, we need to determine the probability for being in state S1 ($P(S = S1)$, see Formula 2). Figure 3 shows the probability for reading an up-to-date object for number of replicas $R = 10$. This number has been taken from a previous analysis of the replication protocol [4], where it has been shown that it guarantees an average object availability $a \geq 99,9\%$, if peer online probability p is higher than 50%. It can be seen that the lower bound of the correct reading probability depends only weakly on the successful update probability $P(U = 1)$, because with or without successful update, the system will contain at least one correct replica (but maybe offline). For example, for a peer online probability of 50%, the correct reading probability with 100% successful updates ($P(U = 1) = 1$) is only 25% higher compared with a system with a probability of zero for successful updates ($P(U = 1) = 0$).

Figure 4 shows how the read probability changes with the increase of the number of replicas ($P(U = 1) = 0.9$). It can be seen that when the number of replicas is greater than 30 ($R \geq 30$), good reading probability ($P(C = 1) \geq 0.9$) can be achieved, even for low-online probabilities of peers ($p \geq 0.28$).

Allowing updates has introduced a possibility that in the system exist many different versions of the same object. As a consequence, our correct reading probability ($P(C = 1)$) is equal to data availability a. In the rest of the cases

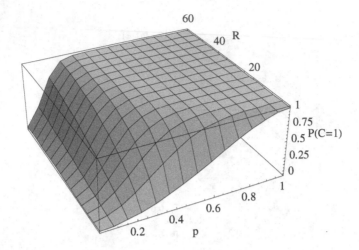

Fig. 4. The probability that correct value is read after update in function of the number of replicas

$(1 - P(C = 1))$, some replicas could be available, but with outdated values. Thus, applications built on top should handle scenarios when returned data are obsolete. However, incorrect replicas will not stay in the system forever; with every new update, or during refreshment round, they will be eventually overwritten with the correct version.

The presented analysis has shown how data availability depends on the given system parameters, i.e. the number of replicas R and the probability that an update was successful $P(U = 1)$. Future research will investigate how $P(U = 1)$ behaves in different application scenarios, and how it depends on the system parameters as well.

4   Related Work

Updates in replicated distributed databases are a widely researched field. As it has already mentioned in Section 2, both optimistic and pessimistic approaches for resolving updates exist [6]. However, they all assume high peer online probability and global system view, e.g. [10] proposes hierarchy-less data distribution, but the approach requires high peer online probability. Our approach is fully decentralized and works under any peer online probability.

The popular P2P filesharing systems (e.g. KaZaA, Gnutella, eDonkey) [11] do not consider updates at all. If a file update occurs, it is not propagated to other replicas. There is no way that a peer that wants to get a file can conclude what is the freshest version.

Oceanstore [12] supports updates and does versioning of objects. An update request is sent first to the object's inner ring (primary replicas), which performs a

Byzantine agreement protocol to achieve fault-tolerance and consistency. When the inner ring commits the update, it multicasts the result of the update down to the dissemination tree. To our knowledge, analysis of consistency guarantees has not been published so far. Also, the inner ring consists of super peers that are highly available.

The paper [13] addresses updates in P2P system, but the aim of the research is to reduce communication costs, data consistency has not been addressed.

Ivy [14] is a peer-to-peer file system that enables writes by maintaining log of changes at every peer with write access. Reading up-to-date file version requires consulting all longs, and that is not very efficient. Additional tool has been provided that can be run manually in order to resolve conflict that could occur during concurrent updates. Our approach does not need to contact all peers in order to find the freshest replica version.

TotalRecall [15] has a peer-to-peer storage system with update support. Files are immutable, so every new version is stored separately in the system, and some garbage collection is needed for removing old version. The system distinguishes master and slave replica copies, and therefore an update is first performed on a master responsible for an object. Then, the master updates all other slaves. If some slaves are offline, new slave peers will be selected and the update will be repeated. Our approach is simpler, we do not distinguish master and slaves, so there is no need to elect new master when the old one goes offline. Even during an update, peers could go offline, and if there is no conflict, the update is successful.

Om [16] is a peer-to-peer file system that achieves data high availability through online automatic regeneration while still preserving consistency guarantees. File access is done by using read-one/write-all quorum, i.e. implicitly high peer online probability is assumed. All writes are first performed at primary replicas that update later secondary replicas.

5   Conclusion and Future Work

The work presented in the paper is adding high data availability feature to any DHT overlay network under consideration of data consistency issues. In particular, versioning and replication of data stored in a DHT are introduced and a preliminary analysis has derived lower-boundaries for the probabilistic data availability guarantees providing consistency in the system. A good probability can be achieved even with moderate costs, i.e. number of replicas ($R = 10$), and with moderate peer online probability ($p > 0.5$), whereas more replicas are needed for systems where peer online probability is low.

The future work will investigate in more details some of the parameter introduced in the model (e.g. update successfulness); their dependency on application patterns and other system parameters. Also, the approach will be investigated in situations when network partitions are allowed. Finally, the approach will be implemented and tested in practice.

References

1. Risse, T., Knežević, P.: A self-organizing data store for large scale distributed infrastructures. In: International Workshop on Self-Managing Database Systems(SMDB). (2005)
2. Knežević, P.: Towards a reliable peer-to-peer xml database. In Lindner, W., Perego, A., eds.: Proceedings ICDE/EDBT Joint PhD Workshop 2004, P.O. Box 1527, 71110 Heraklion, Crete, Greece, Crete University Press (2004) 41–50
3. W3C: Document Object Model. (2002) http://www.w3.org/DOM/.
4. Knežević, P., Wombacher, A., Risse, T., Fankhauser, P.: Enabling high data availability in a dht. In: Grid and Peer-to-Peer Computing Impacts on Large Scale Heterogeneous Distributed Database Systems (GLOBE'05) (submitted). (2005)
5. Dabek, F., Zhao, B., Druschel, P., Stoica, I.: Towards a common api for structured peer-to-peer overlays. In: 2nd International Workshop on Peer-to-Peer Systems. (2003)
6. Özsu, M.T., Valduriez, P.: Principles of Distributed Database Systems. Prentice Hall (1999)
7. Jiménez-Peris, R., Patiño-Marténez, M., Alonso, G., Kemme, B.: Are quorums an alternative for data replication? ACM Trans. Database Syst. **28** (2003) 257–294
8. Berry, D.A., Lindgren, B.W.: Statistics: Theory and Methods. Duxbury Press (1995)
9. Tijms, H.C.: Stochastic Models: An Algorithmic Approach. John Wiley (1994)
10. Kemme, B., Alonso, G.: Don't be lazy, be consistent: Postgres-r, a new way to implement database replication. In: The VLDB Journal. (2000) 134–143
11. Milojičić, D., Kalogeraki, V., Lukose, R., Nagaraja, K., Pruyne, J., Richard, B., Rollins, S., Xu, Z.: Peer-to-peer computing. Technical report, HP (2002) http://www.hpl.hp.com/techreports/2002/HPL-2002-57.pdf.
12. Rhea, S., Wells, C., Eaton, P., Geels, D., Zhao, B., Weatherspoon, H., Kubiatowicz, J.: Maintenance-free global data storage. IEEE Internet Computing **5** (2001) 40–49
13. Datta, A., Hauswirth, M., Aberer, K.: Updates in highly unreliable, replicated peer-to-peer systems. In: Proceedings of the 23rd International Conference on Distributed Computing Systems, IEEE Computer Society (2003) 76
14. Muthitacharoen, A., Morris, R., Gil, T., Chen, B.: Ivy: A read/write peer-to-peer file system. In: Proceedings of the 5th USENIX Symposium on Operating Systems Design and Implementation (OSDI '02), Boston, Massachusetts (2002)
15. Bhagwan, R., Tati, K., Cheng, Y.C., Savage, S., Voelker, G.M.: Total recall: System support for automated availability management. In: First ACM/Usenix Symposium on Networked Systems Design and Implementation. (2004) 337–350
16. Yu, H., Vahdat, A.: Consistent and automatic replica regeneration. ACM Transactions on Storage **1** (2005) 3–37

Caching Indices for Efficient Lookup in Structured Overlay Networks

Vasilios Darlagiannis[1], Nicolas Liebau[1], Oliver Heckmann[1],
Andreas Mauthe[2], and Ralf Steinmetz[1]

[1] Multimedia Communications Lab (KOM), Technische Universität Darmstadt,
Merckstr. 25, 64293 Darmstadt, Germany
{bdarla, liebau, heckmann, steinmetz}@kom.tu-darmstadt.de
[2] Lancaster University, Computing Department, Lancaster, LA1 4YR, UK
andreas@comp.lancs.ac.uk

Abstract. Structured overlay networks for Peer-to-Peer systems (e.g.
based on Distributed Hash Tables) use proactive mechanisms to provide
efficient indexing functionality for advertised resources. The majority of
their occurrences in proposed systems (e.g. Chord, Pastry) provide upper
bounds (logarithmic complexity with respect to the size of the graph representing the network) on the communication cost in worst case scenarios
and their performance is superior compared to unstructured alternatives.
However, in particular (empirically observed) scenarios where the popularity of the advertised resources follows a distribution considerably
different from the uniform distribution, structured P2P networks may
perform inferiorly compared to well designed unstructured P2P networks
that exploit effectively the resource popularity distribution. In order to
address this issue, a very simple caching mechanism is suggested in this
paper that preserves the theoretical superiority of structured overlay networks regardless of the popularity of the advertised resources. Moreover,
the churn effect observed in Peer-to-Peer systems is considered. The proposed mechanism is evaluated using simulation experiments.

1 Introduction

Structured overlay networks for Peer-to-Peer (P2P) systems, e.g. Chord [27],
Pastry [24], Tapestry [29] and Omicron [7], use proactive mechanisms to provide
efficient indexing functionality for advertised resources. The majority of their
implementations provide theoretical upper bounds on the communication cost
in worst case scenarios, assuming that the maintenance of the topology heals the
divergence (caused by the dynamic participation of the peers) from the "ideal"
network structure. Modeling the topology of a P2P network with a graph, the
maximum distance between any two nodes is equal to the *diameter* of the graph.
In graphs representing networks such as Chord (each node maintains $O(log(N))$
neighbors, where N is the number of nodes), the diameter of the network is
$D_{CH} = O(log(N))$. The number of nodes may be equal to the population of
the peers, e.g. in the case of Pastry or Chord or equal to the number of the

Z. Despotovic, S. Joseph, and C. Sartori (Eds.): AP2PC 2005, LNAI 4118, pp. 81–93, 2006.
© Springer-Verlag Berlin Heidelberg 2006

constructed clusters of peers, e.g. in the case of the two-tier architecture of Omicron ($D_O = O(log(N/l))$, where l is the average population of each cluster). However, a more useful metric to evaluate the communication cost for routing messages in structured overlay networks is the *average inter-peer distance*. The average cost for graphs such as the one representing Chord is $\mu_{D_{CH}} = D_{CH}/2$ [27]. On the other hand, the average inter-peer distance for networks such as Omicron based on de Bruijn graphs [8] is $\mu_{D_O} \simeq D_O - (k-1)^{-1}$, where k is the degree of the nodes [13]. However, since the graph nodes in Omicron represent clusters of peers, the actual average inter-peer distance is smaller than the average inter-peer distance in Chord.

Structured overlay networks have been designed mainly to overcome the intrinsic scalability issue of *flat* and *unstructured* networks, such as Gnutella v0.4 [20]. However, for several reasons, structured overlay networks have not been utilized in widely-deployed P2P systems (with the exception of the Kademlia network [18]). Instead, system designers opt for *hierarchical* or *hybrid* approaches where a subset of peers (usually termed as *super-peers*, or *ultra-peers*) is responsible for indexing and finding the advertised resources. Moreover, a number of mechanisms have been suggested to improve the performance of unstructured networks, e.g. expanding rings or multiple random walks [16]. The success of these mechanisms is based on the assumption of uneven popularity of the available resources. In fact, this assumption is validated by a number of empirical observations of file sharing systems (cf. [26], [9] and [4]) where the popularity of the resources is reported. While there is a disagreement on the exact distribution that describes the popularity of the resources (Zipf, lognormal, etc.), it can be safely concluded that it is not uniform.

Therefore, an interesting debate has arisen lately on whether structured overlay networks can perform efficiently if non-uniform popularity of resources is observed [15]. Apparently, structured networks perform equally well in any lookup request, thus, providing upper bounds, though not exploiting effectively the query frequency. Some hybrid approaches have been suggested to address this issue, such as hybrid PIER [14] or OceanStore [22]. Though, in these hybrid approaches the formation of two separate overlay networks is suggested, a structured one and an unstructured one to deal with unpopular and popular queries, respectively. The shortcomings and weaknesses of these solutions are mainly (i) the increased complexity, (ii) the additional maintenance cost that is out-of-band, (iii) the lack of adaptability to both uniform and non-uniform distributions and (iv) the increased delay when the initial overlay network selection for searching the resource fails and the fall-back alternative must be followed.

The aforementioned concerns are taken into account in the solution investigated in this paper. A simple though efficient mechanism is suggested that capitalizes on the adequateness of caching resources following non-uniform distributions and the higher interest of the P2P users to a relatively small subset of the available resources. It extends the capabilities of structured overlay networks without any additional maintenance effort and very low additional routing cost compared to the original algorithms of structured networks in worst case scenarios where the cache is not properly updated. No extension of their signalling protocols is required, thus, avoiding increasing further the complexity of their operation[1]. Merely, we invest on existing information collected through the normal network operation to improve the routing performance. The observed churn rate of the P2P networks, which is the most critical factor (together with the popularity distribution) is considered in our simulation experiments. While caching methods have been proposed for unstructured or hybrid overlay networks (cf. [17], [12]), they lack investigation on the structured counterparts. Moreover, several caching mechanisms have been extensively used for increasing the performance of Web technologies [1].

The rest of the paper is organized as follows. In Section 2 the proposed mechanism and its advantages, together with the related algorithms are presented. Afterwards, the simulation experiments are described in Section 3, followed by the related work in Section 4. The paper is concluded in Section 5.

2   Index Caching Mechanism

2.1   Basics

In the common design approaches of structured overlay networks, e.g. based on Distributed Hash Tables (DHTs) [2], queries are forwarded via intermediate peers towards the destination peer that is responsible for the part of the DHT which includes the globally unique identifier (GUID) characterizing the query. It is only the destination peer(s) that has the required information to reply to the query. Such design is suitable for evenly popular items since there is non-ambiguous mapping of the resources to the system and the workload is evenly distributed. Thus, in such designs it is necessary to follow the whole path before it is possible to match the query.

The common core functionality provided by the majority of structured overlay networks could be described by the following basic operations:

1. The *Routing* operation that requires the construction of a routing table for selecting the most "promising" neighbor to forward the queries.
2. The *Indexing* operation that constructs and updates the necessary distributed data structures for replying to queries.
3. The *Maintenance* operation that maintains the ideal network topology so that the theoretical upper bounds for the communication cost in worst case scenarios can be met.

Chord, Pastry and Tapestry are examples of structured networks that offer the aforementioned functionality. However, Omicron [7] suggests an additional function, that of *caching* to offer more efficient services, though it is proposed as an optional functionality for systems dealing with non-uniformly popular resources. The exploitation of the adequate design of the caching mechanism for structured P2P networks is the focus of this paper.

---

[1] Usually structured networks have more complex operation than their unstructured counterparts.

2.2   Mechanism Design

The rationale behind the caching mechanism is described as follows. Since peers participate both in generating queries and routing them towards the destination, it may be advantageous to reuse the information gained from the replies they received from locally generated queries. Thus, peers may provide directly the position of the requested resource instead of forwarding the query until it reaches the final DHT destination. Moreover, if peers monitor the popularity of forwarded requests, they could additionally consider caching the most popular of them provided that they hold the necessary indexing information. A simple mechanism to develop such indexing knowledge is to modify the semantics of the routing procedure. For popular requests, intermediate peers may consider storing locally the incoming queries and generate identical ones (though originated at the intermediate peer) and forward them instead of the original queries. The received replies can be used both to reply the stored pending queries and to populate the local cache with useful and popular information. However, the gathered information may be used for a maximum amount of time t_{Th} that depends on the peer uptime distribution [5]. In fact, t_{Th} defines the maximum time a cache entry can be used, thereby, providing a simple mechanism deal with the high churn rate. Expired entries are removed from the cache after the t_{Th} time.

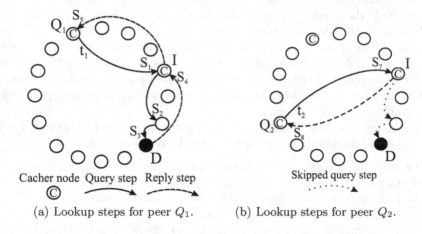

(a) Lookup steps for peer Q_1.   (b) Lookup steps for peer Q_2.

Fig. 1. Lookup operation using cache indices

The proposed scheme is illustrated in Figure 1 using a Chord-like structured network. There, at time t_1 peer Q_1 queries for a resource indexed at peer D (Figure 1(a)). Assume that peer I considers that the specific query is popular. Then, instead of forwarding the query, peer I generates an identical query that eventually arrives at peer D. Peer D replies to peer I, which both updates the local cache and provides the reply to peer Q_1. Apparently, peer Q_1 may also update its local cache if it considers the query popular. Afterwards, assume that at time t_2, with $t_1 < t_2 < t_1 + t_{Th}$ (where t_{Th} is the threshold time indicating that the cache content is valid with high probability), peer Q_2 queries for the same item and peer I is in the path towards peer D. In that case peer I provides the cached information to peer Q_2 immediately skipping the rest of the lookup steps towards D (Figure 1(b)). Furthermore, peer Q_2 may update its local cache if it considers the query popular. However, in the latter case it is important to consider the "aging" of the information as it is not directly provided by peer "D", but from a cached index. Peer Q_2 has to set the lifetime of the entry in the cache to $T'_{Th} = T_{Th} - (t_2 - t_1)$.

Two important factors drive the design mechanisms of caching. First, the scalability of the solution can be only provided if the size of the information that is additionally requested by each peer is *constant*. However, this constraint is not necessarily a practical limitation since this mechanism is designed to operate in systems where a small portion of the resources is frequently requested. Thus, each peer can locally decide which resources are popular by simply using a counter and the elapsed time since the first accounted appearance to estimate the rate of querying them and maintain the c most popular resources.

The second critical factor that has to be considered is the high churn rate of the peers. Nonetheless, conditional reliability mechanisms [5] may reduce the side-effects. Naturally, popular resources are being held by several peers. Assuming that the responsible DHT nodes can provide back either the complete set of these peers or an adequate subset of them, the intermediate peers have sufficient information for locating a reliable peer that is still alive.

Key	Expiration	Frequency	Window reset	Indices	Pending queries	Marked
...	...	...	...	...	...	...

$\left.\vphantom{\begin{array}{c}a\\b\\c\end{array}}\right\}c$

Fig. 2. Abstract description of the cache structure

The proposed cache structure is illustrated in Figure 2. Each row contains information for a single advertised resource. The first field includes the *key* of the resource. The second field contains the *Expiration* timer set to the maximum lifetime of the cache entry. As it has already been mentioned, to set the value of the expiration time the "age" of the index has to be considered. This mechanism assumes that also the indexing mechanism uses an expiration timer to remove old advertisements[2]. The third field is the *Frequency* field, which is a local counter that indicates how many times a query for that item has arrived on the particular intermediate peer. The value of the counter is reset periodically and the *Window reset* field stores that time. The fifth field includes the list of collected *Indices* about peers that posses the requested resources and may be directly contacted.

---

[2] JXTA [28] is an example of a widely acceptable system that utilizes expiration timers to remove old advertisements. The owners of the advertisements are responsible to re-advertised their services and resources.

The subsequent field contains the list of the *Pending queries* for this resource. Finally, the *Marked* field indicates that the cache replacement algorithm has selected this entry to be removed from the cache. However, the list of pending queries for this resource is not empty and the deletion of the selected entry has to be delayed until the reply will be received and the pending queries replied.

Further, an additional characteristic that may be successfully exploited to increase the efficiency of the structured networks is the fact that peers are also owners of resources. In cases where the requested resource is being hold locally on the intermediate peer it can be safely provided to the requestor. It may be additionally argued that instead of developing the index caching mechanism, intermediate peers can provide the requested resources themselves. Nevertheless, this possibility is application depended and many factors (e.g. copyrights, technical limitations, system design) have to be considered. Moreover, if further constraints apply (e.g. find a resource or service provider in the closest vicinity to the requestor) this solution may not provide optimal performance.

2.3 Algorithms

Several cache replacement policies have been developed to fit to the requirements of different problems (cf. least frequently used (LFU) [23], least recently used (LRU) and LRU-K [19]). In fact, the replacement policy adopted for the indices cache on each peer is a variation of the LFU algorithm, which is further enhanced with timeouts on the maximum lifetime of each entry. The latter improvement is mandatory for capturing the dynamics of P2P overlay networks. The pseudo-code of the LFU variation is provided in Algorithm 2.1. If there is an entry with 0 popularity and no pending queries, then this entry is removed. Otherwise, the least popular entry is returned[3].

Algorithm 2.1: LFU_REPLACEMENT($cache, pendingQueries$)

$found = cache.get(1)$
for $i \leftarrow 2$ **to** $cache.size()$
do $\Big\{$ $queryList = pendingQueries.remove(i)$
    if $(cache.get(i).popularity == 0$ **and** $queryList.isEmpty())$
        then $\Big\{$ $cache.remove(i)$
                return $(null)$
    else if $(found.popularity > cache.get(i).popularity$ **and**
        $($ **not** $cache.get(i).isMarked()))$
        then $\{found = cache.get(i)$
return $(found)$

The pseudo-code for filling a cache entry with information obtained from a reply is listed in Algorithm 2.2. Upon the reception of the reply all the pending

---

[3] The popularity of an entry on a particular peer is calculated by the number of related queries traversing this peer over the last time window.

Algorithm 2.2: FILLCACHEENTRY(*cache, entry, pendingQueries*)

$queryList = pendingQueries.remove(entry.ID)$
for $i \leftarrow 1$ **to** $queryList.size()$

do $\begin{cases} lookupMsg = queryList.remove(1) \\ lookupMsg.setDestination(lookupMsg.initiator) \\ lookupMsg.setSender(localGUID) \\ lookupMsg.setValue(entry.value) \\ replyMessage(lookupMsg) \end{cases}$

if $(entry.isMarked())$
  then $\{cache.remove(entry)$
  else
    $entry.setValue(srcs)$

Algorithm 2.3: GETCACHEENTRY(*cache, id, pendingQueries, msg*)

$entry = cache.get(id)$
if $(entry == null)$
  then $\begin{cases} entry = createNewCacheEntry(id, null) \\ cache.put(id, entry) \\ \textbf{return } (entry) \end{cases}$
if $(entry.hasExpired()$ **and** (**not** $entry.isMarked()))$
  then $\begin{cases} cache.remove(id) \\ entry = createNewCacheEntry(id, null) \\ cache.put(id, entry) \end{cases}$
  else
    $entry.updateUsage()$
if $(entry.frequency > FREQUENCY\_THRESHOLD$ **and**
    $entry.getValue == null)$
  then $\begin{cases} queryList = pendingQueries.get(id) \\ \textbf{if } (queryList.isEmpty()) \\ \quad \textbf{then } \begin{cases} lookupMsg = createLookupMessage(id) \\ forwardMessage(lookupMsg) \end{cases} \\ queryList.add(msg) \end{cases}$
if $(cache.size() - marked >= MAX\_CACHE\_SIZE)$
  then $\begin{cases} removed = LFU\_Replacement(cache) \\ queryList = pendingQueries.remove(removed.ID) \\ \textbf{if } (queryList.isEmpty) \\ \quad \textbf{then } \{cache.remove(removed) \\ \textbf{else} \\ \quad removed.mark() \end{cases}$
return $(entry)$

---

queries are further replied. Moreover, if the cache entry is not marked, it is filled
with the received indexing information.

Finally, the pseudo-code for retrieving a stored entry from the cache is listed
in Algorithm 2.3. If the stored entry is older than a safety time threshold (that

is set based on the expected peer uptime) the entry is removed and a new one is created, otherwise the frequency field is updated. Further, if the frequency of the query is higher than a threshold then, the message is stored as a pending query and a new lookup message is being created for the queried GUID, if this is the first pending message[4]. Moreover, if the size of the cache has exceeded its maximum value, the least frequently used entry is either removed if no pending queries are present or is marked for deletion at the arrival of the reply.

3   Evaluation

3.1   Experiments Description

The goal of the simulation experiments is to evaluate the performance improvement of the Chord network using the proposed indices cache mechanism and compare to the original network.

The simulation experiments have been performed using a general purpose discrete event simulator for P2P overlay networks [6]. The population of the peers is consisted of 4096 peers distributed randomly over a Chord ring with key range of 65536. Peers and resources share the same key range. Each experiment lasts approximately 30 minutes of simulation time. Peers randomly select a resource to query every 20 seconds (asynchronously from each other). The process is repeated for 80 times resulting to a total number of approximately 327000 queries.

Peers start requesting the resources after a certain stabilization period. The probability distribution of the resource selection follows a lognormal distribution with parameters $\mu = 0.82$ and $\sigma = 2.9$ following the guidelines in [4]. The selection of the lognormal distribution over the Zipfian distribution is motivated by the greater challenge of the former since the popularity of the resources is more widely distributed. The implemented lognormal generator produces randomly selected GUIDs limited to the aforementioned key range. On average, approximately $4000 - 4100$ different keys are generated on each run.

Figure 3 displays a representative cumulative distribution of the resource popularity, where the resources are sorted from the most to the least popular. From this figure, it can be concluded the first 25 most popular resources contribute to approximately 80% of the query load. Thus, an equivalently small cache size is adequate to store them and achieve high performance, provided that the popularity identification algorithm operates correctly. Nevertheless, in real experiments, the cache size may have to be bigger to capture effectively the popular resources since the key range may be considerably larger.

3.2   Results

In this section the measurement observations of the simulative experiments are reported. Figure 4 displays the reduced routing communication cost in terms

---

[4] In this case, it should be noted that the returned entry contains no indexing information to indicate the status of the query to the routing mechanism.

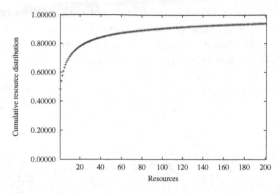

Fig. 3. Cumulative resource popularity distribution

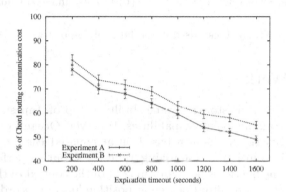

Fig. 4. Cache routing load as a percentage of the original Chord network

of required overlay traverse steps as the percentage of the communication cost of the original Chord network, as a function of the expiration timeout. Two different experiments have been selected:

1. Experiment A, where the $FREQUENCY\_THRESHOLD$ is 5, the maximum cache size is set to 80 and the frequency counter is reset every 200 seconds.
2. Experiment B, where the $FREQUENCY\_THRESHOLD$ is 3, the maximum cache size is set to 300 and the frequency counter is reset every 100 seconds.

We can observe that the total communication load for query routing can be considerably reduced using the caching mechanism down to 50% of the original load.

Moreover, peers responsible for popular resources may become "hot spots" and potential bottlenecks of the system. By utilizing the cache mechanism the load for replying to the queries is getting more evenly distributed. Figure 5(a) displays the load balance in the original Chord network, while Figure 5(b) shows the query replying in the cache-enhanced Chord network. It should be noted that the vertical axis is logarithmically scaled. Moreover, many peers reply with cached values which are not considered in this figure.

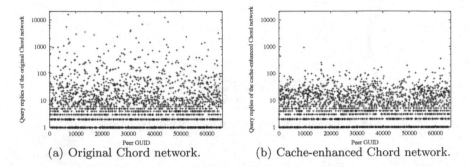

(a) Original Chord network.   (b) Cache-enhanced Chord network.

Fig. 5. Load distribution for replying queries

4   Related Work

OceanStore [11] is a P2P storage system built on top of Tapestry [29] to take advantage of its scalable lookup capabilities. However, OceanStore, employs an additional probabilistic mechanism based on attenuated Bloom Filters [3], resulting to a hybrid solution for improving Tapestry's routing performance when the popularity of the queries is not uniform [22]. In the context of the OceanStore algorithm, the first Bloom filter (located at position '0') is a record of the objects contained locally on the current node. The ith Bloom filter is the union of all of the Bloom filters for all of the nodes a distance i through any path from the current node. An attenuated Bloom filter is stored for each directed edge in the network. A query is routed along the edge whose filter indicates the presence of the object at the smallest distance. When the fast probabilistic algorithm fails to provide the requested results, OceanStore activates the Tapestry routing mechanism to forward the request to the final destination. However, the routing cost is increased when Bloom Filters provide false replies. Moreover, the maintenance of two different overlay networks increases considerably the operational cost of the system (both overlays are based on proactive mechanisms).

Hybrid PIER [14] is an overlay network designed to improve the performance of PIER [10] when looking up for popular resources. It is composed of two components, (i) an UltraPeer-based Gnutella network[5] and (ii), a structured Content Addressable Network (CAN) [21] where only UltraPeers participate. The hybrid search infrastructure utilizes selective publishing techniques that identify and publish only rare items into the DHT (decided by the UltraPeers). The search algorithm uses flooding techniques for locating popular items, and structured (DHT) search techniques for locating rare items.

---

[5] Based on Gnutella v0.6 protocol.

Caching mechanisms have been also utilized in P2P storage systems such as PAST [25], which is deployed on top of Pastry, a structured overlay network. The goals of the caching mechanism in PAST are (i) to minimize client access latencies, (ii) to maximize the query throughput and (iii) to balance the query load in the system. However, the utilized caching management system deals with the stored content and not with the indexing mechanism, which is the focus of this paper.

In addition, the use of caching has been investigated for the case of unstructured P2P overlay networks. Markatos [17] exploits network locality in unstructured networks (i.e. Gnutella) using caching mechanisms. Peers cache received replies and provide them to other peers sending similar queries instead of further forwarding the queries. Therefore, the overall traffic is reduced. Similarly, Liu et al. [12] investigate the reduced traffic and response time when caching the results, using simulation based experiments. Boykin et al. [4] study the statistical properties of queries in Gnutella-like systems and provide analytical results on query cache performance.

5   Conclusions

While caching has been extensively used in Web technologies and in unstructured P2P overlay networks, it has not received sufficient attention for structured P2P network approaches. The adequacy of caching popular indices in intermediate peers along the paths towards the responsible indexing peer(s) for structured networks is demonstrated in this paper.

The proposed caching mechanism reduces significantly the routing cost in structured P2P networks. Compared to alternative proposals, the achieved performance improvement is combined with a set of attractive features. Since the mechanism is locally applied to peers it can be incrementally deployed. Moreover, there is no need to introduce multiple specialized overlay networks operating in parallel or additional protocols to update the cached information.

Though this work identifies the critical parameters that have to be considered for the caching problem, there are several issues that can be further developed. Selecting the optimal values for the critical parameters can improve even further the observed performance. Moreover, a mechanism to adapt the values of the parameters to the dynamics of the network has significant practical and theoretical interest. Finally, different cache operation algorithms may provide better results in certain scenarios. The problem requires further analytical investigation to understand better its dynamics.

Acknowledgements

This work has been performed partially in the context of the project Premium "Preis- und Erlsmodelle im Internet - Umsetzung und Marktchancen" where TU Darmstadt has been funded by the German Bundesministerium fuer Bildung und Forschung (BMBF).

References

1. M. Arlitt, R. Friedrich, and T. Jin. Performance evaluation of Web proxy cache replacement policies. *Performance Evaluation*, 39(1-4):149–164, 2000.
2. H. Balakrishnan, M. F. Kaashoek, D. Karger, R. Morris, and I. Stoica. Looking up Data in P2P Systems. *Communications of the ACM*, 46(2):43–48, 2003.
3. B. H. Bloom. Space/time trade-offs in hash coding with allowable errors. *Communications of the ACM*, 13(7):422–426, 1970.
4. P. O. Boykin, J. S.A. Bridgewater, and V. Roychowdhury. Statistical Properties of Query Strings. Preprint, January 2004.
5. V. Darlagiannis. *Overlay Network Mechanisms for Peer-to-Peer Systems*. PhD thesis, Department of Computer Science, Technische Universität Darmstadt, Germany, June 2005.
6. V. Darlagiannis, A. Mauthe, N. Liebau, and R. Steinmetz. An Adaptable, Role-based Simulator for P2P Networks. In *Proceedings of the International Conference on Modeling, Simulation and Visualization Methods*, pages 52–59, June 2004.
7. V. Darlagiannis, A. Mauthe, and R. Steinmetz. Overlay Design Mechanisms for Heterogeneous, Large Scale, Dynamic P2P Systems. *Journal of Networks and System Management*, 12(3):371–395, 2004.
8. N. G. de Bruijn. A combinatorial problem. In *Proceedings of the Koninklije Nederlandse Academie van Wetenshapen*, pages 758–764, 1946.
9. K. P. Gummadi, R. J. Dunn, S. Saroiu, S. D. Gribble, H. M. Levy, and J. Zahorjan. Measurement, Modeling, and Analysis of Peer-to-Peer File Sharing Workload. In *Proceedings of 19th ACM Symposium on Operating Systems Principles*, October 2003.
10. R. Huebsch, J. M. Hellerstein, N. Lanham, B. Thau Loo, S. Shenker, and I. Stoica. Querying the Internet with PIER. In *Proceedings of VLDB'03*, September 2003.
11. J. Kubiatowicz, D. Bindel, Y. Chen, S. Czerwinski, P. Eaton, D. Geels, R. Gummadi, S. Rhea, H. Weatherspoon, C. Wells, and B. Zhao. OceanStore: an Architecture for Global-scale Persistent Storage. In *Proceedings of the 9th International Conference on Architectural Support for Programming Languages and Operating Systems*, pages 190–201. ACM Press, 2000.
12. Y. Liu, L. Xiao, and L. M. Ni. Building a Scalable Bipartite P2P Overlay Network. In *Proceedings of the 18th International Parallel and Distributed Processing Symposium*, April 2004.
13. D. Loguinov, A. Kumar, V. Rai, and S. Ganesh. Graph-Theoretic Analysis of Structured Peer-to-Peer Systems: Routing Distances and Fault Resilience. In *Proceedings of ACM SIGCOMM'03*, pages 395–406, August 2003.
14. B. Thau Loo, R. Huebsch, I. Stoica, and J. M. Hellerstein. The Case for a Hybrid P2P Search Infrastructure. In *Proceedings of the 4th International Workshop on Peer-to-Peer Systems (IPTPS04)*, February 2004.
15. E. Keong Lua, J. Crowcroft, M. Pias, R. Sharma, and S. Lim. A Survey and Comparison of Peer-to-Peer Overlay Network Schemes. *IEEE Communications Survey and Tutorial*, March 2004.
16. Q. Lv, S. Ratnasamy, and S. Shenker. Can Heterogeneity Make Gnutella Scalable? In *Proceedings of the 1st International Workshop on Peer-to-Peer Systems (IPTPS02)*, March 2002.
17. E. P. Markatos. Tracing a large-scale Peer-to-Peer System: an hour in the life of Gnutella. In *Proceedings of the 2nd IEEE/ACM International Symposium on Cluster Computing and Grid*, pages 65–74, May 2002.

18. P. Maymounkov and D. Maziéres. Kademlia: A Peer-to-peer Information System Based on the XOR metric. In *Proceedings of the 1st International Workshop on Peer-to-Peer Systems (IPTPS02)*, 2002.

19. E. O'Neil, P. O'Neil, and G. Weikum. The LRU-K Page Replacement Algorithm For Database Disk Buffering. In *Proceedings of the 1993 ACM SIGMOD International Conference on Management of data*, pages 297–306, 1993.

20. M. Portmann, P. Sookavatana, S. Ardon, and A. Seneviratne. The cost of peer discovery and searching in the Gnutella peer-to-peer file sharing protocol. In *Proceedings of the International Conference on Networks*, pages 263–268, 2001.

21. S. Ratnasamy, P. Francis, M. Handley, R. Karp, and S. Schenker. A scalable Content Addressable Network. In *Proceedings of the 2001 Conference on Applications, Technologies, Architectures, and Protocols for Computer Communications*, pages 161–172. ACM Press, 2001.

22. S. Rhea and J. Kubiatowicz. Probabilistic location and routing. In *Proceedings of the 21st Annual Joint Conference of the IEEE Computer and Communications Societies*, June 2002.

23. J. Robinson and M. Devarakonda. Data cache management using frequency based replacement. In *Proceedings of the 1990 ACM SIGMETRICS conference on Measurement and modeling of computer systems*, pages 134–142, 1990.

24. A. Rowstron and P. Druschel. Pastry: Scalable, distributed object location and routing for large-scale peer-to-peer systems. In *IFIP/ACM International Conference on Distributed Systems Platforms (Middleware)*, pages 329–350, 2001.

25. A. I. T. Rowstron and P. Druschel. Storage management and caching in PAST, a large-scale, persistent peer-to-peer storage utility. In *Symposium on Operating Systems Principles*, pages 188–201, 2001.

26. S. Saroiu, P. K. Gummadi, and S. D. Gribble. A Measurement Study of Peer to-Peer File Sharing Systems. In *Proceedings of Multimedia Computing and Networking 2002 (MMCN '02)*, 2002.

27. I. Stoica, R. Morris, D. Liben-Nowell, D. Karger, M. F. Kaashoek, Frank Dabek, and Hari Balakrishnan. Chord: A scalable Peer-to-Peer Lookup Service for Internet Applications. *IEEE Transactions on Networking*, 11(1):17–32, February 2003.

28. B. Traversat, A. Arora, M. Abdelaziz, M. Duigou, C. Haywood, J.-C. Hugly, E. Pouyoul, and B. Yeager. Project JXTA 2.0 Super-Peer Virtual Network. http://www.jxta.org/project/www/docs/ JXTA2.0protocols1.pdf, May 2003.

29. B. Y. Zhao, L. Huang, J. Stribling, S. C. Rhea, A. D. Joseph, and J. Kubiatowicz. Tapestry: A Resilient Global-scale Overlay for Service Deployment. *IEEE Journal on Selected Areas in Communications*, 22(1):41–53, 2004.

A Semantic Marketplace of Negotiating Agents

Theodore Patkos and Dimitris Plexousakis

Institute of Computer Science, FO.R.T.H.
Vassilika Vouton, P.O. Box 1385, GR 71110
Heraklion, Greece
Fax: (+30) 2810391638
{patkos, dp}@ics.forth.gr

Abstract. Achieving interoperability and automation in job execution is of utmost importance for next generation e-Commerce applications. This paper proposes a design that integrates three prominent technologies: intelligent software agents, peer-to-peer networking and the Semantic Web. SeMPHoNIA is an architecture for an agent-based marketplace, utilizing knowledge from RDF product repositories, in an open peer-to-peer environment. The platform defines the basic stages of the process of e-trading, facilitating users in closing deals in automated manner. The implementation of our approach is demonstrated in the context of auction scenarios. A performance evaluation of the system is also presented.

1 Introduction

The emergence and rapid development of electronic commerce has influenced many fields of human activity and business industry, providing a gravity well, which pulls a variety of diverse technologies and novel research efforts into closer collaboration. Recent years have seen an enormous increase in the role of information technology in markets, in particular the emergence of electronic marketplaces [2]. The current economic trading sphere is structured on top of an open, distributed, heterogeneous and, most often, unreliable environment.

Human participants are still actively involved in all stages of the buying process. As the trend of e-Commerce continues though, an inevitable growth in the number and features of on-line markets is observed, causing the task of monitoring and effective decision-making to become trivial and time-consuming for humans. The increasing degree of heterogeneity and sophistication on both the business and the customer side will cause interoperability and automation of execution to become the most challenging tasks that next generation e-Commerce applications will face.

In this paper we introduce the design and implementation of a system, called SeMPHoNIA (Semantic Marketplace of Peers Hosting Negotiating Intelligent Agents), for addressing issues of current e-trading [13]. The system integrates and exploits three enabling technologies, namely intelligent software agents, peer-to-peer systems and the Semantic Web, into a unified platform. It is an architecture for an agent-based virtual marketplace structured on top of a peer-to-peer

Z. Despotovic, S. Joseph, and C. Sartori (Eds.): AP2PC 2005, LNAI 4118, pp. 94–105, 2006.
© Springer-Verlag Berlin Heidelberg 2006

network, utilizing semantic approaches. SeMPHoNIA could be considered as what [6] describes as the third key actor in agent-mediated e-Commerce applications, apart from buyers and sellers: the market owner, an environment that sets and controls the rules, in which buyers and sellers trade. The implementation of our approach is demonstrated in the context of auction scenarios. The platform is intended to facilitate users in discovering and bidding across multiple interrelated auctions with varying start and end times and protocols.

The rest of the paper is structured as follows. Section 2 presents an analysis of SeMPHoNIAs architecture and components. Section 3 introduces a number of additional functionalities. An evaluation of the platforms performance is presented in Section 4. Related work is discussed in Section 5 and the paper concludes in Section 6 with final remarks.

2   SeMPHoNIA Platform Architecture

The SeMPHoNIA platform models aspects of market mechanisms that represent a common interaction medium for users on the Internet. It integrates three preexisting technologies; JXTA [8] for configuring the peer-to-peer network, Grasshopper[1] [4] for managing the multi-agent character of the system and ICS-FORTH RDFSuite [7] for exploiting technologies of the Semantic Web. The JXTA Engine module is responsible for implementing JXTA protocols to allow the application to function as a peer, collaborate with other peers and deploy peer-to-peer services. The Grasshopper Middleware module is the component that undertakes the role of automating the negotiation procedure by creating, controlling and monitoring software agents that represent human users. Finally, the Semantic Search Engine module facilitates semantic publish and discovery of products on the network, exploiting software tools provided by the ICS-FORTH RDFSuite, such as RDF validation, storage and querying [1].

Three distinct layers of functionality synthesize the platforms behavior; its semantic, its multi-agent and its peer-to-peer character. Before going into details regarding the platform as a whole, we elaborate on the different layers and their role in the system.

2.1   Semantic Character

Traditional Web-based product searching based on keywords seems insufficient and inefficient in the "sea" of information [10]. Especially in e-auction sites, the current trend of searching numerous catalogues of available products is a rigorous procedure. Instead, next generation e-markets should be able to handle customer queries, such as "Find all running English or Vickrey auctions of

---

[1] IKV++ Technologies AG has recently announced its desire to abandon further development efforts concerning the Grasshopper platform (fall 2004). This has no impact on SeMPHoNIA whatsoever, since it does not depend on any specialized aspects of Grasshopper. In fact, our next version of the system is developed using JADE (http://jade.tilab.com/), which is also a FIPA-compliant multi-agent platform.

paintings created by impressionists of the 16th century". Ontologies have shown to be the right answer to knowledge structuring.

The SeMPHoNIA project applies to an open and heterogeneous environment. For that purpose, we have developed two types of ontologies; process ontologies, which are specifically about auction-related concepts and relations, as well as domain ontologies, which enrich product descriptions with metadata to accurately describe their features. The former type serves transactional needs, while the latter covers informational needs for product specifications. More specifically, each item or auction session, is semantically described by a set of ontologies. Retailers relate products with a specific domain and provide metadata about them in the corresponding domain ontology. The auction ontology, on the other hand, captures the characteristics of a particular auction session combining knowledge from auction protocols and other common trading concepts to specify the context, in which the system operates. It is used to model all information needed by an auctioneer to initiate a new auction session and for a customer to determine a desired session based on criteria, such as brokers identity, payment etc.

It has been argued that until now systems based on centralized ontology schemes suffer from difficulties concerning development and maintenance [16]. Instead, the SeMPHoNIA infrastructure takes advantage of locally stored ontologies sharing common schema representation. The concept behind this design is to use RDF-based reasoning for discovering, matching and filtering auction sessions between peers. Ontologies structured in the platforms environment provide the necessary semantics for all entities and agents, both human and software, to share a common understanding of the world and the rules that govern it. RDFS as a means of knowledge representation, as well as RDF schemas sizes and morphologies have been studied in [11].

To allow product searching and enhance communication, ontology publishing and querying techniques have been developed. Ontologies are published on the network using both the products domain and URI. Thus, general searching is supported that can result to a collection of domain-specific ontologies, each of which is linked with the corresponding auction ontology, or on the other hand, focused searching is possible, which returns specific product descriptions and auction sessions. Querying is performed using RQL [9], a typed language following a functional approach, which supports generalized path expressions, featuring variables on both labels for classes and properties. RQL is considered the most complete RDF query language in comparison to other popular ones, according to elicitations extracted from recent evaluations ([5]). Software agents forward RQL queries directly to the desired local ontologies.

2.2   Multi-agent Character

Agent technology represents a flexible way of conceptualizing and implementing e-Commerce transactions. The ability of agents to exhibit automation in job execution, mobility, communication and collaboration with other agents is exploited in SeMPHoNIA to reduce the tremendous time and human resources invested in on-line trading. Specifically, agents are used to facilitate the connection of buyers and sellers and to automate the process of negotiation in the context of auction scenarios. In SeMPHoNIA, users may decide to participate in multiple auctions at the same time, when the result of one auction may affect the action taken for the other. Agents automate bidding actions and make inferences for determining the optimum path, when interrelated auctions are involved, based on the human users preferences and on their local knowledge.

We identify three types of agents operating in the SeMPHoNIA platform: A-, C- and CL-agents. The *A-agent* (Auctioneer agent) is the auctioneers representative in the SeMPHoNIA network. It surveils and coordinates the execution of a specific auction and is responsible for the enforcement of rules governing the negotiation among all involved parties. The A-agent is aware of its owner's preferences, such as the auction's type, reserve price, etc. This information is captured at the ontology that the user publishes. The agent also declares auction termination and announces winning offers, according to the negotiation rules.

Customers in SeMPHoNIA may initiate one or more auction sessions, participating concurrently in one or more auctions in each of them. Each session has one coordinator agent, the *C-agent* (Customer agent), whose role is to manage the distinct sub-tasks that a session is decomposed into. This agent represents the users intelligent interface to the system, because it performs the necessary actions to achieve the goal of purchasing the desired product with the best to its owner profit among all auctions that it monitors. The C-agent controls the allocation of bids across auctions, relying on information about their progress and on its internal strategy, but does not participate in any of them directly.

CL-agents (Clone agents) are the actual participants in auctions conducted in the SeMPHoNIA marketplace. These agents are created by the C-agent, inheriting the initial knowledge concerning the users preferences, i.e., the maximum price they are allowed to spend for an item, the number of items they should intend to acquire etc. They react to notifications sent by both the A-agent, informing them about the progress of the auction they participate in, and the C-agent, instructing them to continue bidding or postpone their execution, in case this serves best the sessions evolution. CL-agents are specialized according to the type of auction that has been assigned to them (English, Vickrey etc.) and the bidding strategy that the user intends to follow (aggressive, last-minute bidding etc.). They all possess the primal attributes and knowledge of the corresponding C-agent, but present specializations in their behavior, justifying their characterization as clones of the C-agent.

The structure of the multi-agent layer, along with the basic interactions between the various components, is presented in Figure 1. The structure of the distributed agent environment is composed of agencies and places. An *agency* is the actual runtime environment for agents and may be initiated on different hosts on the network. A *place* provides a logical grouping of functionality inside an agency. An important aspect of the multi-agent layer is that it takes advantage of the mobility features of agents for enhancing performance. CL-agents migrate to the place, where the auction is conducted, in order to communicate

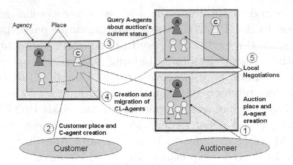

Fig. 1. The multi-agent component

locally with the A-agent, eliminating network latencies. Therefore, a C-agent may have multiple clones scattered across different agencies on different peers.

2.3   Peer-to-Peer Character

The functionality of the previously mentioned multi-agent layer is superimposed on a peer-to-peer network structure, that harnesses the computing power of capable peers (resource sharing) and impels efficient ontology distribution across nodes (knowledge sharing). SeMPHoNIAs peer-to-peer network is a typical asynchronous-message-passing super-peer system that implements the auction marketplace environment. Performance measurements in super-peer networks ([18]) have revealed the potential to combine the efficiency of a centralized search with the autonomy, load balancing and robustness provided by distributed searching. Since computing demands focus on agent operations, our concern is to distribute agencies across peers in the network.

Three are the basic types of SeMPHoNIA peers: customer, auctioneer and operator peers. *Customer* and *auctioneer* peers serve as single end users. Auctioneer peers have the additional functionality of publishing their ontologies on the network. Therefore, they are always accompanied by an ontology database, along with the corresponding RDFServer, which acts as a mediator between the database and the network. All simple peers are able to cache messages and route them over all other peers in the cluster that they are connected to.

The third type of peer is the *operator* peer that acts as super-peer and provides zero or more agencies to the platform. Simple peers are connected to one or more operator peers to ensure greater reliability and scalability. Since heterogeneity is a feature of peer-to-peer networks that can become profitable, if taken into account, we consider operator peers to be nodes with high availability and computing resources. Thus, they supply the medium, where all auction operations take place. Operator peers interconnect forming a backbone of peer clusters, so that whenever an operator peer leaves the network all agents running on its agencies migrate to another operator. Besides, this interconnection allows bridging remote clusters and permits the application of message propagation algorithms to the underlying peers of each cluster, avoiding message flooding to the entire network.

SeMPHoNIA peers advertise their services in language-neutral metadata structures, represented as XML documents, called *advertisements*. Advertisements are the basic unit of data exchanged between peers providing information about available resources. All peers contribute to increasing the level of connectivity to the overall network, by caching locally XML advertisements and automatically delivering them to interested peers upon request, without any need for human intervention. Advertisements are published inside a peer cluster and are additionally broadcasted between operator peers. Thus, a simple peer searching for available ontology advertisements of a specific domain broadcasts the request to peers in its cluster and to the operator peers that is connected to.

An important notion of the SeMPHoNIA peer-to-peer architecture is its peer grouping concept. Peer groups are used to promote trusted services, by segmenting the network space into distinct communities of peers participating in an auction. For every auction listed on the network a new peer group is created by the auctioneer peer and whenever a customer decides to participate in an auction, it must first join the corresponding peer group. Only after the admission is granted, the peer is allowed to send agents to the auction place. This authentication mechanism applied for joining peer groups before registering in auctions can be extended to restrict entrance to specific members, provisioning the creation of private or secure auctions, based on criteria, such as peer reputation. We believe that security issues are better handled at the peer-to-peer layer than at the multi-agent layer, due to the ability to combine restriction mechanisms from both the lower physical level (encryption, authentication) and the higher software level (trust models, trust content).

2.4 SeMPHoNIA Platform

The previously described functionalities of the system are integrated in the SeMPHoNIA platform to implement a complete and well-defined e-trading environment. This section presents how the different layers of functionality co-exist and collaborate to synthesize the overall system infrastructure.

Figure 2 displays a snapshot of the system state at a random moment. The middle part shows a fraction of the peer-to-peer network. Simple peers connect with operator peers, which in turn interconnect with each other to form a network of main channels. Advertisements travel between peers on the same cluster or between operator peers and are cached at various nodes throughout their path. These advertisements may describe resources, such as product domains, ontologies, auction peer groups, agency addresses or just the presence of peers. The lower part of the image depicts the correspondence between auctioneer peers and their own auction peer groups, indicated by dashed-dotted lines. Auctioneers may create multiple peer groups, one for every auction they conduct. This layer also shows the virtual presence of customer peers in each peer groups. Last, the upper part displays the multi-agent layer of the system, which is the component that implements all auction sessions. The dashed-dotted line here implies the

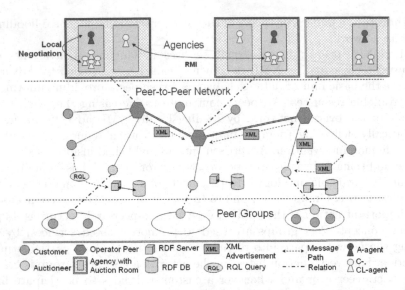

Fig. 2. SeMPHoNIA platform elements, relations and interactions

relation between an operator peer and the agencies it offers. The other peers create places for supporting negotiations and agents that travel between agencies.

3   Advanced Features

SeMPHoNIA is a virtual market architecture that includes numerous advanced features for supporting users in accomplishing electronic negotiation tasks. This section discusses some additional facilities that the platform integrates, which provide the supplementary infrastructure needed to become a complete system.

3.1   Statistical Information Support

The history of bidding of a product and the auction statistics have gained importance over the years, due to the increase in Internet-based auctions. This information is valuable for future auctions, for assisting bidders in specifying appropriate bids and sellers in setting the base prices. Currently, none of the on-line auction sites give any information of such kind.

The SeMPHoNIA platform provides a special type of agent, whose role it to yield feedback of previous auctions and produce valuable auction statistics. This agent, named as S-agent (Statistical agent), automates the process of monitoring auctions. It follows the same interaction mechanism as C-agents; it creates CL-agents that travel to the remote place, where the auction is running, recording its progress, while the master agent coordinates the session and extracts statistical data obtained by all the clones. Auction statistics may include average winning bids, price convergence behavior, equilibrium price, progress of bidding etc.

3.2   Agent Reasoning

SeMPHoNIA agents exhibit intelligent behavior. Regardless of their type, their most important components are the *communication module* and the *inference engine*. Due to space restrictions we only examine the latter.

In SeMPHoNIA, the most challenging task that agents are called to accomplish is that of bidding across multiple auctions with varying start and end times and varying protocols, attempting to ensure that at most one of the desired items will be purchased , thus procuring the best deal for the customer. The agent responsible for managing this task is the C-agent. Therefore, the implementation of a sophisticated reasoning behavior for the C-agent is of vital importance for the success of a profitable auction participation.

Our current approach is indicative and can be used as a reference point for implementing more advanced strategies. The C-agent is designed to manage multiple CL-agents and decide which of them should bid and which should wait, according to the progress of their auction. Four are the basic constraints that the C-agents logic mechanism is designed to comply with: *Singularity Constraint*; among clone agents, only one is allowed to be active at any particular moment and, thus, permitted to place bids in its auction. The rest are set at a stand-by mode, waiting for the C-agent to activate them. *Exclusiveness Constraint*; while the active clone holds the maximum bid in its auction, no other clone can be set active, ensuring that no purchase at more than one sessions can be accomplished. *Optimum Path Constraint*; the intention is to always select as active the agent that stays on the optimum path among all bidding sessions, meaning that it is the one that maximizes the C-agents utility function. *Eligibility Constraint*; clones, while active, persistently pursues to hold the maximum bid of their auctions, until reaching the offer limit, ensuring that if a purchase is profitable and it will be accomplished.

3.3   Flexibility in Applying Custom Strategies

The design of SeMPHoNIAs agent architecture offers flexibility and extensibility. Program developers can build custom strategies by creating new CL-agents with advanced reasoning mechanisms. Application developers can manipulate CL-agents as black boxes and utilize custom-built CL-agents to enhance interaction with the system, without any need to re-design the entire negotiation template.

As a proof of concept of this design, apart from the popular iterative English auction and the single-cycle Vickrey auction, both of which rely on a central auctioneer to direct the session, in the context of the SeMPHoNIA project we have developed a peer-to-peer continuous auction. The vast majority of on-line auction houses perform centralized auctions, in which clients do not negotiate with each other, but rather with the auctioneer exclusively, who distributes information about offers among them. However, peer-to-peer auctions receive increasing attention, due to the absence of a central role and the drawbacks that this scheme implies, as identified in [12]. In our peer-to-peer auction agents negotiate in pairs. Participants register in the auction and seek a random party to negotiate with. The negotiation between any two agents is private, the winning offer, though, is announced to the other participants and to the A-agent, in order to update, if necessary, the current maximum offer of the auction. The A-agent, throughout the evolution of the auction, preserves a passive role, guarding the valid execution of the auction rules.

What is interesting is that the extension of the system with new negotiation protocols, even when they present such vast differences as centralized and peer-to-peer auctions, requires no modification in the platform. For the generation of the peer-to-peer auction the only action required is the creation of the specialized peer-to-peer CL-agent and the expansion of the A-agents auction ontology to acknowledge the existence and features of such auctions. Neither the C-agent nor the A-agent needs to have the protocol hard-coded explicitly beforehand.

4   Performance Evaluation

This section discusses the performance study of SeMPHoNIAs agent design. We limit the demonstration of our evaluation on the multi-agent layer, for the sake of clarity and expressiveness of results. The hypothesis that we seek to evaluate is that our proposed negotiation scheme is scalable and performs efficiently in a wide range of conditions. We measure the performance of our platform in terms of negotiation rate and utilization factor (messages processed per second). Following are the results obtained by running several test cases, including simultaneous progression of multiple auctions.

To retain a common base line for our evaluations, each C-agent was given a random maximum asking price ranging from 1 to 500 units and all English and Peer-to-Peer auctions were evolving using an incremental step of 5 units (we refer to such auctions with the abbreviation 500/5). All participants join the auctions before their opening. In addition, we chose to implement the most demanding scenario, where CL-agents inform their C-agents at every new bid notification, reducing their performance, but increasing efficiency.

Our first measurement concerned memory demands. For a typical Java Virtual Machine memory allocation (64Mb) a single operator peer can handle up to 600 agents, before running out of memory. If we consider the fact that the majority of auctions held on eBay, the largest consumer-to-consumer auction site, have an average of 20 to 40 bidders [19], then a single operator peer can host up to 15 parallel auctions. This we believe is a very satisfactory number for a distributed system, such as SeMPHoNIA, which is designed to allocate services at multiple peers across the network. Besides, it is also possible to extend the amount of memory that JVM utilizes during a single execution, depending on the hosts specifications.

The first set of test cases investigates how the behavior of the system changes as we increase the number of agents negotiating, during a single auction. We consider the English 500/5, the Peer-to-Peer 500/5 and the Vickrey auctions. Figures 3a and 3b display the time needed for each auction to converge to the equilibrium price and the computational needs, respectively. Although time itself

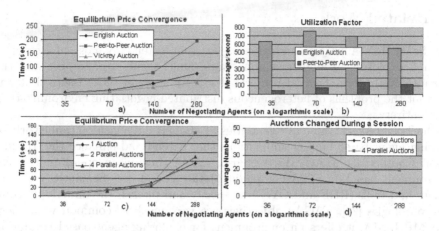

Fig. 3. a) Single-auction convergence rate, b) Utilization factor for a single auction, c) Multi-auction convergence rate, d) Number of active clones changed in a session

is not a metric, since it depends on the hosts characteristics, the diagrams are useful in studying the systems scaling, when reaching its memory limits. What is interesting in these diagrams is that the systems performance as load increases is satisfactory, even when it reaches its limits. In particular, the utilization factor increases up to a certain upper limit and then starts diminishing. This upper limit is the point at which the maximum number of messages can be processed, maximizing the performance gain. Below that point, the computational needs are so great that no resources are available for handling all messages arriving or departing. We measured that the utilization factors upper limit is reached at around 90 agents for the English auction and 200 agents for the peer-to-peer auction (we note that the behavior of these two type of auctions agree with observations made in [12] simulating negotiations with 2,500 to 160,000 agents).

The second set of test cases considers the parallel execution of multiple English 500/5 auctions that start simultaneously. Figure 3c compares the convergence rate in 2 and 4 parallel auctions. No significant difference is observed when few bidders are present. When this number increases, though, we see that bidding in only two auctions is less efficient than bidding in four. To understand why this holds, we need to investigate the behavior of agents in each case. Figure 3d explains how they behave in parallel auctions. When only two auctions are running, C-agents tend to focus on only one of them, resulting in a scheme where bidders are split between the two and behave as if only one were active. This causes the auctions to take more time to converge. Increasing the number of concurrent auctions, parallelism is improved. The reason why parallelism is not promoted with two auctions is because new offers are accepted faster than required for an agent to infer whether to change its current auction or not. Especially when the number of participants becomes high (more than 160), the computational needs increase as well, causing greater latencies in the time it takes for an agent to decide on an action.

5   Related Work

The SeMPHoNIA project addresses issues that extend to most phases of e-trading, exploiting technologies concerning multi-agent, peer-to-peer and the Semantic Web areas. Several projects deal with some of those issues, but few confront the problems of heterogeneous distributed negotiating environments in their entirety.

The Travel Agent Game in Agentcities (TAGA) [14] is a general framework for running agent-based market simulations that extend and enhance the Trading Agent Competition (TAC) [17] scenario. TAGA runs on an open, multi-agent environment based on FIPA compliant platforms and uses Semantic Web languages and tools (RDF and OWL) to specify and publish the underlying common ontologies [20]. TAGAs objectives are very much in common with those of SeMPHoNIA; it offers an environment for exploring agent-based trading in dynamic markets, it supports semantic querying and publishing and it allows users to create their own reasoning mechanisms for their agents. TAGA offers a controlled environment, specialized in settled trading scenarios and based on a centralized infrastructure. SeMPHoNIA, on the other hand, provides openness and interoperability and is based on a peer-to-peer structure that approximates more realistic matchmaking and trading mechanisms. Moreover, SeMPHoNIA places emphasis on local negotiations between agents of remote peers, achieving efficiency in trading, as well.

Outside of, but related to, the auction scenario, automated negotiation represents an important issue of the SeMPHoNIA project. [15] attempts to address the problem of automated agent negotiations in open environments, where the negotiation protocols are not known beforehand, but instead the host advertises the type of protocol regulating the interaction. A shared ontology of protocols is defined based on the idea that some general concepts are present in any negotiation protocol. Moreover, a method ontology, written in DAML+OIL, aims at modelling knowledge about the interactions between agents on how to perform a task. SeMPHoNIA is able to integrate similar techniques. It should be noted, though, that it is still at an early stage of development and other issues need to be investigated, such as completeness of ontological protocol representations.

6   Conclusions

We have presented the design and implementation of SeMPHoNIA, a system that integrates three emerging technologies; intelligent software agents, peer-to-peer networking and the Semantic Web. Our primary motivation has been to demonstrate the power of combining these three technologies in facilitating human participation in next-generation e-Commerce transactions. The system realizes auction scenarios as a general negotiation framework, while maintaining a flexible design that allows experimenting with new techniques.

References

1. Alexaki, S., Christophides, V., Karvounarakis, G., Plexousakis, D., Tolle K.: The ICS-FORTH RDFSuite: Managing Voluminous RDF Description Bases. Proc. of the 2nd International Workshop on the Semantic Web (SemWeb'01) in conjunction with 10th International World Wide Web Conference (WWW10), Hong-Kong (2001) 1-13
2. Bichler, M., Field, S., Werthner, H.: Introduction: Theory and Application of Electronic Market Design. Electronic Commerce Research Journal, Vol. 1 (2001) 215-220
3. FIPA Specifications, http://www.fipa.org/specifications/
4. Grasshopper web site, http://www.grasshopper.de
5. Haase P., Broekstra J., Eberhart A., Volz R.: A Comparison of RDF Query Languages. S.A. McIlraith et al. (Eds.): ISWC (2004), LNCS 3298 (2004)
6. He, M., Jennings, N. R., Leung, H. F.: On Agent-Mediated Electronic Commerce. IEEE Transactions on Knowledge and Data Engineering, Vol. 15, No. 4 (2003)
7. ICS-FORTH, The ICS-Forth RDFSuite web site, http://139.91.183.30:9090/RDF
8. JXTA Project, http://www.jxta.org
9. Karvounarakis, G., Alexaki, S., Christophides, V., Plexousakis, D., Scholl, M.: RQL: A Declarative Query Language for RDF. 11th International World Wide Web Conference (WWW02) Honolulu, Hawaii, USA (2002)
10. Lee, R. S.T., Liu, J. N.K.: iJADE eMiner - A Web-Based Mining Agent Based on Intelligent Java Agent Development Environment (iJADE) on Internet Shopping. D. Cheung, G.J. Williams, and Q. Li (Eds.): PAKDD 2001, LNAI 2035 (2001) 28-40
11. Magkanaraki, A., Alexaki S., Christophides V., Plexousakis, D.: Benchmarking RDF Schemas for the Semantic Web. In: First International Semantic Web Conference (ISWC'02), Sardinia, Italy, June 9-12 (2002) 132-146
12. Ogston, E., Vassiliadis, S.: A Peer-to-Peer Agent Auction. AAMAS02, Bologna, Italy, (2002)
13. Patkos, T., Plexousakis, D.: A Semantic Marketplace of Peers Hosting Negotiating Intelligent Agents. Proceedings of the CAiSE'05 Forum, O. Belo, J. Elder, J. Falcao e Cunha, O. Pastor (Eds.), Portugal (2005) 3-8
14. TAGA web site, http://taga.umbc.edu (2004)
15. Tamma, V., Wooldridge, M., Blacoe, I., Dickinson, I.: An Ontology based Approach to Automated Negotiation. In Proceedings of the 4th International Workshop on Agent-Mediated Electronic Commerce, Bologna, Italy (2002)
16. Terziyan, V., Zharko, A.: Semantic Web and Peer-to-Peer: Integration and Interoperability in Industry. In: International Journal of Computers, Systems and Signals, IAAMSAD, ISSN 1608-5655, Vol. 4, No. 2 (2003) 33-46
17. Wellman, M. P., Greenwald, A., Stone, P., Wurman, P. R.: The 2001 Trading Agent Competition. 14th IAAI Conference, Edmonton (2002)
18. Yang, B., Garcia-Molina, H.: Designing a Super-Peer Network. IEEE International Conference on Data Engineering, San Jose, California, (2003)
19. Yang, I., Jeong, H., Kahng, B., Barabasi, A. L.: Emerging behavior in electronic bidding. Physical Review E 68, 016102, The American Physical Society (2003)
20. Zou, Y., Finin, T., Ding, L., Chen, H.: Using Semantic Web Technologies in Multi-Agent Systems: a case study in the TAGA trading agent environment. Proceedings of the 5th International Conference on Electronic Commerce, Pittsburgh, Pennsylvania (2003) 95-101

Semantic Web Service Composition Through a P2P-Based Multi-agent Environment

Peep Küngas[1] and Mihhail Matskin[2]

[1] Norwegian University of Science and Technology
Department of Computer and Information Science
Trondheim, Norway
`peep@idi.ntnu.no`
[2] Royal Institute of Technology
Department of Microelectronics and Information Technology
Kista, Sweden
`misha@imit.kth.se`

Abstract. This paper describes a multi agent system (MAS) for distributed composition of Semantic Web services. Since our system is intended to function in highly dynamic environments, where heterogeneous agents rapidly join and leave the system, we consider P2P approach as most suitable for facilitating agent and service discovery. The MAS is based on Chord P2P network, which allows the MAS to dynamically publish and locate available Semantic Web services, which are specified with OWL-S. In order to compose new Web services from existing ones, agents apply symbolic reasoning in a cooperative problem solving manner.

Keywords: Semantic Web services, multi-agent systems, P2P.

1 Introduction

The increasing popularity of P2P systems (such as Overnet, Kazaa and Gnutella) for file sharing, indicates general interest in resource sharing. However the current P2P systems suffer at least from two drawbacks. First, they are mostly designed for sharing either data or CPU power, but not both in the same system. Moreover, in the case of CPU sharing, the executable computational processes are expected to be known *a priori* for each participant (like in SETI@Home). Second, the current P2P network nodes still lack a degree of proactivity, which would provide higher degree of autonomy, rationality and fairness.

In contrary, multi agent systems (MAS) still seem to lack enough capabilities to reorganise themselves in dynamic environments. In particular, despite of the intelligent behaviour assigned to agents, MAS architectures are currently mostly designed manually. Therefore combining MAS-s and P2P networks would extend the capabilities of both architectures.

Recently many articles, related to automated composition of (Semantic) Web services [1, 2], agent technologies and P2P networks [3, 4, 5, 6, 7] (see Section 7 for a review) have been published. Although many of them [8, 9, 10, 11, 12] discuss a combined approach, to the best of our knowledge there are currently no systems available,

Z. Despotovic, S. Joseph, and C. Sartori (Eds.): AP2PC 2005, LNAI 4118, pp. 106–119, 2006.

which apply agent technologies to distributed composition of Semantic Web services over structured P2P networks.

Our goal is to construct a system, which would allow users to seamlessly integrate the available Web services and support the exchange data. Emergence of the Semantic Web has resulted in a uniform view to data and computational resources. Describing both data and Web services as semantic objects allows to move from data sharing and service sharing to resource sharing in a unified infrastructure. We are going to exploit this uniform view while discovering particular resources in our system.

In this paper we describe an implementation of a MAS where agents cooperatively apply distributed symbolic reasoning for discovering and composing Semantic Web services. A structured P2P network is used to self-organise MAS infrastructure for efficient resource discovery.

Using a Semantic Web service description in an OWL-S-like language significantly increases to amount of semantic information available for discovering requested services. In addition, if no services satisfying user requirements are found, then cooperative problem solving (CPS) is applied for dynamic construction of new composite Web services. The general structure of our system, supporting Semantic Web services composition, is depicted in Figure 1.

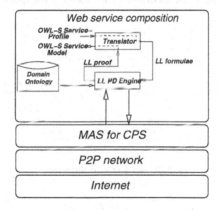

Fig. 1. The system architecture

Our Web service composition process reads input (available atomic Semantic Web services and the requested one) from OWL-S ServiceProfile, transforms it into Linear Logic (LL) formulae and applies Partial Deduction (PD) to find (partial) solutions for a request. During PD attached domain ontologies are used to reason over the semantics of Web services' inputs and outputs. Partial solutions can be extended through our CPS framework until a complete solution has been found. Complete solutions are transformed into OWL-S ServiceModel and the result is returned to the requester.

This approach allows exploitation of Web services in a MAS, which is expected to be distributed over the Internet. The usage of agent technologies allows us to take advantage of agent communication languages, which are well-suited for delivering semantic information. Additional agent techniques could be used as means for controlling access to Web services and other resources that agents possess.

The rest of the article is structured as follows. In Section 2 we briefly introduce our method for (distributed) composition of Web services. Section 3 describes how we are going to use Chord P2P network in our application. The architecture of our MAS is presented in Section 4. Section 5 demonstrates the usage of our system, while our composition method is evaluated in Section 6. The latter section discusses in which cases the usage of P2P is justified in our MAS. Section 7 reviews related work and Section 8 concludes the paper and discusses further research.

2   Distributed Composition of Semantic Web Services

Recently Rao et al [13] presented a Semantic Web service composition process, which applies linear logic (LL) [14] for Semantic Web service representation and LL theorem proving for Semantic Web service composition. They also described mappings from DAML-S language to LL and from a LL proof to BPEL. This formal framework has been applied in a distributed way [11] in a mediator-based MAS with multiple mediators. The general topology of the previously proposed architecture is depicted in Figure 2, where agoras represent mediators with extended capabilities.

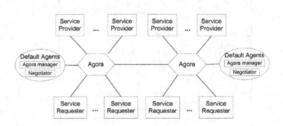

Fig. 2. Agora agent architecture

However, the paper [11] does not explain how Web service provider agents select mediators where to register themselves and how new mediator agents are selected and organised. In this paper we extend the former framework and show how new mediators are selected and organised in P2P manner. We also show that P2P approach gives greater scalability of the system with many nodes compared to a manual approach of setting up mediators.

In order to understand better how we represent Semantic Web services, agents' goals, and how service composition works, let us consider a scenario, where we have two agents—a traveller ($\mathcal{T}$) and a flight company ($\mathcal{F}$). Let S, G and Γ denote respectively available resources, goals and capabilities (Semantic Web services) of agents. Available resources and goals represent respectively the inputs and outputs of a (composite) Web service, which is required by an agent.

The goal of $\mathcal{T}$ is to make a booking (*Booking*) for a specific itinerary. Initially $\mathcal{T}$ knows only its starting (*From*) and final (*To*) location. Additionally the agent has

2 local Web services running, *findSchedule* and *getPassword*, for finding a schedule (*Schedule*) for a journey and retrieving a password (*Password*) from its internal database for a particular Web site (*Site*).

From the overall set of LL operations, the following example contains multiplicative conjunction ($\otimes$), linear implication ($\multimap$) and "of course" operator (!). In terms of resource acquisition the logical expression $\vdash A \otimes B \multimap C \otimes D$ means that resources C and D are obtainable only if both A and B are available. If the implication is applied, A and B are consumed and C and D are produced. Formula $!C$ means that the usage of resource C is unbounded.

Goals, resources and capabilities of agent $\mathcal{T}$ are described in LL with the following formulae.

$$G_\mathcal{T} = \{Booking\}, S_\mathcal{T} = \{From \otimes To\},$$

$$\Gamma_\mathcal{T} = \begin{array}{l} \vdash From \otimes To \multimap_{findSchedule} Schedule, \\ \vdash Site \multimap_{getPassword} Password. \end{array}$$

For booking tickets, traveller agent $\mathcal{T}$ should contact an airline company. The airline company $\mathcal{F}$ does not have any explicit declarative goals (that is common for companies, whose information systems are mainly based on business process models). The only fact that $\mathcal{F}$ exposes, is the company Web site (*Site*). Since the fact is unbounded it can be delivered to customers any number of times (this is denoted by ! in the example).

Agent $\mathcal{F}$ has 2 local Web services running—*bookFlight* for booking a flight, and *login* for identifying customers and creating secure channels for information transfer. We assume that a customer has created a personal profile at the airline company including customer's credit card information. Therefore the customer does not have to provide this information explicitly. Goals, resources and capabilities of the airline company $\mathcal{F}$ are described in LL with the following formulae.

$$G_\mathcal{F} = \{1\}, S_\mathcal{F} = \{!Site\},$$

$$\Gamma_\mathcal{F} = \begin{array}{l} \vdash SecureChannel \otimes Schedule \multimap_{bookFlight} Booking, \\ \vdash Password \multimap_{login} SecureChannel. \end{array}$$

In the preceding we used linear logic (LL) to encode the capabilities of agents. LL is a refinement of classical logic introduced by J.-Y. Girard to provide means for keeping track of "resources". In LL two assumptions of a propositional constant A are distinguished from a single assumption of A. This does not apply in classical logic, since there the truth value of a fact does not depend on the number of copies of the fact. Indeed, LL is not about truth, it is about computation.

3   P2P Network Layer

Since we assumed that in our application we can map each resource to an integer key, we chose to take advantage of a structured P2P network, namely Chord [15]. Structured

P2P systems provide scalable resource-location mechanism compared to non-structured networks, where the network is flooded with messages in order to locate resources.

Generally, the Chord protocol consist of a consistent hashing function to provide unique key assignments for each node/object in the network. With the key's value each node can determine its logical position in the system. In Chord the logical position of a node is a point in a circular key space. For example, Figure 3 presents an instance of a Chord network topology for a key space with length 32. Black dots represent nodes in the network and white dots represent keys that are not used.

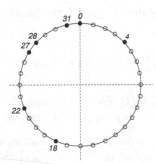

Fig. 3. A Chord network example

In order to maintain the ring structure of the network, each node constantly updates its predecessor and successor nodes in the network. These are the nodes which immediately precede or succeed, respectively, a node in the circular key space. As long as predecessors and successors of all nodes are updated, nodes are guaranteed to be found in the network. Thus if one node has to locate a peer holding a particular key, a message could be sent either to its successors or predecessors in the circular key space until it reaches the correct location. This process is made more efficient by using routing tables, which allow to bypass many nodes at once when forwarding a message to its destination.

Each node in the network maintains its personal routing table with N records for 2^N key space. Each record points to a successor of a key, which is at distance of 2^i, $i = 0 \ldots N - 1$ from the key, which identifies the node. A routing table of node 27 of Chord network in Figure 3 is represented for example in Table 1. Now, if peer with key 27 wants to deliver a message to the peer with key 22, then according to this routing table the message would be sent initially to a peer with key 18 (the peer with a closest preceding key to 22) and the peer with key 18 would forward the message further.

In order to apply Chord network and its object location mechanism for Semantic Web service composition, we have to implement a mapping from objects to indices. In this article we consider objects to be the names of inputs and outputs of Semantic Web services. Additionally we assume that agents share the same ontology. Thus we can just apply a hash function from an object name to an integer key such that the objects with the same intended meaning would have the same key.

However, in large P2P networks different agents tend to use different ontologies. Therefore we recognise the need for a function, which would transform concepts from

Table 1. Routing table of node 27 in Figure 3

Index	Key	Node
1	$27 + 2^0 = 28$	28
2	$27 + 2^1 = 29$	31
3	$27 + 2^2 = 31$	31
4	$27 + 2^3 = 3$	4
5	$27 + 2^4 = 11$	18

different ontologies, but with the same meaning, to the same key or to similar keys. One way to overcome this problem might be to annotate all concepts with sets of keywords. Then *Latent Semantic Indexing* or some other information retrieval algorithm [16] could be applied for computing a unique value to a particular set of keys.

Alternatively, if objects have been annotated with keywords, Hilbert space filling curves (SFC) could be applied for mapping an n-dimensional keyword space to 1-dimensional hash value space. This approach has been used by Schmidt and Parashar [17] for locating Web services at Chord P2P network. Unfortunately we could not apply their results directly in our system, since Schmidt and Parashar described Web service *classification* with keywords, while we need to annotate the *inputs* and *outputs* of Web services.

4 The MAS Architecture

Our MAS architecture is designed as a layer on top of Chord P2P network. While P2P handles issues related to indexing and efficient location of resources, agents initiate these actions in P2P networks. In our case agents use the P2P network for discovering other agents, whose Web service descriptions include particular literals (names of inputs and outputs). Thus our MAS could be seen as an application layer of a P2P network, whereas P2P network is just another medium for MAS.

In order to facilitate efficient location of related agents, one agent per each literal is designated to mediate access to other agents interested in particular literals. Since an agent specification usually includes more than one literal, a single agent may mediate several keys. When an agent joins the network, it first determines whether there are already agents mediating some of its keys. If there is no mediator for particular keys, the agent joins the network as a mediator for these keys. In the case there exists a key mediator, the agent registers itself at the particular mediator. Mediators are organised according to Chord algorithm.

A mediator could be seen as a kind of superpeer, which facilitates communication between agents sharing a particular key. In order to apply Chord P2P network for our purposes, literals in Web service specifications are transformed into integer keys, where a key is the result of the mapping from a literal (concept name). An instance of our network topology is presented graphically in Figure 4. The inner circle there represents mediators in the Chord network while auxiliary nodes represent mediated agents.

If an agent has to send a task to other agents, then literals in the task are identified, transformed to keys and the task would be delivered to mediators taking care of

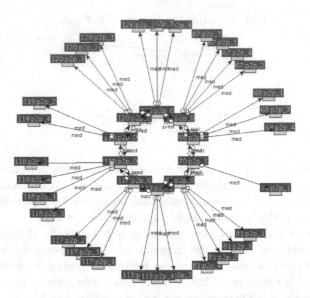

Fig. 4. Example P2P network topology

particular keys. Then these mediators shall multicast the message to agents, which are registered at these mediators. If the mediated agents would like to deliver a message to other mediators, then they first send a message to their mediator and this mediator shall forward the message to other mediators. If an agent has registered itself at several mediators, then the messages would be sent to the most preceding mediator of a particular key. In this case multicast is implemented on top of a P2P network. If a mediator considers leaving the system, then it delegates its tasks to one of the agents which is registered at this mediator. However, if a mediator does not have any agents registered at itself, then the key disappears from the network.

Since the network of agents and the set of literals is constantly evolving, we would not be able to manually set up mediators, unless we would designate a single agent for mediating all others. The manual approach could work in small or static systems but not in large and dynamic ones.

One disadvantage of P2P networks is that extra efforts are needed to keep them stable and consistent. A Chord network is defined to be stable if successors and predecessors of all nodes are correct. If a network is not stable, then it may break into clusters and there is no guarantee anymore that required resources will be located.

In order to keep the network stable, we would still like to preserve some degree of centralisation in future. Namely, we envisage that there are entities, which monitor the evolution of the network and try to detect and resolve anomalies. Anyway, indexing and search would be still organised in the distributed manner.

5   Elaboration of an Example

Let us consider again the agent/service specifications from Section 2. The specifications of agents T and F form a domain, which consists of 7 literals—*From, To,*

SecureChannel, *Booking*, *Schedule*, *Site* and *Password*. The 4 last literals are shared by both agents. This means that they shall compete for the right to mediate these literals.

Let us assume that these 7 literals are mapped to keys 0, 4, 18, 22, 27, 28 and 31, respectively. To demonstrate the interaction between agent- and P2P-related concepts we additionally assume that agent $\mathcal{T}$ would mediate keys 0, 4, 22 and 28, while $\mathcal{F}$ would mediate 18, 27 and 31. This configuration is summarised in Table 2.

Table 2. Keys and mediators of literals

Literal	Key	Mediator
From	0	$\mathcal{T}$
To	4	$\mathcal{T}$
SecureChannel	18	$\mathcal{F}$
Booking	22	$\mathcal{T}$
Schedule	27	$\mathcal{F}$
Site	28	$\mathcal{T}$
Password	31	$\mathcal{F}$

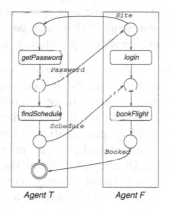

Fig. 5. The composite Web service

Given its specification, agent $\mathcal{T}$ derives and sends out the following task (see [11] for how this and the following tasks were derived):

$$Schedule \vdash Booking.$$

This task would be sent to mediators of literals *Schedule* and *Booking*, which are Chord nodes 27 and 22. These mediators would start solving the task and also multicast the task to registered agents. Since we have currently only 2 agents in the network, then the message would be sent only to agent $\mathcal{F}$.

Agent $\mathcal{F}$ merges the task with its current state $!Site \vdash 1$ and as a result achieves task $!Site \otimes Schedule \vdash Booking$. Since $\mathcal{F}$ cannot satisfy the proposal, it derives a new task and forwards it to agent $\mathcal{T}$:

Site ⊢ Password.

Agent T deduces the task further and constructs the final composite Web service. Thereby T produces, with help of $\mathcal{F}$, a composite service, whose execution achieves the goal of agent T. The resulted composite service is graphically represented in Figure 5. The service composition is finally translated to a process description languages like OWL-S process model or BPEL4WS. The exact translation process is described in [13].

6   Empirical and Analytical Evaluation

In order to evaluate our architecture and the CPS method, we chose to measure the number of messages, which were sent by agents until all agents solved their problems (each agent had to compose a Web service). We considered 4 different methods for message distribution:

1. multicast—each agent delivers its messages through a mediator to agents, whose domain includes any of the literals in a derived partial solution
2. broadcast—each agent deliveres its messages to all other agents in the system
3. simple P2P—before delivering each message, the mediators of potentially interested agents are located and then the message is delivered to them
4. P2P with caching—the same as simple P2P with the only difference that the location of each mediator is discovered only once per runtime and is cached for further use

While data for multicast and broadcast was acquired through experiments, the results for the P2P versions are estimated analytically. For analytical evaluation we assumed that our P2P architecture performs equally with the mediator-based agent architecture with a difference that extra messages should be sent to discover particular mediators. Additionally we assumed that our key space is 1024 to accommodate 1000 concepts. This implies that in order to discover a mediator, generally $log_2 1024 = 10$ messages should be sent in Chord network. Therefore, to evaluate the maximum cost of P2P, we multiplied the number of messages, exchanged during multicast, by 10. However, if we assume that each peer applies caching, then we could use a function $max(N*A+m, p)$ to evaluate the message burden. N, A, m, p in the formula represent respectively the numbers of concepts, agents, multicast messages and worst case P2P communication messages sent. This function reflects that in the worst case each peer has to discover and cache the locations of all keys/concepts in the systems. We do not consider the number of stabilisation messages, while evaluating the cost of using P2P.

Experiments with multicast and broadcast were performed with 10, 20, 50 and 100 agents. With each set of agents the same set of service and task specifications was used with both broadcast and multicast. We ran each experiment with each set of agents 5 times. The overall domain, where the names of services' inputs and outputs were randomly selected, consisted of 1000 concepts. We made experiments with 2 configurations:

1. each agent published 4 Web services, a required composite Web service consisted of at least 3 Web services
2. each agent published 5 Web services, a required composite Web service consisted of at least 5 Web services

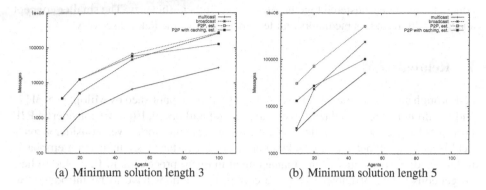

(a) Minimum solution length 3   (b) Minimum solution length 5

Fig. 6. Messages sent during problem solving

The results of configuration 1 and 2 are respectively summarised in Figure 6(a) and Figure 6(b). Both figures show how many messages in average were sent during problem solving, before all agents found their solutions. Figure 7 demonstrates the exponential complexity of the problem solving methodology (with 10 agents), which is bound to the complexity of LL. Although there exist logics with polynomial complexity [18] for solving the similar problem, their expressive power is far behind LL.

Figure 6(a) and Figure 6(b) show clearly that with few agents in a network (less than 50 in Figure 6(a)) broadcast is generally better than P2P topology. However, if the number of agents and services increases, P2P with caching becomes a better choice than broadcast. Moreover, both figures show a tendency that while the number of agents and services grows in the network, the difference between P2P with caching and multicast becomes proportionally smaller. Therefore we conclude that if the number of concepts in the network is constant and the number of peers approaches infinity, P2P is almost as good as multicast, if we do not consider the number of messages sent during Chord stabilisation procedure. Anyway, the assumption that the number of concepts is fixed and the number of agents grows, could be interpreted as that in small networks several

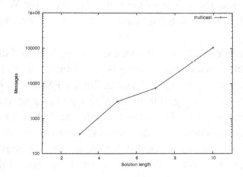

Fig. 7. Problem solving complexity

concepts should be clustered together to achieve higher efficiency. The smaller concept space would mean less mediators and less messages for mediator discovery.

7   Related Work

A thorough analysis of major P2P technologies has been published by Milojicic et al [7] and would not be reviewed here. Anyway, several authors [9, 10] have considered P2P networks for Web service applications. Additionally some works even consider semantical issues in P2P networks. Broekstra et al [5], for instance, set their main emphasis to knowledge representation and management in query processing in P2P. Due to heterogeneous nature of knowledge there certain conventions have to be introduced to semantic reasoning process.

Crespo and Garcia-Molina [6] consider the construction of semantic overlay networks for P2P systems. Their contribution is a method for automatic clustering of P2P networks to semantic overlay networks according to agent properties given by the semantics of their content. A peer may belong to several overlay networks if it encapsulates data with different semantics. Such a clustering allows query routing according to its content. Since the message is sent directly to affected parties, the number of messages for resource location is significantly decreased.

Bawa et al [4] propose a P2P network topology, where the network is clustered into segments by topics. In this case short distance links connect peers sharing the same topic, while long distance links connect peers at different segments. For each topic a centroid is constructed, which represents a centerpoint for a topic. In our network a centroid is represented with a literal. Thus each literal in the system represents a centroid. Peers may be connected to several centroids simultaneously. Thus although we apply Chord [15] ideology and protocols for managing our P2P network, we have a subnetwork for each literal. Each peer may have several identification codes—one for each subnetwork.

Verma et al [19] consider a P2P infrastructure for publishing and discovering semantically enriched descriptions of Web services. Anyway, they still use UDDI mechanism for publishing Web services, whereas UDDI structures are used for storing semantic information about inputs and outputs of Web services similarly to Paolucci et al [20]. Our approach allows to bypass the usage of centralised servers for Web service discovery though we do not neglect their possible usage, if they could provide semantic content as well.

Paolucci et al [12] implement a P2P service discovery mechanism through the usage of Gnutella P2P network. Discovery process is based on reasoning over DAML-S descriptions of Web services. Java Expert System Shell (JESS) is applied as a DAML-S inference mechanism and is engaged to determine whether a service satisfies a query. The approach is suitable in cases where atomic Semantic Web services are known *a priori* and semantically equivalent or similar services have to be discovered. Anyway, during automated composition it is not known, which atomic services would be included in the a resulting composite service. Thus their approach is not particularly suitable for automated composition as we consider it here.

Arpinar et al [8] apply similarily to us automated Web service composition over a P2P network. In their P2P architecture peers are organised into communities such that each community involves peers, which represent the same domain. DAML-S is used for describing Web services and queries (composite Web service interfaces). The major difference between our ideology and the one presented by Arpinar et al is that they try to determine links between Web services at publishing time, while we do it at composition time. While our approach is more flexible and suits better to highly dynamic networks with a moderate amount of queries, their approach is definitely more suitable for more stable networks with massive amounts of queries. Anyway, their method does not consider the non-monotonicity of Web services, which is handled by our methodology.

Finally, research on symbolic reasoning over P2P has been considered by Adjiman et al [3], who implemented a P2P network for distributed theorem proving over propositional classical logic clauses. The underlaying network is based on *small world* topology, where each peer has a list of other peers, who share the same literals (parts of a theory) as the agent does.

8 Conclusions and Future Work

In this paper we described an implementation of a MAS for distributed composition of Semantic Web services. The MAS applies P2P networking for reorganising and configuring its mediators. The main purpose of the mediators is to group agents which share a part of a domain. From service composition point of view these are agents, whose services' inputs or outputs include a common object (literal at the formalisation level). If agents have been gathered in such a way, their location over a distributed system is more efficient and reliable than in nonstructured distributed systems.

Although our system can function without the P2P architecture, we believe that P2P would give some added value to our MAS, especially when it comes to balancing message load between agents. In fact, our empirical/analytical results show that in a system with an increasing number of Semantic Web services and agents, our P2P approach would mean almost the same message load as a system with mediator-based multicast. However, with P2P architecture message load between agents is balanced more evenly compared to a system with multicast, where all messages are routed through a central mediator. Additionally, the usage of P2P would eliminate the central point of failure in the whole system.

In order to facilitate semantic reasoning during the composition process, we would like to design a function, which would map objects with the similar meaning to a similar integer key. This would allow us to be sure that the objects/concepts with the same meaning are in the same neighborhood. One possible solution has been proposed by Tang et al [21] who consider semantics in P2P systems. They adopt Latent Semantic Indexing (LSI) for information retrieval in Content-Addressable Networks (CAN). The semantics of a document is described with a set of keywords.

Currently we are considering options for mapping the entire structure of LL formulae to P2P networks instead of inputs and outputs only. Such a method would obviously allow us to exploit richer structural semantics of Web services already at P2P level. Another thread of our current research is devoted to meaning negotiation between agents.

Given the heterogeneity of ontologies in agent systems, meaning negotiation would provide means for mapping ontologies on the fly during agent interaction.

Acknowledgements

This work was partially supported by the Norwegian Research Foundation in the framework of Information and Communication Technology (IKT-2010) program—the ADIS project. The authors would like to thank the anonymous referees for their comments.

References

1. McIlraith, S., Son, T.C.: Adapting Golog for composition of Semantic Web services. In: Proceedings of the Eighth International Conference on Knowledge Representation and Reasoning (KR2002), Toulouse, France, April 22–25, 2002, Morgan Kaufmann (2002) 482–493
2. Wu, D., Parsia, B., Sirin, E., Hendler, J., Nau, D.: Automating DAML-S Web Services composition using SHOP2. In: Proceedings of the 2nd International Semantic Web Conference, ISWC 2003, Sanibel Island, Florida, USA, October 20–23, 2003. (2003)
3. Adjiman, P., Chatalic, P., Goasdoué, F., Rousset, M.C., Simon, L.: Distributed reasoning in a peer-to-peer setting. Technical report, LRI, Université Paris Sud, France (2004)
4. Bawa, M., Manku, G.S., Raghavan, P.: SETS: Search enhanced by topic segmentation. In: Proceedings of 26th Annual International ACM SIGIR Conference (SIGIR 2003), Toronto, Canada, July 28–August 1, 2003, ACM Press (2003) 306–313
5. Broekstra, J., Ehrig, M., Haase, P., van Harmelen, F., Kampman, A., Sabou, M., Siebes, R., Staab, S., Stuckenschmidt, H., Tempich, C.: A metadata model for semantics-based peer-to-peer systems. In: Proceedings of the WWW'03 Workshop on Semantics in Peer-to-Peer and Grid Computing. Budapest, Hungary, May 20, 2003. (2003)
6. Crespo, A., Garcia-Molina, H.: Semantic overlay networks for P2P systems. Technical report, Department of Computer Science, Yale University (2002)
7. Milojicic, D.S., Kalogeraki, V., Lukose, R., Nagaraja, K., Pruyne, J., Richard, B., Rollins, S., Xu, Z.: Peer-to-peer computing. Technical Report HPL-2002-57, Hewlett-Packard (2002)
8. Arpinar, I.B., Aleman-Meza, B., Zhang, R., Maduko, A.: Ontology-driven web services composition platform. In: Proceedings of IEEE International Conference on E-Commerce Technology, CEC'04, San Diego, California, USA, July 6–9, 2004, IEEE Press (2004) 146–152
9. Benatallah, B., Dumas, M., Sheng, Q.Z., Ngu, A.H.H.: Declarative composition and peer-to-peer provisioning of dynamic Web services. In: Proceedings of the 18th International IEEE Conference on Data Engineering, ICDE'02, San Jose, USA, February 2002. (2002) 297–308
10. Ermolayev, V., Keberle, N., Kononenko, O., Plaksin, S., Terziyan, V.: Towards a framework for agent-enabled Semantic Web service composition. International Journal of Web Services Research 1 (2004) 63–87
11. Küngas, P., Rao, J., Matskin, M.: Symbolic agent negotiation for semantic web service exploitation. In: Proceedings of the Fifth International Conference on Web-Age Information Management, WAIM'2004, Dalian, China, July 15-17, 2004. Volume 3129 of Lecture Notes in Computer Science., Springer-Verlag (2004) 458–467
12. Paolucci, M., Sycara, K., Nishimura, T., Srinivasan, N.: Using DAML-S for P2P discovery. In: Proceedings of the First International Conference on Web Services, ICWS'03, Las Vegas, Nevada, USA, June 23–26, 2003, CSREA Press (2003) 203–207

13. Rao, J., Küngas, P., Matskin, M.: Logic-based Web services composition: From service description to process model. In: Proceedings of the Second International Conference on Web Services (ICWS 2004), San Diego, California, USA, July 6–9, 2004. (2004) 446–453
14. Girard, J.Y.: Linear logic. Theoretical Computer Science **50** (1987) 1–102
15. Stoica, I., Morris, R., Karger, D., Kaashoek, M.F., Balakrishnan, H.: Chord: A scalable peer-to-peer lookup service for internet applications. In: Proceedings of ACM SIGCOMM 2001, San Diego, California, USA, August 27–31, 2001, ACM Press (2001) 149–160
16. Raghavan, P.: Information retrieval algorithms: A survey. In: Proceedings of the Eighth Annual ACM-SIAM Symposium on Discrete Algorithms, New Orleans, Louisiana, United States, January 5–7, 1997, SIAM (1997) 11–18
17. Schmidt, C., Parashar, M.: A peer-to-peer approach to Web service discovery. World Wide Web Journal **7** (2004) 211–229
18. Lämmermann, S.: Runtime Service Composition via Logic-Based Program Synthesis. PhD thesis, Department of Microelectronics and Information Technology, Royal Institute of Technology, Stockholm (2002)
19. Verma, K., Sivashanmugam, K., Sheth, A., Patil, A., Oundhakar, S., Miller, J.: METEORS WSDI: A scalable P2P infrastructure of registries for semantic publication and discovery of Web services. Journal of Information Technology and Management (2004) To appear.
20. Paolucci, M., Kawamura, T., Payne, T.R., Sycara, K.: Importing the Semantic Web in UDDI. In: Proceedings of the CAiSE 2002 International Workshop on Web Services, E-Business, and the Semantic Web, WES 2002, Toronto, Canada, May 27-28, 2002, Revised Papers. Volume 2512 of Lecture Notes in Computer Science. Springer-Verlag (2002) 225–236
21. Tang, C., Xu, Z., Dwarkadas, S.: Peer-to-peer information retrieval using self-organizing semantic overlay networks. In: Proceedings of ACM SIGCOMM'03, Karlsruhe, Germany, August 25–29, 2003, ACM Press (2003) 175–186

A Low-Latency Peer-to-Peer Approach for Massively Multiplayer Games

Jin Zhou[1], Li Tang[1], Kai Li[1], Hao Wang[1], and Zhizhi Zhou[2]

[1] University of Tsinghua, Beijing, China
{zhoujin00, tangli03, li-k02, wanghao02}@mails.tsinghua.edu.cn
[2] Renmin University of China, Beijing, China
zhouzz@ruc.edu.cn

Abstract. This paper focuses on the latency reduction problem in massively multiplayer games (MMGs). As the client-server (CS) architecture in use today in most commercial MMGs applications are exposing its weakness in scalability as the number of players increases, researchers start to consider the peer-to-peer (P2P) model that has inherent high scalability for MMGs. However, existing P2P models generally lead to high latency that significantly detracts from the playing experience. To improve this, we present a novel communication model intended to reduce the latency of network communication on game states. The model, based on DHT protocol, can select the best candidate node to perform server's role for a game zone. In contrast, existing P2P models designate 'peer servers' randomly without considering latency effects. The simulation shows that our approach obtains much lower latency than existing P2P models. The performance of our approach is shown to be even better than that of CS models.

Keywords: MMGs, P2P, Low latency, DHT, Smart manager.

1 Introduction

Developing *massively multiplayer games* (MMGs) is much harder than traditional PC games because of the requirement of network programming and certain cross-session infrastructures for managing and maintaining the game communities. Besides, to avoid losses caused by service- stoppage, service providers have to add and update many servers to cope with increasing players. As a result, only few companies can afford the cost of establishing, maintaining and updating a large number of servers and telecom service. The peer-to-peer (P2P) approach has been considered to be a possible solution to reduce such costs by using the spare resources (i.e. CPU, memory, bandwidth) on clients.

The latency in network communication seriously hampers the P2P approach's ability to achieve high scalability for MMGs: There is usually a high frequency of communications in MMGs. This paper presents a novel P2P approach which is capable for communicating with low latency; the latency is shown to be lower than that of the client-server model. The approach has the potential of reaching optimal latency by selecting peer servers for game zones.

Z. Despotovic, S. Joseph, and C. Sartori (Eds.): AP2PC 2005, LNAI 4118, pp. 120–131, 2006.

2   Related Work

Existing communication architectures for MMGs can be conceptually summarized into the following four categories:

2.1   Client-Server Model

In *client-server model*, each client sends game events to a central server, and then the server sends updated game states to the related clients. The server's capacity needs to correspond to the player numbers; insufficient server capacity detracts from the game experience while too many servers waste resources. In addition, the fixed location and limited bandwidth of the servers also increase communication latency.

2.2   Fully-Connected Model

In a *fully-connected model* [1], every node stores a global latest game state. Any event caused by a node is broadcasted to all others. Supposing the number of players is N, the number of total messages needed for each event is $O(N^2)$. So this model may not scale well when N becomes large.

2.3   Hybrid Model

In MMGs, each node needs to obtain only the necessary game states relating to itself rather than the overall states. Therefore the game world may be divided into several autonomous zones according to the game rules. In *hybrid model* [1], players are grouped according to the zones. Group members communicate with each other the same way described above in the fully-connected model, while the communication between different zones is realized by means of multicast. This model improves scalability to some extent, but how to optimize the grouping algorithm still remains a difficult problem. However, over-grouping leads to much inter-zone communication while under-grouping results in heavy intra-zone communication.

2.4   DHT-Based Peer-to-Peer Model

Current P2P models used in MMGs [2], which obtains routing efficiency by means of *distributed hash tables* (DHT), convert the data search into a key lookup problem. They designate the management privilege of the zone data to a randomly selected node, called coordinator, to take charge of recording TCP/IP addresses of the zone members, storing or modifying the game states in the zone, receiving queries and broadcasting updated states. We name such an approach the *random manager* (RM) model. The coordinator in RM has to organize the zone members and manage zone data simultaneously. Since the selection of the coordinator has no consideration of communication latency, the latency between the coordinator and the zone members may be very high.

At the present, the CS model is the most popular, while the structured DHT model of P2P has the highest potential of further development due to its scalability and availability. We propose a novel DHT-based P2P model using the 'Smart Manager' to achieve low latency that can be shown to be consistently better than that of the CS model.

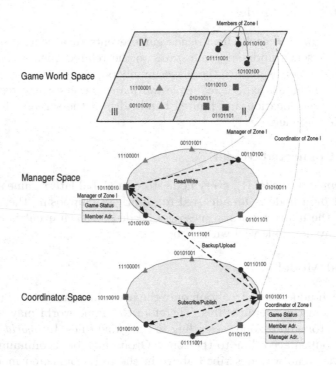

Fig. 1. Role spaces of smart manager model

3   Smart Manager

3.1   Main Idea

The essential difficulty in optimizing the selection of the coordinator in RM comes from its random identification mechanism that ignores and conceals the actual topology of the physical networks. The nodes are never able to discover the network distance between each other unless using probe message that may require significant extra bandwidth.

We propose a novel model, *Smart Manger* (SM), to solve the latency problem of the RM model (Fig.1). Compared with having only one coordinator to take charge of managing the zone work in RM model, two roles in the SM model, named as manager and coordinator respectively, cooperate to carry out such mission. The coordinator is responsible for organizing zone members, while the manager holds the zone data and only itself has the modification privilege. To read or modify the zone data, members in a certain zone must request the manager to carry out the actions for them. Such mechanisms guarantee the consistency of global game states and correct order of communication messages. The procedures of selecting manager and coordinator of a zone are independent with each other. Similar to the RM model, the coordinator in the SM model is also designated randomly. However, the manager is selected by the coordinator of the same zone, with the principle that the maximal latency between the zone manager and other zone members should be minimal. As the instance shown in Fig.1, members of zone I in game world space, say 00110100, 01111001 and 10100100, find out the zone coordinator using DHT protocol in coordinator space first, say 01010011, to get the address of the zone manager, say 10110010 in manager space; and then communicate with the manager directly for sending requests and receiving updates.

3.2   Location-Based Node Identifier Assignment

To select the manager with the consideration of reducing latency, the SM model needs to transform the identifier (ID) of each node to its network location and vice versa. Our previous work LENS (Locality-Embedded Naming Strategy) [3], in which the ID of a node reflects its network location, is a solution for this requirement.

The LENS embeds the locality information into the node ID to keep the neighborhood of locality in the ID space. That is, if two nodes are near in the network, their IDs are adjacent as well. LENS is lightweight and does not require the nodes to store the global location information all the time. Instead, it computes it at runtime immediately.

LENS benefits from an ability of Global Network Positioning (GNP) [4] to predict round-tip times to other host nodes without having to contact them first. GNP assigns synthetic coordinates in D-dimension *hypercube* to nodes such that the distance between the coordinates of two nodes accurately predicts the communication latency between the nodes. To compute the coordinate, each node is required to offer its network distance to some landmark nodes by sending ping/pong messages.

Each dimension of the hypercube is divided into 2^k equal parts, and the hypercube will be totally divided into 2^{kD} parts, named as *grid*. Then we traverse all the grids with Hilbert curve with Moore version which is one kind of Discrete Space Filling Curve (DSFC) [5].

An important characteristic of DSFC is to maintain the relative locations of the points, that is, if the points are near multi-dimensional space, they remain near in one dimensional space [6]. We identify the passed grids with $0 \sim 2^{kD}$ (binary format) in turn along the Hilbert curve. Fig.2 gives an example of the identifying procedure of Hilbert curve in two-dimensional hypercube, where $k = 2$.

Each node takes the ID of the grid where it is located as the prefix of the node ID and takes a random value as the suffix which is generated with a hash function to assure the uniqueness of the node ID.

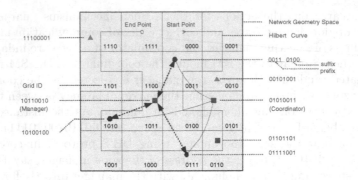

Fig. 2. Identifying nodes based on grids of network geometry space

3.3 Model Design

On MMGs, nodes do not have to share all global states. Therefore, we divide the whole global states into several zones and make each zone governed by some nodes. The zone's boundary is defined by the game program.

Along with the concept of zones, we introduce three roles of the node: zone member, zone coordinator and zone manager. Each node may play one or more such roles.

Zone Member. Zone member is one of the nodes intending to read or modify the states of the specific zone. To read or modify the global states of some zone, the node must become a zone member first, for which it may seek out the coordinator of the destined zone on the DHT overlay, send it joining-request message and wait for its authorization.

Zone Coordinator. Zone coordinator is the node in charge of organizing the zone member nodes. The SM model selects the zone coordinator randomly as shown in Fig.1. The SM model maps some character of the zone to a key, and uses DHT to find the nearest node to the key to act as the zone coordinator. The coordinator node is responsible for recording the TCP/IP addresses of the members and the manager (described later), selecting the manager node for the zone, notifying the manager's address to the members, backing up data and temporarily playing the role of manager when the manager is vacant.

From the coordinator, zone members get the addresses of the manger in order to request reading or modifying states; on the other hand, the manger gets the addresses of the zone members in order to send them updated states.

Zone Manager. The zone manger is the node possessing the management privilege, such as storing/modifying the global states and sending update message to the zone members. Any MMG has the potential to define a criterion function to qualify the manager candidates, for example, requiring enough idle computing time or good reputation. According to specific criterion function, the most qualified node would be selected as the manager. Our SM model defines the criterion function to be the maximal latency between the manager and each of the zone members, called the zone latency, which should be minimized during the selection of the manager.

The key process of the SM model is selecting the zone manager by the zone coordinator. The coordinator will select what minimizes the criterion function out of the qualified nodes to be the manager. The criterion function of the SM model, the zone latency, can be depicted as follows:

$$L_{Net}(z, m) = \max_{i \in S(z)} \{D_{Net}(m, i)\} \tag{1}$$

where m stands for the manager, i stands for certain zone member, $S(z)$ stands for the member set of zone z, and the dual function D_{Net} stands for the communication latency between two nodes.

The manager is selected with the following steps:

1) The coordinator sends messages to all zone members to obtain their GNP coordinates.
2) The coordinator optimize the criterion function according to all the received GNP coordinates to figure out the coordinate m^* of the ideal manager.
3) The coordinator converts m^* to its corresponding key with a hash transformation, searches the key using DHT protocols, and designates the result to be the zone manager.

As the role in the game may frequently change its location in the game world, for example from one city to another, the coordinator has to periodically execute the manager-selection procedures so as to minimize the intra-zone communication latency.

The manager should download all data of the zone it manages from the coordinator immediately after it assumes the post. Then the manager's local copy becomes the standard game state of the zone. The zone members should require the manager to perform their read or modification demands. When a node enters a new zone, it will find the zone coordinator with the DHT protocol, request to join and get the address of the zone manager, and then create and maintain a direct communication connection to the manager until it quits that zone. The DHT protocol provides mechanisms for the zone members, the coordinator and the manager to communicate and find their demanded objects. The manager periodically backs up the game state data of the zone to the coordinator so as to avoid data loss. If the current manager drops out, the coordinator would temporarily take up the role of the manager until a new manager is selected.

It should be noted that in practice there may not be such an appropriate node whose coordinate is m^* exactly. Thus, the DHT protocol may need to approximate m^* with a candidate node as accurate as possible.

4   Simulation

The simulation measures the latency of the CS, RM and SM models under the same conditions. Here, the latency is defined as the network communication time without considering the processing time for computing and displaying.

4.1 Methodology

We assume all nodes have enough band width and computing ability. The zone managers can use multiple threads to communicate with several zone members in parallel, and the number of the threads does not affect latency.

Network Topology. We use GT-ITM [7] software to randomly construct an Internet-like virtual network. The simulation uses the Transit-Stub model because it most resembles the present Internet structure.

We simulate a network containing 9600 hosts. These hosts act as clients or servers in CS model, while as P2P nodes in the SM and RM models. Some of the hosts are randomly selected to construct different scale MMGs networks. The detailed configuration in the GT-ITM is given in Table1.

Table 1. Parameter Values

Symbol	Value	Meaning
T	1	Total number of transit domains
N_T	4	Average number of transit nodes per transit domain
K	3	Total number of stub domains
N_S	8	Average number of stub nodes per stub domain
L	1	Average number of LANs per stub domain
N_L	100	Average number of hosts per LAN
N_R	100	Total number of routing nodes
N_H	9600	Total number of hosts
E_{TT}	100ms	Latency between transit nodes
E_{TS}	20ms	Latency between stub node and transit node
E_{SS}	5ms	Latency between stub nodes
E_{SL}	1ms	Latency between stub node and LAN

Node ID. The nodes in the CS or RM model get their IDs by hash functions in a random way. While the SM model generates the nodes IDs with LENS that can embed the location information into the node ID.

Zone Arrangement and Node Distribution. The game space can be divided by grouping the nodes, each group corresponding to a zone. The number of groups can be calculated from the number of the nodes in the game space and the average size of the groups. Each node has to choose a group and join it to become a member of the corresponding zone.

In order to analyze the performance of the SM model deeply, we consider two different node distributions in the game world.

a) Location-independent distribution
   In this case, the nodes randomly choose their own group.
b) Location-dependent distribution
   Under this distribution, a node chooses the group based on its network address. It is common for the relationship of the players in real world to affect

their relationship in the game world. For example, players in the same net bar battle together in the same RPG game; students on campus play board&card in the same competition; and the multiplayer-online-community games bring more affiliation between the real world and the game world. So, it is spontaneous to group the near nodes into the same group in the locality dependent distribution. As shown later, the SM model has lower latency in both distributions than the CS and RM model, especially in the locality dependent distribution.

Assignment of Zone Coordinator and Zone Manager. In the CS model, the only central server plays double roles as the coordinator and manager for all zones. In the RM model, the zone coordinator is randomly assigned by the hash function, meanwhile it also acts as the manager role for the same zone. Zone coordinator in SM model is also randomly assigned by the hash function, but the zone manager is selected according to the latency metric mentioned in previous section.

Simulation Criterion. We define the zone latency as the maximal latency between the manager and each of the zone members, which is consistent with the latency criterion function defined in Eq.(1). We use the average zone latency of all zones to evaluate the CS, RM and SM models.

4.2 Procedure of Simulation Program

A detailed procedure for the simulation program is shown below. The procedure requires the parameters, such as communication model (CS/RM/SM), total of nodes and group scale to be preset.

1) Building the topological network with 9600 hosts by GT-ITM.
2) Computing the routing latency among each pair of hosts, with the assumption that the routing path between any two nodes has the lowest latency.
3) Defining the node number N and the group scale G, then randomly choosing N nodes from the hosts as system nodes.
4) Identifying the node ID for each specific model independently.
5) Grouping all the nodes in the game space.
6) Selecting the zone coordinator and manager for each model.
7) Computing the zone latency and storing the average latency for all zones.

Each experiment is run ten times with different random seeds, and the mean values are presented.

4.3 Results

Latency vs. System Scale. Table2 shows the average latency of the three models against different system scales under location-independent distribution with group scale being 2.

First, we can see an obvious reduction of the latency in the SM model, whose latency is respectively 60% and 80% of that of RM and CS model. In practice,

Table 2. Latency for Different System Scales

N	104	201	531	933	1977	4556
CS	140.6538	140.9801	141.7269	143.8853	144.7633	144.7452
RM	193.5385	189.6119	191.1394	196.7621	193.7891	191.6198
SM	116.3077	116.4229	119.2335	118.2401	118.1639	117.7259

the game server in the CS model is often located as near as possible to the backbone network to reduce the average latency. However, compared to SM, CS is limited to select only one node to act as the manager for all zones, which restricts the optimization. Meanwhile, SM is able to select the manager that is optimal for each specific zone, and the managers of different zones can be either the same or distinct. From the view point of GNP space, CS selects the exclusive manager in the whole node set, while SM is able to select respective managers in the center of each specific zone.

Second, Table2 indicates that increasing the number of nodes has little effect on the latency in all the three models. When we raise the node number from 104 to 4556, the latency rises only 2.91%, -0.99% and 1.22% respectively in the CS, RM, and SM model. That is because we assume that the latency is not affected by the requirement of computing and bandwidth. Actually, the increase of the node number will add the number of the parallel threads in the memory which may make the manager process requests of multiple threads in batch and increase the game latency. Note that game latency is different from network latency: the increase of game latency comes from the limited computing capacity that is unable to process the tasks of computing and networking at the same time. From the perspective of increasing the scalability of the computing capacity and bandwidth, the SM and RM model belonging to the P2P model have more potential than the CS model [8]. Detailed discussion of this, however, is out of the scope of this paper, for we primarily focus on the latency problem.

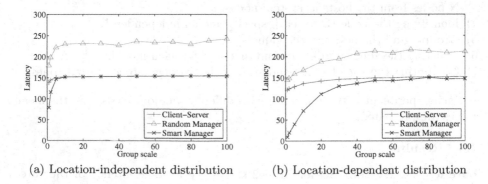

(a) Location-independent distribution   (b) Location-dependent distribution

Fig. 3. Latency as a function of group scale

Latency vs. Group Scale. Fig.3 shows the latency of the CS, RM and SM models with different group scales. In Fig.3, (a) and (b) respectively shows the results of location-independent distribution and the location-dependent distribution. There are 1008 nodes in Fig.3(a) and 1001 in Fig.3(b).

In Fig.3 we can find that the curves of the CS, RM and SM models have the same trend whether we use location dependent or independent distribution. Both the graphs indicate:

a) The average latency of the CS, RM and SM all increase as the increment of group scale. The rate of increase gradually slows down, and reaches a stable value when the number of groups becomes large.
b) With different group scales, the relationship of the latency of the three models is always the same, SM$\leq$CS$\leq$RM.
c) The curves of CS and SM approach approximately the same value as the group scale increases, and the two curves are always superior to the curve of RM.

Because the zone latency is the maximal latency between the manager and the members, adding new members to a zone will either increase or retain the zone latency. So it is reasonable for the zone latency to increase together with the group scale in general. When the group scale is small, the distribution of the members has a large effect on the latency, and each newly joined node will have significant effect on the distribution. When the groups scale increases, the distribution of zone members is analogous to the whole system. That is, the center of a large zone is very near the center of all the nodes in the game world. In this case, a newly joined node would change the zone latency slightly.

The three models are independent with the group scale. That is why the comparison result of the latency of the three models remains the same. And we have analyzed the reasons for the comparison result order in previous paragraphs. As we have presented above that the center of a large zone is very near to the center of the whole system, although the SM can select different manager for each zone, the best one may be the same as the server of CS model. That's why the latency curves of the SM and CS model become nearly identical at last.

Comparing Fig.3(a) with Fig.3(b), we can find that the differences mainly appear where the group scale is small. As the group scale increases, the latency curve of the location dependent distribution gradually rises up, while the latency curve of the location-independent distribution rises up steeply at the beginning and slows down afterwards. We can also explain this by comparing the distribution of the zone members and the nodes in the system. With the location-independent distribution, the zone members distribute randomly in network geometry space, no large group scale (e.g. 5 in Fig.3(a)) may make the zone members' distribution analogous to that of all the nodes of the whole system; for the other, the zone members are a group of nearby nodes in network geometry space, only large group scale (e.g. 50 in Fig.3(b)) can satisfy the distribution. Based on the mechanisms of CS, RM and SM, it is easy to find that the node distribution in the game world only has effects on SM. Because

SM takes advantage of the affiliation between the node distribution and game grouping, it becomes possible for it to achieve a much lower latency with the location-dependent distribution.

5   Conclusion

In summary, the SM model has the following features:

a) Scalability and reliability
   The SM model implements the P2P overlay with the DHT protocol that has seen rapidly progress in recent years. It provides high reliability and scalability.
b) Latency optimization
   The SM model assigns the work of organizing the zone members to the zone coordinators and let the zone manager maintain the zone data. The zone manager is selected by the zone coordinator based on the principle of minimizing the zone latency.
c) Consistency and time correctness
   The SM model uses the interest management approach. Only the manager possesses the privilege to modify the game ,eq:one states. All the outer requests for reading and modifying game states of the zone are performed by the manager so as to guarantees the consistency of the game states and correct order of messages.

These advantages and preliminary simulation results help demonstrate that the SM model is capable of achieving low latency for MMGs.

In future work, we will implement the SM model on a game platform named Freegame which is intended to provide a generic network platform using P2P technologies for board&card games and various desktop games, offering services of scoring, recording fee and chatting.

Acknowledgement

This work was supported by a research grant from NEC Laboratories China.

References

[1] Fiedler Stefan, Wallner Michael, and Weber Michael. A communication architecture for massive multiplayer games. In: Proceedings of the first workshop on Network and system support for games. ACM Press, 2002. 14-22
[2] Knutsson B., Lu H., Xu W. and Hopkins B. Peer-to-Peer Support for Massively Multiplayer Games. In: IEEE Infocom. 2004.
[3] ZHOU Jin, TANG Li, LI Kai, and ZHOU Zhizhi. Freegame: A Testbed for Peer-to-peer Techniques in Massive Multiplayer Online Games. ResearchReport-2004-11-1. 2004.

[4] Eugene Ng T. S. and Zhang Hui. Predicting Internet network distance with coordinates-based approaches. In: IEEE INFOCOM 2002. IEEE Press, 2002.
[5] H. Sagan. Space-filling curves. New York : Springer-Verlag, 1994.
[6] Gotsman C. and Lindenbaum M. On the Metric Properties of Discrete Space-Filling Curves. In: Proceeding of ICPR9'4. 1994.
[7] Zegura, E., Calvert, K. L., and Bhattacharjee, S. How to model an internetwork. In: Proceedings of the IEEE Infocom'96. IEEE Computer Society Press, 1996. 594-602
[8] Bauer Daniel, Iliadis Ilias, Rooney Sean and Scotton Paolo. Communication Architectures for Massive Multi-Player Games. Research Report. IBM Research, Zurich Research Laboratory, Switzerland. 2003.

An Agent-Based Collaborative Framework for Mobile P2P Applications

Mengqiu Wang, Heiko Wolf, Martin Purvis, and Maryam Purvis

University of Otago, Dunedin, New Zealand
{mwang, hwolf1, mpurvis, tehrany}@infoscience.otago.ac.nz

Abstract. The design of ad-hoc, wireless, peer-to-peer applications for small mobile devices raises a number of challenges for the developer, with object synchronisation, network failure, and device limitations being the most significant. In this paper, we introduce the FRAGme2004 framework for mobile P2P application development. To address data availability and stability problems, we have devised an agent-based fostering mechanism to protect applications against data losses in cases of peers dropping out. In contrast to most current literature, we focus on small scale P2P applications, especially gaming applications.

1 Introduction

Peer-to-peer computing architectures go beyond currently popular client-server architectures and stand to become the dominant form of distributed computing in the coming years. Typical P2P systems are characterized by decentralized control, scalability and robustness. Despite the popularity of Internet-based large scale P2P systems, smaller scale P2P applications that run on small, mobile devices are becoming increasingly popular as well [17]. The absence of centralized control and thus no single failure-point, extreme dynamism in structure, and full mobility and flexibility are all desired features in many application domains, which can be achieved via mutual exchange of information and services over ad-hoc, wireless, P2P networks. But challenging problems arise in the development of such applications [5], [14], [15]. Firstly, wireless, ad-hoc networks face problems such as stability, data integrity, routing, notification of joining and leaving peers, and in case of peer failure, fault tolerance. In such networks, the connections of the devices may be highly variable, as devices may hop from online to offline unpredictably, and thus affect reliability. Secondly, since the peers exist in a collaborative environment without central control, synchronisation of peers and the distribution of resources become significant issues. Thirdly, for the applications to run smoothly on the small devices we intend, efficient management of local computing resources is a necessity.

When developing new applications, these issues happen repeatedly, since there is no generic infrastructure which addresses all the aforementioned problems. In this paper we present the "FRAGme2004"[1] framework, which is designed

---

[1] FRAGme2004 stands for Framework for Realtime Ad-hoc Games micro edition 2004.

Z. Despotovic, S. Joseph, and C. Sartori (Eds.): AP2PC 2005, LNAI 4118, pp. 132–144, 2006.

for mobile P2P applications, and concentrate particularly on its agent-based mechanism supporting collaboration among peers, called the "peer fostering" mechanism.

2   Background

Milojicic *et al.* [16] provide a good review for P2P systems. An important topic in this domain is data availability. Cooper *et al.* [5] argue that "a complete system must ensure that important data remain preserved even if the creator or publisher leaves the system" (p.2), and they developed a reliable preservation service built on a P2P architecture, on top of which digital library applications could be built. Another strategy, the "dissemination tree", is used by Chen *et al.* [4] to reduce the number of replicas and the bandwidth needed for updates. Finally, Lin *et al.* [14] introduce a protocol to handle the loss and rebuilding of replicas. All those approaches are aimed at applications such as file sharing, where data loss and node failure can harm the performance, but not the overall functioning of the system. In contrast with their approaches, our concern is with small-scale P2P networks where every node failure can be a fatal threat to the functioning of the system.

There have been several earlier efforts to develop a framework for P2P applications. Akehurst *et al.* [1] and Kato *et al.* [13] have proposed frameworks which include group management and multicasting support to assist the design of complex applicactions. With respect to the domain of applications, even though most P2P applications have so far been restricted to file sharing or instant messaging, Gerke *et al.* [10] have introduced a framework that supports P2P services of any kind. In contrast with all these frameworks, FRAGme2004 aims at highly interactive small-scale P2P applications, such as gaming over wireless ad-hoc networks. In this domain of small scale and volatile wireless systems, there are challenges that have not been covered by previous research.

The use of agent technologies in P2P systems has been investigated by several researchers. Dasgupta [6], [7] proposed a P2P architecture in which mobile agents are used as peer mediators, replacing traditional message-based protocols to achieve higher efficiency, robustness, and scalability. Babaoglu *et al.* [2] designed and implemented the Anthill framework, which supports the design, implementation and evaluation of P2P applications based on agent concepts. In the P2P architecture proposed by Homayounfar *et al.* [11], peers are modelled as agents with some intelligence (e.g., calculating the success probability of data search in order to improve search efficiency) to enhance the capability and autonomy of peers. The agent-based fostering mechanism in FRAGme2004 has some similarities with the concepts in Homayounfar *et al.*'s work. Peers in a FRAGme2004 application are equipped with on-host service agents which are autonomous and have the intelligence to organize and reconstruct the collaboration relationship among peers. These collaboration relationships are crucial for data availability purposes, and will be discussed in Section 4.

3   The FRAGme2004 System

The FRAGme2004 framework is written in Java and represents a redesign and extension of earlier work by Nagel [18]. The framework has a three-layer architecture, in which layers communicate with each other through well-defined interfaces. The bottom layer is the Infrastructure Layer, which consists of the basic building blocks that address the communication requirements. A layer above the Infrastructure Layer is the Object Layer. An "object" is the smallest entity that is distributed among the peers. The information and data that must be shared in the applications is encapsulated into objects, and the agents associated with each peer take care of the delivery, synchronization and life-cycle management of objects. The top layer is the Application Layer.

The FRAGme2004 framework frees application developers from networking and resource management. This includes the establishment of the underlying network infrastructure, notification of joining and leaving peers, communication and object exchange. As a consequence, application developers can focus their attentions on the higher-level operation of the applications. To make applications run reliably at all times, the agents that take care of object synchronization and distribution also use a novel fostering mechanism that makes use of data redundancy to achieve overall integrity and robustness even in cases of node failure.

3.1   Infrastructure Layer

Currently, the communication layer of FRAGme2004 is based on the middleware architecture JGroups [12], which is used in a number of P2P projects to provide reliable multicasting. JGroups was chosen as a foundational infrastructure, because it provides reliable and standardized unicasting and multicasting, which frees us from having to reimplement those low level details. Although all P2P applications require efficient communication, it is especially true with complex applications such as games, which is a special concern for FRAGme2004. Unicasting (point to point communication), although used in many situations such as file sharing applications, does not suffice here. In circumstances where peers in a group share the same resource or need to be notified at the same time for synchronization purposes, multicasting is needed.

Two communication approaches for FRAGme2004 were originally tested, one based on simple Remote Method Invocation (RMI) unicasting and one based on multicasting, to determine the more efficient communication mechanism. We observed that multicasting is more efficient than RMI calls in group communications, a difference that is magnified with an increasing number of peers. Although RMI and JGroups are not totally comparable due to their different marshalling mechanisms, the performance differences can be partially attributed to the fact that in the case of RMI, a sender has to contact every other peer, one by one, in order to share information with his group; whereas in multicasting it only needs to send one message.

A further reason for using JGroups in our architecture is that it provides needed group management functions, for example, the creation and deletion of groups, the notification of change of membership (joined/left/crashed peers), etc. The value gained from group management support is significant: while group management appears to be simple, it conceals a number of low level details, such as the establishment of the network structure and communication channels and the identification for groups.

Another feature of JGroups is that it provides support, albeit limited, for guaranteed delivery. In wireless communication, virtually no routing protocols can provide one hundred percent guarantee of delivery success. But with some failure detection and retransmission mechanisms that are included in JGroups, we can be reasonably confident concerning the success of message delivery. Such a near guarantee is important in terms of object-level protocol design. It has allowed us to implement high level protocols (for example the interaction protocols used by agents in the Object Layer) with less overhead and therefore higher efficiency. One of the tradeoffs associated with such a "guarantee" of delivery is that the scalability of the P2P system is restricted. In order to maintain reasonable efficiency under this guaranteed delivery policy, the network is constrained to be tightly-coupled. But within the target application domain of FRAGme2004 (small-scale gaming applications), such a tradeoff is acceptable.

3.2   Object Layer

The Object Layer comprises functionalities for object sharing, exchange and synchronization of change. In case of peer failure, protection mechanisms are put in place to avoid data loss and the malfunctioning of other peers. To achieve this, several on-host service agents are created for each peer. Currently there are three kinds of agents that provide simple services in the framework: the object managing agent, the synchronizing agent and the fostering agent.

The object managing agent is in charge of the life-cycle management of any shared objects. When a new object(resource) is requested from the application layer, the object managing agent will locate the appropriate factory for creating instances of this object. It will gather all the required information for creating such an object, issue commands to the factory for creating the object, and return the object to the application layer. The object managing agent will also notify the synchronizing agent that a new object has been created, and the synchronizing agent will distribute the object to other peers. Upon receiving signals from the application layer indicating that an object is not used anymore, the object managing agent is responsible for checking the memory status. Depending on the amount of free memory available, it makes decisions concerning whether to cache the object for future use (by returning it to the factory) or to garbage collect it. Once objects are created and handed back to the application layer, changes may be invoked on these objects, both locally and remotely. In FRAGme2004, objects are assigned ownership, and, by default, objects are always owned by the peer that created them. To avoid cases where multiple peers invoke changes to the same object at the same time, we rely on synchronizing agents to synchronize the change events. The change request is treated as a service request and is handled by the local synchronizing agent. The agent will first try to identify the ownership of the objects. If the object is owned locally, then it will simply invoke the change on the object, and then locate synchronizing agents residing on other peers and inform them. If the object is not owned by the current peer, the synchronizing agent will locate the owner of the object and request an object-changing service on the synchronizing agent of the owning peer. The synchronizing agents use a specific protocol that has the following packet format:

| Performative | Sender Agent ID | Receiving Agent ID | Message Type | Content |

The fostering agents serve a special purpose, "Peer Fostering". Due to the high volatility of wireless ad-hoc networks, special care must be taken to protect applications from information loss and potential problems associated with it. In this connection, we have devised a "peer fostering" mechanism to increase the fault-tolerance of applications in case of peer failure, by introducing a dependence relationship among peers. When a new peer joins the group, the fostering agents of all existing peers will negotiate among themselves to elect an agent with the least amount of fostering workload, to be the *fosterer* of the new peer. When a peer leaves the group intentionally or accidentally, the peer fostering mechanism comes into effect. As every peer's objects are fostered by another peer's fostering agent, they will not be lost. If the dropping-out peer was holding any objects that are important to other peers (for example, the ball in a sports game) the fostering agents will negotiate ownership transfer and delegate the ownership of such objects to a new peer. In the case where the previously dropped out peer rejoins, fostering agents will negotiate for the ownership to be transferred back to the rejoining agent. When a new peer joins, the existing fostering agents will negotiate among themselves to elect the agent with the lightest workload, and assign the new peer to be the chosen agent's *fosteree*. This is described in more detail in Section 4.

3.3 Application Layer

Because the bottom two layers take care of all communication and resource management, application programmers can focus on the domain-specific aspects of the application without worrying about generic problems that come with P2P networks. A clearly defined API is provided to the programmers at this layer to interact with the framework. The interaction mainly goes through an access point, the "Control Center". Factory design patterns are used to connect applications to the framework. Programmers are responsible for implementing appropriate factories for resources (objects) that are to be shared across the network. More information about the API is available at [9].

4   Agent-Based Peer Fostering

Compared to cable-bound communications, wireless communication poses additional challenges, primarily in connection with packet loss. At a low level,

JGroups provides reliable uni- and multicasting, but it doesn't offer protection from higher-level problems that affect applications. Temporary disconnection of devices can occur frequently, especially in dynamic real-world environments. This problem can seriously impact the basic usability of applications. In games, for instance, it is generally not satisfactory if a player is not able to continue the game simply because of some temporary connection loss (e.g., he walks into a lift). The problem becomes more serious when not only that player suffers from a temporary disconnection, but also other peers are affected. Consequently, it is important to ensure the integrity of data and continuity of the execution under these uncertain circumstances. Furthermore, it is also desirable to afford the disconnected peer the capability of rejoining the application without loss of its previously-held data.

4.1   Introduction to "Peer Fostering" Mechanism

To address these problems, we introduced the "Agent-Based Peer Fostering" mechanism into FRAGme2004. Inspired by the schemes used in some P2P applications (Gnutella, Napster), peer fostering is built on the idea that there exists some degree of data redundancy in all P2P systems. Most of the other systems don't have any special scheme that optimizes the degree of redundancy, but rather rely on the highly redundant data in the system. This works for systems where peers are heavy-duty computational resource nodes, such as PCs. But for our applications, all devices are assumed to be limited in terms of available memory. Therefore, expecting such a high degree of redundancy could significantly constrain the performance of applications. As the number of peer failure instances increases, the accretion and management of redundant data could lead to unacceptable system performance.

In order to enable all peers to make sensible decisions about what to do in case of other peers' failures, the peers need to be able to collaborate, and this process can be modelled effectively using agents. Each fostering agent is autonomously acting on behalf of its owner peer, and through negotiation and collaboration, the agents can help balance the workload (the number of *fosterees*) with other agents.

4.2   Peer Fostering Relationship

We define the set of existing peers in a system $\mathcal{P} = \{p_1, p_2, \ldots, p_n\}$. a_i is the fostering agent of p_i, and $\mathcal{A} = \{a_1, a_2, \ldots, a_n\}$ is the set of vertices in a graph. If $n > 1$, the Peer Fostering State (*PFS*) is defined as:

Definition 1. *the peer fostering state of a system is a simple directed closed loop* $\mathcal{C}_{pfs}$

$$\mathcal{C}_{pfs} = \{\langle a_{i_1}, a_{i_2}\rangle, \ldots, \langle a_{i_{n-1}}, a_{i_n}\rangle, \langle a_{i_n}, a_{i_1}\rangle\}$$

where each occurrence of $\langle a_{i_a}, a_{i_b}\rangle$ *is a directed edge in the loop from vertex* a_{i_a} *to vertex* a_{i_b}. *For any particular* $\mathcal{C}_{pfs}$, *the set* $\{a_{i_1}, a_{i_2}, \ldots, a_{i_n}\}$ *is a permutation of the set* $\{a_1, a_2, \ldots, a_n\}$.

Each edge $\langle a_{i_a}, a_{i_b} \rangle$ denotes a "fostering" relationship between the fostering agent of peer p_{i_a} and the agent of peer p_{i_b}. In such a relationship, we say a_{i_a} is "fostering" a_{i_b}, with a_{i_a} being the *fosterer* and a_{i_b} being the *fosteree*.

When a peer drops out and the objects that it owns are not needed by the others, these objects still have to be sustained to allow possible rejoining later. In our system, instead of having these objects taking up memory storage on every peer, only the *fosterer* of the dropped out peer needs to store them. The *fosterer-fosteree* relationship is illustrated in Figure 1.

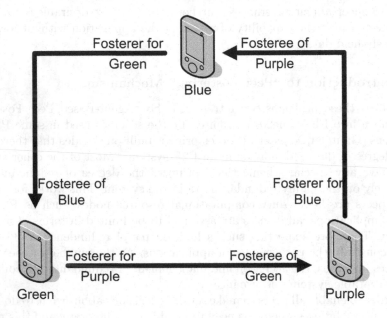

Fig. 1. Illustration of Fosterer-Fosteree Relationship

In the "Peer Fostering" scheme, each participating fostering agent not only knows who its *fosteree* is, but also knows whom its *fosteree* is fostering. The local knowledge of a fostering agent can be expressed as:

Definition 2. *the knowledge of peer* a_i *is*

$$K(a_i) = \langle F(a_i, a_j), F(a_j, a_k), Adopt(\{a_{x_1}, \ldots, a_{x_m}\}) \rangle$$

where the set $\{a_{x_1}, a_{x_2}, \ldots, a_{x_m}\}$ *contains the agents that* a_i *has temporarily "adopted", and where* F *denotes a fostering relationship.*

The reason for storing this extra information will be evident when the drop-out scenario is described in Section 4.3.

Note that such relationships among fostering agents are updated every time a new peer joins, or an existing peer drops out. In the case of a new peer joining, the existing fostering agents will negotiate among themselves to determine which agent is to foster the new agent. The fostering agents follow a set of interaction protocols that allow the agents to make conversations to build the relationships. These conversations are initiated by the "active" agent — the *fosterers*. Although the reader will notice that every single fostering agent is a *fosterer* in some relationship, the agents don't have such global knowledge, and such knowledge is not required. Each agent only makes sure that the relationship in which it is the "active" party is properly pursued. It can be seen that when all agents finish building their own relationships, each agent will be fostered by some other agent. In order to correctly build the fostering relationships, we make the assumption that new peers join the network one at a time.

Each agent has its own thread of execution to secure its autonomy, thus the acquision of information and negotiation among agents happens behind the scene of the main gaming thread, and thread-safety measures are taken in our implementation. This relationship-building phase is essential, but it generates a very small amount of traffic in the network and therefore has negligible impact.

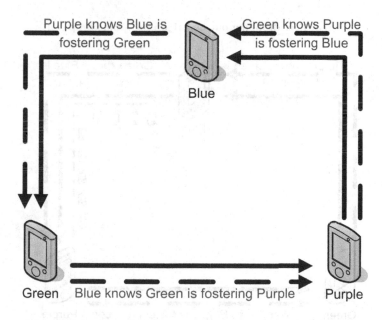

Fig. 2. Peer dropping out and rejoining - initial configuration

4.3   Peer Drop-Out Handling

In this section we describe the procedure that fostering agents take when another peer drops out, and use Figures 2 - 4 for illustration. In the initial configuration, the local knowledge of a_{purple} is:

$$K(a_{purple}) = \langle F(a_{purple}, a_{blue}),$$
$$F(a_{blue}, a_{green}), Adopt(\emptyset)\rangle$$

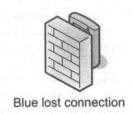

Blue lost connection

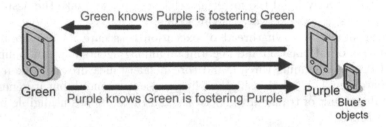

Green knows Purple is fostering Green

Green   Purple knows Green is fostering Purple   Purple
Blue's
objects

Fig. 3. Peer dropping out and rejoining - Blue drops out

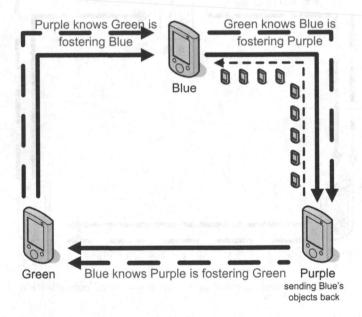

Purple knows Green is
fostering Blue

Green knows Blue is
fostering Purple

Blue

Green   Blue knows Purple is fostering Green   Purple
sending Blue's
objects back

Fig. 4. Peer dropping out and rejoining - Blue rejoins

and the local knowledge of a_{green} is:

$$K(a_{green}) = \langle F(a_{green}, a_{purple}),$$
$$F(a_{purple}, a_{blue}), Adopt(\emptyset) \rangle$$

When a peer (p_{blue}) drops out, all other peers will be notified. a_{purple} will notice that a_{blue} matches the *fosteree* in one of the relationships ($F(a_{purple}, a_{blue})$) that it knows it's engaged in. And because the *fosterer* in that relationship is a_{purple}, itself, a_{purple} will first store all a_{blue}'s objects, updating the adopting set to be $Adopt(\{a_{blue}\})$, and then notify other fostering agents that the ownership of a_{blue}'s objects has been changed to a_{purple}. Knowing that a_{blue} was fostering a_{green}, a_{purple} will then take the initiative of reconstructing relationships by sending a_{green} a fostering request. Upon receiving such a request, a_{green} will send information about its own *fosteree*, which in this case is a_{purple}. The local knowledge of a_{purple} will now be updated to be:

$$K(a_{purple}) = \langle F(a_{purple}, a_{green}),$$
$$F(a_{green}, a_{purple}), Adopt(\{a_{blue}\})\rangle$$

On the other hand, when a_{green} was notified that a_{blue} dropped out, it will notice that a_{blue} matches the *fosteree* in one of the relationships ($F(a_{purple}, a_{blue})$) that it knows locally. And because a_{purple} is its current *fosteree*, it foresees that a_{purple} will be fostering some other peer after the relationship has been reconstructed, and therefore it sends a request to a_{purple} to get the updated *fosteree* of a_{purple}. After a_{purple} sends back the reply, the local knowledge of a_{green} will be updated to be:

$$K(a_{green}) = \langle F(a_{green}, a_{purple}),$$
$$F(a_{purple}, a_{green}), Adopt(\emptyset)\rangle$$

When a_{blue} rejoins, all peers will be notified of the joining event, and a_{purple} will notice that it is adopting a_{blue}'s previous objects. If a_{blue} requests to have its previous data back (it has the alternative option to rejoin as a completely new peer), a_{purple} will send a_{blue}'s objects back, and transfer the ownership of these objects back to a_{blue}. This scheme can be scaled up to an arbitrary number of peers.

5   The Games

As a proof-of-concept, three networked games that run on the PDA Sharp Zaurus SL-C700 [8], [21] were developed based on FRAGme2004:

- a space shooter game, called "SpaceBattle",
- a strategic tank game, called "BOOM!"
- and the Bomberman-like arcade game, called "RoboJoust".

A screenshot of RoboJoust can be seen in Figure 5 [20]. The implementation demonstrates that memory and communication bandwidth constraints were handled well enough by FRAGme2004 to allow fast action games on a limited device such as the Sharp Zaurus. Also, minimal knowledge of the framework was required, which allowed novice developers to focus on the gameplay design. "BOOM!" and "RoboJoust" were developed from scratch by a group of eight senior undergraduate students as a course project.

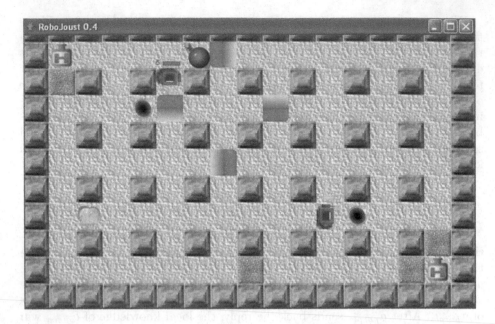

Fig. 5. Screenshot of RoboJoust

6   Evaluation of Agent-Based Fostering Mechanism

Based on the three games, we performed two experiments for the purpose of evaluating the fostering mechanism. Both experiments were performed on both PCs with LAN connections and Sharp Zaurus PDAs with WiFi connections. The first experiment had a game with five players. During play, we let randomly chosen players drop out, one after another until there was only one player left. We observed that each time after a player droped out, the remaining player could continue without any problem or noticeable lag. All the game-critical objects were kept intact by the framework, without the application programmer having to write any additional code. Then we let the formerly dropped-out players rejoin the game. Again, we observed that players could rejoin without experiencing problems, and each time a player rejoined, the gameplay flow was not affected. The second experiment took the first experiment one step further. Before each peer that dropped out rejoins, we select an additional randomly chosen peer to drop out, and let them all rejoin afterwards. Again, there was no negative impact on the performance of the game. In both experiments, the workload (number of *fosterees*) of fostering agents were balanced over time. Although these operations are qualitative, they do give suggestive evidence that the fostering mechanism works in the case of one peer dropping out at a time. Our implementation will not be so effective if two peers drop out at the same time, because the fostering pair will not maintain a complete closed loop. The two peers at the ends of the path are not protected by the fostering mechanism, but fostering will still function for the peers on the rest of the path.

7   Conclusion

The development of mobile P2P applications must overcome a number of obstacles, with object synchronisation, network failure and device limitations being the most significant. With FRAGme2004, we have developed a system that tackles those problems using agent technologies and offers a more reliable framework for P2P application development. By separating the application layer strictly from the framework infrastructure, FRAGme2004 allows developers to implement applications with minimal knowledge of the framework and to concentrate on the application functionality. The negative impact of network failure and peer dropout is reduced by our agent-based peer fostering mechanism.

For future development, the range of FRAGme2004 enabled devices can be further expanded. The development took place on the Sharp Zaurus SL-C700, which runs Java Personal Profile. It would be desirable to extend the implementation platform domain to include smaller devices running Java Mobile Information Device Profile (MIDP). The agent-based fostering mechanism can also be enhanced to handle cases in which two peers drop out at the same time. The agents can be further enhanced to incorporate more capabilities, such as taking security and trust measures when communicating with other agents.

References

1. Akehurst, D.H., Waters, A.G., and Derrick, J. (2004). "A Viewpoints Approach to Designing Group Based Applications", In Herwig Unger, editor, *Design, Analysis and Simulation of Distributed Systems 2004*, Advanced Simulation Technologies Conference, pp. 83-93, Arlington, Virginia, April 2004.
2. Babaoglu, O., Meling, H., and Montresor, A. (2002). "Anthill: A Framework for the Development of Agent-Based Peer-to-Peer Systems", *Proceedings of the 22nd International Conference on Distributed Computing Systems(ICDCS)*, pp. 15-22, Vienna, Austria, 2002.
3. Bruegge, B., and Dutoit, A.H. (2004). *Object-oriented Software Engineering: Using UML, Patterns, and Java.* Upper Saddle River, NJ, USA: Prentice Hall.
4. Chen, Y., Katz, R. H., and Kubiatowicz, J. (2002). "Dynamic Replica Placement for Scalable Content Delivery", *IPTPS '01: Revised Papers from the First International Workshop on Peer-to-Peer Systems*, Springer-Verlag, pp. 306-318, March 2002.
5. Cooper, B., Bawa, M., Daswani, N., Marti, S., and Garcia-Molina, H. (2003). "Authenticity and Availability in PIPE Networks", *Future Generation of Computer Systems*.
6. Dasgupta, P. (2003). "A Peer-to-Peer System Architecture for Multi-agent Collaboration", *Advances in Soft Computing, (Proceedings of the 3rd International Conference on Intelligent Systems and Design Automation, Tulsa, OK)*, Springer-Verlag, pp. 483-492, August 2003.
7. Dasgupta, P. (2003). "Improving Peer-to-Peer Resource Discovery Using Mobile Agent Based Referrals", *Proceedings of the 2nd Workshop on Agent Enabled P2P Computing (co-located with AAMAS)*, pp. 41-54, Melbourne, Australia, July 2003.
8. Device preview: Sharp Zaurus SL-C700 VGA resolution PDA, http://linuxdevices.com/articles/AT5295837592.html

 9. FRAGme2004 System Documentation,
    http://secml.otago.ac.nz/Documents/FRAGme_documentation_2004.pdf
10. Gerke, J., Hausheer, D., Mischke, J., and Stiller, B. (2003). "An Architecture for
    a Service Oriented Peer-to-Peer System (SOPPS)", *Praxis der Informationsverar-
    beitung und Kommunikation (PIK)*, 2/03, pp. 90-95, April 2003.
11. Homayounfar, H., Wang, F., and Areibi, S. (2002). "Advanced P2P Architecture
    Using Autonomous Agents", *CAINE*, San Diego California, pp. 115-118, November
    2002.
12. JGroups Project, http://www.jgroups.org
13. Kato, T., Ishikawa, N., Sumino, H., Hjelm, J., Yu, Y., and Murakami,. S. (2003)
    "A Platform and Applications for Mobile Peer-to-Peer Communications",
    http://www.research.att.com/ rjana/Takeshi_Kato.pdf.
14. Lin, S.-D., Lian, Q., Chen, M., and Zhang, Z. (2004). "A Practical Distributed
    Mutual Exclusion Protocol in Dynamic Peer-to-Peer Systems", *IPTPS04*, Springer-
    Verlag.
15. Margaritis, M., Fidas, C., Avouris, N., and Komis, V. (2003). "A Peer-To-Peer
    Architecture for Synchronous Collaboration over Low-Bandwidth Networks", in
    K. Margaritis, I. Pitas (ed.) *Proc 9th PCI 2003*, Thessaloniki.
16. Milojicic, D. S., Kalogeraki V., and Lukose R. (2002). "Peer-to-peer computing",
    Technical Report HPL-2002-57, HP Lab, 2002.
17. Moore, D., and Hebeler, J. (2002). *Peer-to-Peer: Building Secure, Scalable and
    Manageable Networks*. Berkeley, CA, USA: McGrawHill/Osborne.
18. Nagel, M. (2003). "FRAG: A Java Framework for Peer-to-Peer Games", Diploma
    Thesis, *Technische Universität München*, Feburary 14, 2003.
19. Pang, X., Catania, B. and Tan K. (2003). "Securing Your Data in Agent-Based
    P2P Systems", *Eighth International Conference on Database Systems for Advanced
    Applications (DASFAA '03)*, Kyoto, Japan, p.55, March 26 - 28, 2003.
20. Wolf, H., and Wang, M. (2004). "Robo Joust Game Documentation",
    http://secml.otago.ac.nz/agents/Assets/documents/robojoust.pdf
21. Freedman, A. (2003). "Zaurus SL-C700 Unofficial FAQ",
    http://avi.freedman.net/zaurus/slc700.html

ACP2P: Agent-Community-Based Peer-to-Peer Information Retrieval – An Evaluation

Tsunenori Mine[1], Akihiro Kogo[2], and Makoto Amamiya[1]

Department of Intelligent Systems, {Faculty[1], Graduate School[2]} of Information
Science and Electrical Engineering, Kyushu University
6-1 Kasuga-koen, Kasuga, Fukuoka 816-8580, Japan
{mine, kogo, amamiya}@al.is.kyushu-u.ac.jp
http://www-al.is.kyushu-u.ac.jp/~mine/mine-e.html

Abstract. The Agent-Community-based Peer-to-Peer Information Retrieval (ACP2P) method[1],[2] uses agent communities to manage and look up information of interest to users. An agent works as a delegate of its user and searches for information that the user wants by communicating with other agents. The communication between agents is carried out in a peer-to-peer computing architecture. Retrieving information relevant to a user query is performed with content files which consist of original and retrieved documents, and two histories: a query/retrieved document history and a query/sender agent history. The ACP2P is implemented using the Multi-Agent Kodama framework.

In this paper, we present some mathematical aspects of the ACP2P method with respect to the relationships between communication loads and the number of records that are stored both in the two histories and retrieved document content files, and discuss the experimental results, for which illustrate the validity of this approach. The results confirm the mathematical conjectures we presented and show that the two histories are more useful for reducing the communication load than a naive method employing 'multicast' techniques, and lead to a higher retrieval accuracy than the naive method.

1 Introduction

Although the rapid growth of the World Wide Web and the spread of the Internet have helped Internet users to access useful resources or services, users often find it difficult to search for the information they need because of the flood of information that needs to be filtered out, and lack of a clear idea of the targets they want. In order to deal with these problems, a lot of studies on information filtering (e.g. [3]), information recommendation (e.g. [4]), expert finding (e.g. [5]), and collaborative filtering (e.g. [6]) have been carried out. Most systems developed in that research are, unfortunately, based on the server-client computational model and are often distressed by the fundamental bottle-neck coming from their central control system architecture. Although some systems based on peer-to-peer (P2P for short) computing architectures have been developed and

Z. Despotovic, S. Joseph, and C. Sartori (Eds.): AP2PC 2005, LNAI 4118, pp. 145–158, 2006.
© Springer-Verlag Berlin Heidelberg 2006

implemented (e.g. [7], [8], [9], [10]) , each node of most of those systems only deals with simple and monolithic processing chores.

Considering these issues, we proposed an Agent Community based Peer-to-Peer information retrieval method called ACP2P method, which uses agent communities to manage and look up information related to a user query.[1],[2] The agent communities can reflect the structures of human groups or societies such as laboratories, departments, institutions, research groups and so force, where the people with the same or similar interests, objectives or aims stay together, and often browse or look for similar information from the Web. In the ACP2P method, considering such environments, an agent works as a delegate of its user and searches for information that the user wants by communicating with other agents. The communication between agents is carried out based on a P2P computing architecture. In order to retrieve information relevant to a user query, an agent uses two histories: a query/retrieved document history (Q/RDH for short) and a query/sender agent history (Q/SAH for short). The former is a list of pairs of a query and retrieved document information, where the queries were sent by the agent itself and the document information includes the addresses of both agents that returned the document and those that created or owned the document. The latter is a list of pairs of a query and a sender agent's address and shows "who sent what query to the agent." This is useful for finding new information sources. Making use of the Q/SAH is expected to have a collaborative filtering effect, which gradually creates virtual agent communities, where agents with the same interests stay together. We have demonstrated through several experiments that the method reduced communication loads much more than other methods which do not employ Q/SAH to look up a target agent, and was useful for creating a "give and take" effect, i.e., as an agent receives more queries, it acquires more links to new knowledge[11], but have not so far discussed any mathematical aspects of the method or the retrieval accuracy of the method.

In this paper, we present some mathematical aspects of the ACP2P method with respect to the relationships between communication loads and the number of records that are stored both in the two histories and retrieved document content files, and discuss the experimental results to illustrate the validity of this approach. The results confirm our mathematical conjectures about the ACP2P method and show that the two histories are more useful for reducing communication loads than a naive method employing 'multicast' techniques, and lead to a higher retrieval accuracy than the naive method. The remainder of the paper is structured as follows. Section 2 considers the ACP2P method. Section 3 discusses the experimental results and Section 4 describes related work.

2   ACP2P Method

2.1   Overview of the ACP2P Method Implemented with Multi-agent Kodama

The ACP2P method employs three types of agents: user interface (UI) agent, information retrieval (IR) agent and history management (HM) agent. A set of three agents (UI agent, IR agent, HM agent) is assigned to each user. Although a UI agent and an HM agent communicate only with the IR agent of their user, an IR agent communicates with other users' IR agents not only in the community it belongs to, but also in other communities, to search for information relevant to its user's query. A pair of Q/RDH and Q/SAH histories and retrieved document content files are managed by the HM agent.

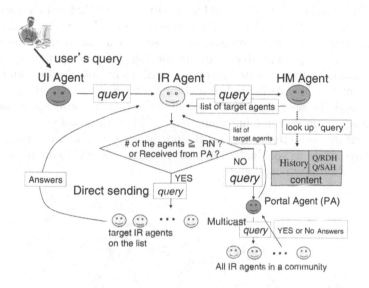

Fig. 1. Actions for Sending a Query

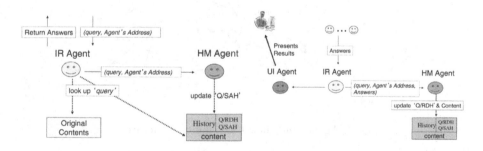

Fig. 2. Actions for Receiving a Query (left) and for Receiving Answers (right)

When receiving a query from a UI agent, an IR agent asks an HM agent to look up target agents with its history or asks a portal agent to multicast a query (Fig.1) . When receiving a query from other IR agents, an IR agent looks up the information relevant to the query from its original document and retrieved document content files, sends an answer to the query-sender IR agent, and also sends a pair of the query and the address of the query-sender IR agent to an

HM agent so that it can update Q/SAH (Fig.2 (left)). The returned answer is either a pair of a 'Yes' message and retrieved documents or a 'No' message indicating that there is no relevant information, although retrieved documents are not returned when the query comes through a portal agent. When receiving answers with a 'Yes' message from other IR agents, the IR agent sends them to a UI agent, and sends them with a pair of a query and the addresses of answer sender IR agents to an HM agent (Fig.2 (right)).

The ACP2P method is implemented with Multi-Agent Kodama (Kyushu university Open & Distributed Autonomous Multi-Agent) [12]. Kodama comprises hierarchical structured agent communities based on a portal agent model. A portal agent is the representative of all member agents in a community and allows the community to be treated as one normal agent outside the community. A portal agent has its role limited in a community, and the portal agent itself may be managed by another higher-level portal agent. A portal agent manages all member agents in its community and can multicast a message to them. Any member agent in a community can ask the portal agent to multicast its message. The portal agent has its role limited in a community, and itself may be managed by another higher-level portal agent.

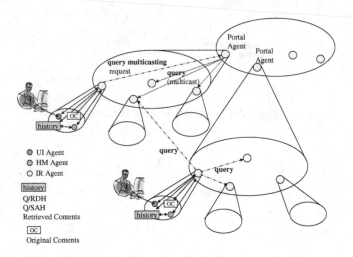

Fig. 3. Agents and their Community Structure

Fig.3 shows an example of the agent community structure which the ACP2P method is based on. A portal agent in the figure manages all member agents' addresses there, where a member agent of a community designates an IR agent. When a member agent wants to find any target agents which have information relevant to a query, the agent looks them up using two histories: Q/RDH and Q/SAH, and content files. If the target agents are found, a query is sent directly to them, and their retrieved results are also returned directly to the query-sender IR agent. If the requested number (N_R) of such agents is not found, the agent asks the portal agent to send the query to all the other member agents in the community by multicasting a query. At that time, all the answers will be returned to the portal agent. If the number of results with a 'Yes' message reaches N_R, without waiting for the rest of answers from other IR agents, the portal agent sends them back to the query-sender IR agent. Even if the number of 'Yes' messages did not reach N_R after all the other IR agents replied, the portal agent still sends the currently held results to the query-sender IR agent.

2.2   Communication Load and History Size

MultiCast: Without Using Two Hisotries. In the ACP2P method, every IR agent sends one query in rotation. Since an IR agent initially has no records in its histories, the IR agent first has to ask a portal agent to multicast the query to all other IR agents in its community. After receiving the query, the IR agents return a 'Yes' or 'No' message with their address to the portal agent. Then the portal agent selects the top N_R IR agents returning 'Yes' messages in the order they are received, makes a list of them and sends the list to the query-sender IR agent without waiting for the rest of other IR agents' answers. After receiving the list, the query-sender IR agent again sends the query to the IR agents on the list. These processes of exchanging messages are shown as follows:

1. QS-IRA $-(1)\rightarrow$ PA $-(N-1)\rightarrow$ All-IRAs
2. QS-IRA $\leftarrow(1)-$ PA $\leftarrow(N-1)-$ All-IRAs
3. QS-IRA $-(N_R)\rightarrow$ T-IRAs
4. QS-IRA $\leftarrow(N_R)-$ T-IRAs

Where QS-IRA, PA, All-IRA and T-IRA represent a query-sender IR agent, a portal agent, all other IR agents, and target IR agents, respectively. The number in the parentheses on the arrow represents the number of messages received by the agent (or agents) pointed by the arrow. N is the number of IR agents in a community. During the period when every IR agent sends one query in rotation, the total number of messages exchanged among all IR agents and a portal agent is at most $2(N + N_R)N$, the number of messages received by a portal agent is at most N^2 and the average number of messages received by an IR agent is $2N_R + N$. Therefore, when the multicast technique is employed, the number of messages received by each IR agent in one routine is proportional to N because $N >> N_R$.

Using Two Histories. As more queries are sent, more records will be accumulated in the two histories of an IR agent. Let N_{RD} be the maximum number of documents returned by target IR agents that received a query. At that time, the maximum number of documents to be stored in a content file holding retrieved documents (# in content for short) will be $N_R \times N_{RD}$, and the maximum number of pairs in Q/RDH of a query and the address of an IR agent that replied to the query (# in Q/RDH for short) will be N_R. Since the number of these records to be stored in a content file or Q/RDH is proportional to the number of queries to be sent by an IR agent, after the IR agent sends N_Q queries, # in content and # in Q/RDH will be $N_Q \times N_R \times N_{RD}$ and $N_Q \times N_R$, respectively. An IR agent receives at most $(N - 1) \times N_Q$ queries when an IR agent happens to receive a query from all the other IR agents. Then, the Q/SAH will hold $(N - 1) \times N_Q$ records, which are pairs of a query and a query-sender IR agent's address. On the average, Q/SAH will hold N_Q records.

When an IR agent sends a query, it searches for N_R target IR agents from both its retrieved document content file and the two histories. When N_R target candidate IR agents or more were found, the query-sender IR agent ranks the IR agents based on the similarity of the query and selects the top N_R IR agents from among them. The similarity measure will be described in Sec. 3.3. Otherwise, the query-sender IR agent has to ask a portal agent to multicast the query to all the other IR agents so that the IR agent can fulfill its quota of target IR agents. For every query sending of each IR agent, $2N_R$ messages will be exchanged in the former case, and $2N_R + 2N$ messages in the latter case, as mentioned earlier. As more queries are sent by IR agents, the number of occurrences of the latter case, i.e. multicasting, will be reduced according to the increase in records in their content files and histories.

3   Experiments

3.1   Preliminaries

We used the Web pages of Yahoo! JAPAN [13] for the experiments as Mine et al. [11] did. The Web pages used are broadly divided into five categories: animals, sports, computers, medicine, and finance. Each of them consists of 20 smaller categories, which are selected in descending order of the number of Web pages recorded in a category. An IR agent is assigned to each selected category, and thus 100 IR agents are created and activated in the experiments. A category name is used as the name of an IR agent, and the Web pages in the category are used as the original documents of the agent. All 100 IR agents are assigned to a single community for simplicity.

We conducted experiments to show how the two histories help to reduce communication loads between agents looking for information relevant to a query and how Q/SAH (a query/sender agent history) helps in searching for new information sources, having a comparable or higher accuracy in retrieving documents han a method without two histories. To perform the experiments, we compared three methods : (1) ACP2P with a Q/SAH (wQ/SAH for short), (2) ACP2P without a Q/SAH (woQ/SAH for short), and (3) a simple method always employing a 'multicast' technique (MulCst for short).

In the experiments, two query sets : QL=1 and QL=2, were used. QL=1 and QL=2 consist of 10 queries, whose query length is one and two, respectively, where query length means the number of terms in a query. When using queries belonging to QL=1, 10 nouns are extracted from every category assigned to each IR agent in descending order of their frequency of occurrence in the category. Each noun is used as a query of the IR agent. When using those belonging to

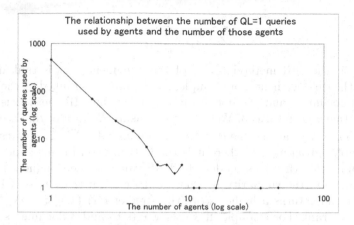

Fig. 4. The relationship between the number of QL=1 queries used by agents and the number of those agents. Both axes are in log scale.

QL=2, 5 nouns are extracted and the combinations of the extracted 5 nouns taken in pairs create 10 queries.

The relationship between the number of QL=1 queries used by agents and the number of such agents is shown in Fig.4, where both axes are in log scale. The relationship almost seems to obey a power law distribution.

3.2 Relevance Judgement and Evaluation

In a P2P network environment, gathering all documents from every peer is not always possible, that is, indexing all documents is quite difficult. Thus the first goal for IR in the P2P network environment is to achieve a result comparable with a Conventional probabilistic IR method using a centralized indexing database (CIR method for short). As the CIR method, we employed a Probabilistic IR method that applies a simplified BM25 [14] weighting function to all the documents collected from every peer. The simplified BM25 is defined as follows:

$$\sum_{T \in Q} \log \frac{n + 0.5}{N - n + 0.5} \frac{2tf}{\frac{dl}{avdl} + tf} \tag{1}$$

Where Q is a query that contains terms T. tf is the frequency of occurrence of the term within a specific document. N and n are the number of items (documents) in the collection[1] and the number of documents containing the term, respectively. dl and $avdl$ are respectively the document length and average document length, where the document length is the number of terms in a document, and a term is a word detected by a morphological analyzer.

In order to compare the ACP2P method with the CIR method, we used the following equation:

---

[1] In the experiment, the documents in the collection are those collected from all peers.

$$\sum_{i=1}^{N_R} \frac{1}{r(i)} / \sum_{i=1}^{N_R} \frac{1}{i}$$

Where $r(i)$ is the CIR method's rank of the document that is ranked by the ACP2P as the ith document. For example, if a document is ranked by the ACP2P as the 2nd document and the document's rank by the CIR method is 3, then this means that $r(2)$ returns 3. We call this measure *Reciprocal Rank Similarity* (RRS for short). We can assume that RRS's denominator $\sum_{i=1}^{N_R} \frac{1}{i}$ represents the ideal value of a given model, where it is the CIR method in this paper. As the ACP2P approaches the given model, the RRS value becomes higher. Thus, the RRS can measure the similarity between ranks generated by the ACP2P and by the CIR and returns a higher score the smaller $r(i)$ $(1 \leq i \leq N_R)$ is, i.e., the higher the rank. For example, if a user wants to find 3 documents relevant to his/her query and we suppose the top 3 ranked documents' rank returned by his/her agent to be 3, 5 and 1, then the RRS returns $\frac{1/3+1/5+1/1}{1/1+1/2+1/3} = 0.84$, and the top 3 ranked documents' rank to be 3, 5 and 2, then the RRS returns $\frac{1/3+1/5+1/2}{1/1+1/2+1/3} = 0.56$.

In the experiment, we use an average RRS: $\frac{1}{N_a} \sum_i^{N_a} RRS(i)$, where N_a is the the number of all IR agents and $RRS(i)$ is the RRS of the ith IR agent.

3.3   Similarity Measure for Detecting Target Agent

In order to find N_R target agents to be sent a query, we calculate $Score(query, t\_agent)$, which returns the similarity value between query $query$ and target agent t_agent, with equation (2); $Score(query, t\_agent)$ becomes higher if t_agent sends a greater number of similar queries and returns more documents related to $query$.

$$Score(query, t\_agent) = \sum_{i=1}^{k} \cos(\boldsymbol{query}, \boldsymbol{qh_{di}})$$

$$+ \sum_{i=1}^{m} (\cos(\boldsymbol{query}, \boldsymbol{qh_{sai}}) + \varphi(i))$$

$$+ max_{1 \leq i \leq n} Sim_d(\boldsymbol{query}, \boldsymbol{doc_i}) \qquad (2)$$

$$\varphi(i) = \begin{cases} \delta \text{ if } qh_{sai} \text{ is a query directly sent by} \\ \quad \text{an other IR agent.} \\ 0 \text{ otherwise} \end{cases}$$

In equation (2), $query$ consists of $w_1, ..., w_m$, and w_i $(1 \leq i \leq m)$ is a term in $query$. $\boldsymbol{query}$ is the term vector whose element is the frequency of occurrence of the term in $query$. qh_d and qh_{sa} represent a query in a record of Q/RDH and Q/SAH, respectively. The first term $\sum_{i=1}^{k} \cos(\boldsymbol{query}, \boldsymbol{qh_{di}})$ returns the total score of the similarities between $query$ and each of k number of queries sent to t_agent. The second term $\sum_{i=1}^{m}(\cos(\boldsymbol{query}, \boldsymbol{qh_{sai}}) + \varphi(i))$ represents the score between $query$ and qh_{sai}, which is the i_th of m queries sent by t_agent in Q/SAH. $\varphi(i)$ is a weight to consider the importance of 'direct sending of a query'. If qh_{sai} is sent directly by t_agent, δ is added to the score. In order to decide the value of φ, we performed a simple pre-experiment that compared $\varphi = 0$ with $\varphi = 0.1$. Since the result of $\varphi = 0.1$ was better than that of $\varphi = 0$, we employed $\varphi = 0.1$. The last term $max_{1 \leq i \leq n} Sim_d(\boldsymbol{query}, \boldsymbol{doc_i})$ is the maximum score of similarity between $query$ and each of n documents originally created by the user of t_agent or just returned by t_agent. $Sim_d(query, doc)$ represents the similarity between $query$ and the content of retrieved document doc. It is calculated with a more simplified of version of BM25, in which $\frac{dl}{avdl}$ in equation (1) is set to 1, and N is the total number of documents a query-sender IR agent has. After calculating $Score(query, t\_agent)$ for each IR agent t_agent in the retrieved document content file and two histories: Q/RDH and Q/SAH, N_R target agents will be selected in the descending order of $Score(query, t\_agent)$, which should be greater than 0. Whenever N_R agents are not found, a query-sender IR agent asks a portal agent to multicast a query to all the other IR agents. If a target IR agent finds information relevant to $query$ from its original or retrieved document content files with Sim_d in equation (2), it returns a 'Yes' message, otherwise a 'No' message. If the similarity value between a document and a query that was returned by Sim_d is greater than some threshold value (0 for the experiments), the document will be judged relevant, otherwise irrelevant.

3.4   Experimental Results

First we compare the change of the average number of messages exchanged by each IR agent for every query input. For the comparison, we use 3 different request numbers: N_R=3, 10 and 20. The results are shown in Fig.5. In the figure the vertical axis is the average number of messages and the horizontal axis is the number of queries sent by each IR agent. The left side in the figure shows the results of using QL=1 and the right side shows those of using QL=2.

The results show that the average number of messages received by each IR agent is, except for MulCst, reduced for every query input. In particular, when using QL=2, the number of received messages decreases more quickly than for QL=1, and almost converges at the third query input because there is a larger number of identical words in QL=2 queries than those of QL=1, and consequently the words in QL=2 queries are more frequently found in two histories and retrieved document files than is the case for QL=1. Furthermore we can see that the graph of the number of messages in woQ/SAH approaches more closely to that in MulCst than that for wQ/SAH, as N_R increases. Thus we can say that Q/SAH history is quite useful for finding target agents related to queries, in particular when a user uses a greater number of different queries which include fewer identical words.

Next we compare the RRS values of the three methods under the same conditions as in the previous experiment. The results are shown in Fig.6. In the figure the vertical axis is the average RRS and the horizontal axis is the number of

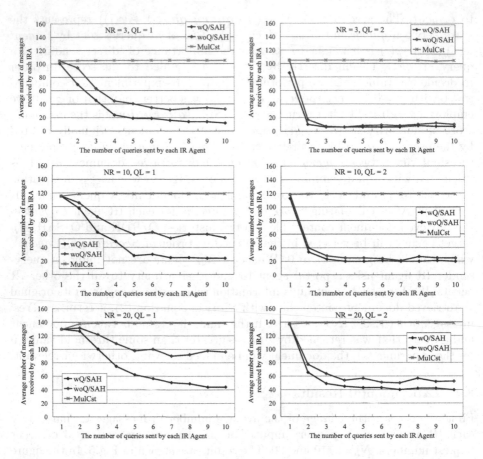

Fig. 5. The comparison of average number of messages received by each IR agent for every query input using 3 diifferent N_R values: N_R=3 (TOP), N_R=10 (MID) and N_R=20 (BTM). The query belongs to either QL=1 (left) or QL=2 (right).

queries sent by each IR agent. As the value of N_R increases, the RRS value also increases and the curve of the graphs becomes flatter. We can see that the RRS value of MulCst increases as the number of queries sent increases. Considering this phenomenon, we surmise that original documents assigned to IR agents will gradually be spread over the community through the document retrieval process of each IR agent. Thus even though a portal agent selects target agents in the order their 'Yes' messages are received, the probability that higher weighted documents will be returned rises. For the same reason, since the RRS value of the MulCst increases as N_R increases, the difference of the three methods decreases. When using QL=1, the wQ/SAH almost achieves higher retrieval accuracy than the other two methods, although the RRS value is unfortunately not so high because the records stored in the content files and the two histories are originally

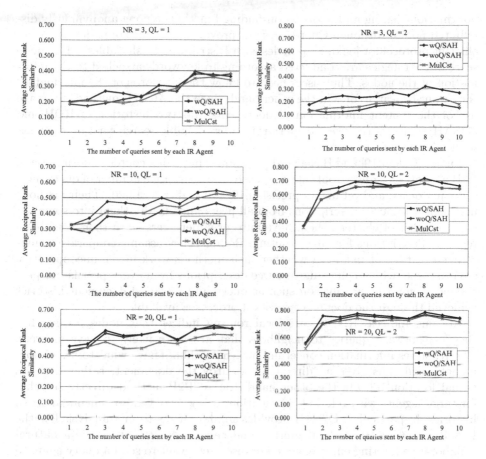

Fig. 6. The comparison of average reciprocal rank similarity (RRS) of each IR agent for every query input using 3 diifferent N_R values : N_R=3 (TOP), N_R=10 (MID) and N_R=20 (BTM). The query belongs to either QL=1 (left) or QL=2 (right).

acquired by a portal agent using the query multicasting technique and its RRS value is not so high. However, when using QL=2, all three methods identically achieve high RRS scores at both N_R=10 and 20.

4   Related Work

There is lots of work related to the topics considered in this paper. Distributed Information Retrieval selects some IR systems to send a query, aggregates the results returned by the selected IR systems, and presents them to a user. Before selecting the IR systems to be sent a query, the resource description of each IR system is often created [15]. In the ACP2P method, Q/RDH incrementally creates an effect similar to the resource description. Freenet [8] and Chord [7] are carried out in a pure P2P computing architecture. Freenet provides information-sharing and information-finding functions among anonymously distributed nodes. Although Chord does not provide anonymity of nodes, it has an efficient protocol for looking up nodes with Distributed Hash Tables. Their node searching strategies are conducted according to keywords attached to the information of the nodes. Thus users need to know the keywords of the information they want to search for. On the other hand, since the ACP2P method can make use of the content information of documents and two histories: Q/RDH and Q/SAH, it allows the users to perform a more flexible search for target agents with relevant information.

Lu and Callan[19] and Bawa et al.[20] shows that using content information in P2P networks for query routing can greatly reduce average number of query messages per query, and get higher precision[19] and higher recall[20]. Their methods first collect resource descriptions from all peers and classify them into some decided number of clusters, then, have hubs or super-peers learn their neighbors' resource descriptions for query routing. Because they assume cooperative environments, it is not unknown whether their methods work in the uncooperative environments where collecting resource descriptions from every peer is not possible and only the information such as query and retrieved document histories achieved through the document retrieval process is available.

Routing Indices (RIs)[16] are local routing indices that nodes use so that they can forward queries to neighbors that are more likely to have answers. The RI stores information concerning which neighbors have what topics of documents, and thus gives a "direction" towards the document, rather than its actual location[16]. On the other hand, the ACP2P method directly searches for target agents with relevant information, using retrieved documents and two histories. In particular, Q/SAH provides similar effects to link analysis like the PageRank[17] or HITs algorithm[18], and can be expected to make a natural collaborative filtering effect emerge because users want to send a query again to the peers that can return results which satisfy them, and vice versa. However, query forwarding like RIs would be able to help the ACP2P search for more relevant information. NeuroGrid[21] is an adaptive decentralized search system which supports distributed search by forwarding queries based on the contents of each network node, and supports a learning mechanism that dynamically adjusts metadata describing the contents of nodes and the files that make up those contents, using users' positive and negative feedback. However, to our knowledge, there is no discussion of the accuracy of NeuroGrid, and it does not use a history like Q/SAH of the ACP2P.

5   Conclusions and Future Work

We presented some mathematical aspects of the ACP2P method and discussed the experimental results that illustrate its validity. To do the experiments, we implemented the method with Multi-Agent System Kodama. We conducted several experiments to show whether or not two histories helped to reduce communication loads between agents in searching for information relevant to a query, and whether or not Q/SAH helped in looking up new information sources. The experimental results showed that the two histories are quite useful for looking up new information source and for reducing communication loads, and have a higher accuracy in retrieving documents than a simple method employing a multicast technique. Although the RRS value of the ACP2P method (wQ/SAH and woQ/SAH) for the conventional probabilistic IR method using a centralized indexing database, which is constructed from all documents collected from every peer, i.e., every agent in the community, was not so high, it is because the records stored in the content files and two histories were originally based on results selected in the order they were received by a portal agent. Therefore if we improve the way a portal agent selects the results, for example, make it wait for a greater number of results than N_R and select N_R of them in order of their weighting score, we will probably be able to achieve a higher similarity, although this method might require more time than the current method. Another method is to employ query routing before asking a portal agent to multicast the query, that is, to let an IR agent ask target IR agents to forward a query to the IR agents which are relevant to the query and are stored in the two histories of the target IR agents.

We are currently continuing experiments to achieve results with more than one hierarchical agent community, and with dynamic community environments which agents freely join and leave, and where agents update their contents so that we can simulate more realistic environments and evaluate the scalability of the ACP2P method. Furthermore, we are investigating how we can make use of user feedback embedded into the results in order to reflect it in ranking of retrieved documents to achieve a higher retrieval accuracy according to some measure specific to the user. We will report these results in the near future.

Acknowledgment

This research was partly supported by the Grant-in-Aid for Scientific Research (C) (16500082) from the JSPS and the SCOPE-C (052310008) from the MIC, Japan.

References

1. Mine, T., Matsuno, D., Takaki, K., Amamiya, M.: Agent community based peer-to-peer information retrieval. In: Proc. of Third Int. Joint Conf. on Autonomous Agents and Multi Agent Systems (AAMAS 2004). (2004) 1484–1485
2. Mine, T., Matsuno, D., Kogo, A., Amamiya, M.: ACP2P : Agent Community based Peer-to-Peer Information Retrieval. In: Proc. of Third Int. Workshop on Agents and Peer-to-Peer Computing (AP2PC 2004). (2004) 50–61
3. Lang, K.: NewsWeeder: learning to filter netnews. In: Proceedings of the 12th International Conference on Machine Learning, Morgan Kaufmann publishers Inc.: San Mateo, CA, USA (1995) 331–339
4. Schafer, J.B., Konstan, J.A., Riedi, J.: Recommender systems in e-commerce. In: Proceedings of the 1st ACM Conference on Electronic Commerce. (1999) 158–166

5. Yimam-Seid, D., Kobsa, A.: Expert finding systems for organizations: Problem and domain analysis and the demoir approach. Journal of Organizational Computing and Electronic Commerce **13** (2003) 1–24

6. Good, N., Schafer, J.B., Konstan, J.A., Borchers, A., Sarwar, B.M., Herlocker, J.L., Riedl, J.: Combining collaborative filtering with personal agents for better recommendations. In: AAAI/IAAI. (1999) 439–446

7. Stoica, I., Morris, R., Karger, D., Kaashoek, M.F., Balakrishnan, H.: Chord: A scalable peer-to-peer lookup service for internet applications. In: Proceedings of the 2001 conference on applications, technologies, architectures, and protocols for computer communications. (2001) 149–160

8. Clarke, I., Sandberg, O., Wiley, B., Hong, T.W.: Freenet: A distributed anonymous information storage and retrieval system. Designing Privacy Enhancing Technologies: International Workshop on Design Issues in Anonymity and Unobservability, http://www.doc.ic.ac.uk/~twh1/academic/ (2001)

9. v6.0, G.P.D.: http://rfc-gnutella.sourceforge.net/ (2003)

10. Napster: http://www.napster.com/ (2000)

11. Mine, T., Matsuno, D., Kogo, A., Amamiya, M.: Design and implementation of agent community based peer-to-peer information retrieval method. In: Proc. of Eighth Int. Workshop CIA-2004 on Cooperative Information Agents (CIA 2004), LNAI 3191. (2004) 31–46

12. Zhong, G., Amamiya, S., Takahashi, K., Mine, T., Amamiya, M.: The design and application of kodama system. IEICE Transactions INF.& SYST. **E85-D** (2002) 637–646

13. Yahoo: http://www.yahoo.co.jp/ (2003)

14. Robertson, S.E., Walker, S., Jones, S., Hancock-Beaulieu, M.M., Gatford, M.: Okapi/keenbow at trec-8. In: NIST Special Publication 500-246: The Eighth Text REtrieval Conference (TREC-8). (1999) 151–162

15. Callan, J., Connell, M.: Query-based sampling of text databases. ACM Transactions on Information Systems **19** (2001) 97–130

16. Crespo, A., Garcia-Molina, H.: Routing indices for peer-to-peer systems. In: the 28th International Conference on Distributed Computing Systems. (2002)

17. Brin, S., Page, L.: The Anatomy of a Large-Scale Hypertextual Web Search Engine. In: Proc. of 7th International World Wide Web Conference:WWW7 Conference. (1998)

18. Kleinberg, J.M.: Authoritative sources in a hyperlinked environment. Journal of the ACM **46** (1999) 604–632

19. Lu, J., Callan, J.: Content-based retrieval in hybrid peer-to-peer networks. In: Proceedings of the twelfth international conference on Information and knowledge management. (2003) 199–206

20. Bawa, M., Manku, G.S., Raghavan, P.: Sets: search enhanced by topic segmentation. In: Proceedings of the 26th annual international ACM SIGIR conference on Research and development in informaion retrieval. (2003) 306 – 313

21. Joseph, S.: Neurogrid: Semantically routing queries in peer-to-peer networks. In: the International Workshop on Peer-to-Peer Computing (co-located with Networking 2002), http://www.neurogrid.net/php/publications.php. (2002)

A Peer Ubiquitous Multi-agent Framework for Providing Nomadic Users with Adapted Information

Angela Carrillo Ramos, Jérôme Gensel,
Marlène Villanova-Oliver, and Hervé Martin

Laboratory LSR – IMAG. B.P. 72
38402 Saint Martin d'Hères Cedex, France
{carrillo, gensel, villanov, martin}@imag.fr

Abstract. In this paper, we describe how *PUMAS*, a framework based on Ubiquitous Agents for accessing *Web Information Systems (WIS)* through *Mobile Devices (MD)* can help to provide nomadic users with relevant and adapted information. Using *PUMAS*, the information delivered to a nomadic user (whose location changes) is adapted according to, on the one hand, her/his preferences, intentions and history in the system and, on the other hand, the limited capacities of her/his *MD*. We describe the extension we propose for handling adaptation in *PUMAS*. We also describe different scenarios which illustrate the way *PUMAS* works, especially when a query is processed.

1 Introduction

Shizuka *et al.* [1] define *Peer to Peer* (*P2P*) systems as systems characterized by a direct communication between the peers with no communication needed through a specific server, and by the autonomy a peer gets for accomplishing some assigned tasks. These *systems* are highly dynamic in that peers join or leave the system. Shizuka *et al.* consider that *P2P* computing is one of the potential communicative architectures and technologies for supporting *ubiquitous/pervasive computing*.

During the last decade, access to *Web Information Systems* (*WIS*) has evolved a lot due to numerous factors: the inherent mobility of nomadic user, the technical advances in *Mobile Device* (*MD*, e.g. *PDA*, phones, laptop), the need to cope with some of their intrinsically limited capacities (e.g., size of screen, memory, hard disk) and the multimedia nature of exchanged data. Nowadays, *Mobile Devices* can be used for accessing distant *WIS* but also for storing small amount of information for (simple) *WIS* or applications. A *WIS* which executes on *MDs* could provide services as accessing, searching and storing resources (files) inside it.

Having to face the reduced capacities of *MDs*, *WIS* designers must use mechanisms and architectures in order to efficiently store, retrieve and deliver data using these *MDs*. The underlying challenge is to provide *WIS* users with useful information based on an intelligent search and a suitable display of the delivered information. In order to reach this goal, *Multi-Agent Systems* (*MAS*) are

Z. Despotovic, S. Joseph, and C. Sartori (Eds.): AP2PC 2005, LNAI 4118, pp. 159–172, 2006.
© Springer-Verlag Berlin Heidelberg 2006

an interesting approach. The *W3C* [2] defines an agent as *"a concrete piece of software or hardware that sends and receives messages"*. These messages can be used for accessing a *WIS* and for exchanging information. Agents can be executed on the *MD* and/or migrate through the net, searching for information on different servers (or *MDs*) in order to satisfy the user's queries. This is the underlying idea of the *Mobile Agent* concept [3].

Many technical and functional aspects have to be considered when designing a *WIS* accessed through *MDs*, especially when addressing the issue of adapting the delivered information to the nomadic user [4][5][6][7]. In a previous work [8], we have defined *PUMAS*, a framework for retrieving information distributed among several *WIS* and/or *MDs* from different types of *MDs*. The architecture of *PUMAS* is composed of four *MAS* (one *Connection MAS*, one *Communication MAS*, one *Information MAS* and one *Adaptation MAS*) each one encompassing several *ubiquitous agents* which cooperate in order to achieve the different tasks handled by *PUMAS* (*MD* connection/disconnection, information storage and retrieval, etc.). In *PUMAS*, data representation, agent roles and rules for controlling their behaviors and data exchange rely on *XML* files. In this paper, we focus on the *Adaptation MAS* whose ubiquitous agents are in charge of performing adaptation. Through *PUMAS*, our final objective is to build and propose a framework which is, beyond the management of accesses to *WIS* using *MDs*, also in charge of performing an adaptation of the information according to the user's profile, the technical features of her/his *MD* and the contextual features.

For adaptation purpose, in *PUMAS*, the emphasis is particularly put on her/his location in her/his profile. Indeed a nomadic user may often change her/his location, which, sometimes, can impact her/his information needs. *PUMAS* focuses on *location dependent queries* defined by Thilliez *et al.* [6] as queries which are evaluated according to the current physical location of the user (e.g. *which are the nearest stores to the user?*). In order to detect the user's location, it is possible to use a *GPS* device or methods like the *Signal Strength*, the *SNMP* (*Simple Network Management Protocol*) or the *Local Access to the MAC* (*Media Access Control*) address of the access point, proposed by Nieto-Carvajal *et al.* in [4].

Regarding the adaptation to the reduced capacities of *MD*, one objective is to anticipate the fact that some retrieved information can not be properly displayed (e.g. the *MD* can not support video). It is necessary to investigate such situations at design time in order to decide which solution to adopt. For instance, considering a query whose result contains video data, these should not be delivered if the user accesses the *WIS* through a *PDA* which does not have enough resources to display them. In this case, the Negotiation vocabulary proposed by Lemlouma [9] can be used for adaptation purpose. It allows describing the user's *MD*, considering the constraints in terms of software and hardware environments and in terms of network.

This paper is structured as follows. We expose in section 2 the motivation for using agents and *P2P approach* in *PUMAS*. Then, section 3 presents *PUMAS* architecture. We describe more particularly the *Adaptation MAS* which extends the previous version of our framework [8]. In section 4, we give some scenarios which show how *PUMAS* works from the connection of a *MD* to the processing of a query. An example which illustrates our proposition is given in section 5. In section 6, we present some related works before we conclude in section 7.

2   A Framework Based on Agents and the P2P Approach

The goal of our work is to provide any nomadic user who accesses a *WIS* through a *MD* with the more relevant information according to her/his preferences, as well as to her/his contextual characteristics and her/his *MDs* features. Our approach is based on the agent technology. In the remainder of the paper, we call an *Agent-Based Web Information System* (*ABWIS*), a *WIS* developed using an agent approach (and accessed by users through *MDs*).

Wooldridge *et al.* [7] have highlighted the flexible and autonomous problem-solving behavior (*autonomy* and *proactivity*) of agents, the richness of an agents interaction (*communication features*) and the complexity of the structure of an agent system organization (*sociality*). An agent interacts with other agents or with the user in order to achieve a common objective or, in order to achieve its own objectives. An agent performs its actions while situated in a particular environment (e.g., computational, physical, ubiquitous one) and it decides for itself what actions it should perform at what time. These authors consider that an agent can also be a stand-alone entity which can perform some task on the user's behalf. Rahwan *et al.* [5] recommend to use the agent technology in *MD* applications: an agent which executes on the user's *MD* can inform the systems it accesses about its contextual information (i.e., time, place and tasks under execution). In such an environment, the user's context is dynamic, since users may move from one place to another (location changes). These location changes could produce changes in the tasks and information needs of the user. Consequently, the agent has to reason about the user's goals and the way they can be achieved.

The applications running on the *MD* must allow users to consult data at any time from any place. This is the underlying idea of the *Ubiquitous Computing* (*UC*). The *W3C* [2] defines *UC*, as an emerging three-fold paradigm of personal computing, characterized by: first, small, handheld, wireless computing devices. Second, the pervasiveness and the wireless nature of devices which require network architectures that support automatic and ad hoc configuration. Third, ubiquitous computing environment is characterized by a high distribution, heterogeneity, mobility and autonomy.

An agent performs its tasks independently from the server and other agents. This is the foundation of *P2P Systems*. A *P2P system* can be *Pure P2P* or *Hybrid P2P* [1]. In a *Pure P2P system*, every peer is able to directly connect to all other peers and messages are sent without the mediation of a server. In a *Hybrid P2P system*, a peer needs to connect to both an index server and other peers. In this connection, some messages are passed via the server and other messages are directly exchanged between the peers. *PUMAS* agents are organized in an *Hybrid P2P* architecture where each agent can connect or disconnect willingly towards and from the system and cooperate with other peer agents and, communicate directly with other agent(s) for performing individual or collective task(s). There are agents which execute on *MDs* and they can communicate through the central platform of *PUMAS* (this platform executes on a server).

Following the *P2P* approach, an *ABWIS* has to represent knowledge required by each agent for accomplishing tasks associated with the different roles they can play (client, server, moderator, coordinator, etc.). The work of Panti *et al.* [10] is an example of a *Peer Multi-Agent System*. However, both the *Agent* and the *P2P* approaches suffer from the lack of expressiveness of the data and services definition languages. The data distribution among the *MDs*, the distributed system problems (e.g., heterogeneity, data consistency) and the changes in contextual features of the nomadic user are not considered by these approaches.

We address these issues in our proposition. *PUMAS* (*Peer Ubiquitous Multi-Agent Systems*) [8] is a framework built on the one hand, for designing, developing and deploying *ABWIS*, and on the other hand, for providing the user with the information (that could be distributed in *MDs* and/or servers) according to her/his characteristics in the system and to the *MD* she/he uses. Each *MD* has at least one agent which informs the system about the user's location (using a *GPS* device or other methods like the ones presented in [4]) and its connection features (e.g., time, connection device, protocol). The agents of *PUMAS* can retrieve information and have the ability to perform tasks (e.g. connections to the system, communications with other agents, analysis of the queries, etc). These agents can, on the one hand, migrate to different servers (or other *MDs*) where *WIS* are executed in order to find the peer agent(s) that will help to answer the queries or, on the other hand, they can use a central platform in order to communicate with other peer agents. Users equipped with *MDs* can use the *PUMAS* central platform in order to communicate together through agents executed on their *MDs*, exchange information or support cooperative work between agents when performing their assigned tasks. In the next section, we describe *PUMAS*. Its architecture is described with a special emphasis on its adaptation features.

3   The PUMAS Framework

In this section, we focus on the description of the *Adaptation MAS* which performs the adaptation of the information for the user. We also present an overview of the *Connection*, the *Communication* and the *Information MAS*.

3.1   Architecture Overview

The original architecture of *PUMAS* [8] is composed of three *MAS*:

- A *Connection MAS* which provides the mechanisms for facilitating the connection from different types of *MD* to the system. It encompasses one or several *Mobile Device Agents* (*MDAs*) and one *Connection Controller Agent* (*CCA*).

- A *Communication MAS* which ensures a transparent communication between the *MDs* and the system, and applies a *Display Filter* for displaying the information to the user in an adapting way according to the constraints of her/his *MD*. For this, it is helped by agents of the *Adaptation MAS* presented in section 3.2. The *Communication MAS* encompasses one *Coordinator Agent* (*CA*), one *MDProfile Agent* (*MDPA*) and one or more *Proxy Agents* (*PAs*).
- An *Information MAS* which receives the user's query, redirects them to the "*right*" *Information System* (the nearest *Information System*, the one which can answer the user's queries, the more consulted one), applies a *Content Filter* (with the help of the *Adaptation MAS* agents) according to the user's profile in the system (preferences, history, intentions) and returns the results to the *Communication MAS*. The *Information MAS* encompasses one *Receptor/Provider Agent* (*R/PA*), one *Router Agent* (*RA*) and one or more *ISAgents* (*ISAs*).

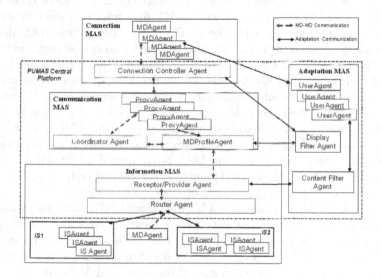

Fig. 1. The *PUMAS* Architecture

The inherent mobility of the user and of the agents is supported by *ubiquitous mobile agents* (the *Mobile Device Agents* in the *Connection MAS* and the *IS-Agents* in the *Information MAS*) which can be transmitted through the network to retrieve some needed information and which can communicate with other agents for performing tasks. In *PUMAS*, the ubiquitous agents are organized in a *Hybrid P2P Architecture* which copes with the following issues: security in the applications (security problems inherent to the agent mobility), communication between agents in a point to point or in a broadcast way, management of the agent's status (e.g., connected, disconnected, killed, etc.) and of the services they provided. A more detailed description of the *Connection, Communication* and *Information MAS* is exposed in [8]. The main contribution of this paper, described in the next section, deals with the introduction of a new *MAS* which supports the adaptation capabilities of *PUMAS*.

3.2   The PUMAS Adaptation MAS

The adaptation capabilities of *PUMAS* rely on a two step filter process which aims at providing the user with adapted information (i.e. "*the right information in the right place at the right time*") according to both the user and her/his *MD*. First, the *Content Filter* allows selecting the more relevant information according to the user's profile defined in the system. Second, the *Display Filter* applies to the results of the first filter and takes into account the characteristics and technical constraints of the user's *MD*.

We introduce a new *MAS*, called the *Adaptation MAS*, in the architecture of *PUMAS*. Similarly to the three other *MAS* of *PUMAS*, the *Adaptation MAS* is composed of some *ubiquitous agents*. The services and tasks of these agents essentially consist in managing specific *XML* files which contain information about the user and her/his *MD*. The agents of the *Adaptation MAS* also have some knowledge (stored in *Knowledge Bases*) which allows selecting and filtering the information for users. This knowledge is acquired by analyzing user's previous experiences in the system, like her/his last connections, queries, preferences, etc. The *Adaptation MAS* agents communicate with the agents of the *Connection*, the *Communication* and the *Information MAS* in order to provide them with information about the user (explicitly extracted from the *XML* files or inferred from their rules and knowledge), connection and communication features, *MDs* characteristics, etc. The *Adaptation MAS* is composed of several *UserAgents* (*UA*), one *DisplayFilterAgent* (*DFA*) and one *ContentFilterAgent* (*CFA*). These agents execute on the central platform of *PUMAS* (see Fig. 1).

Each *UserAgent* (*UA*) manages a *XML* file (*User Profile XML* file) which contains personal user's characteristics (*user ID*, location, etc.) and her/his preferences (e.g., the user wants only video files). This file is obtained by means of the *Mobile Device Agent*. There is only one *UA* which represents a user at the same time. Since a user can access the system through several *MDs*, the *UA* communicates with the *Mobile Device Agents* and the *Proxy Agents* (which respectively belong to the *Connection* and the *Communication MAS*) for analyzing and centralizing all the characteristics of the same user. The *UA* communicates with the *CFA* for sending the *User Profile XML* file. When the *CFA* receives this file, it stores this information as facts in its *Knowledge Base* (this agent stores a register of user's preferences). When the *Receptor/Provider Agent* (which belongs to the *Information MAS*) asks the *CFA* for the user's preferences, the latter sends it the latest *XML* file received from the *UA*. If the *UA* did not send this file (e.g., there are only general user's preferences valuable for all sessions), the *CFA* takes into account for this user her/his preferences from previous sessions.

The *DisplayFilterAgent* (*DFA*) manages a *Knowledge Base* which contains general information about the characteristics of different types of *MDs* (e.g., format files supported) and acquired knowledge from previous connections (e.g., problems and capabilities of networks according to data transmissions). The *Connection Controller Agent* (of the *Connection MAS*) communicates with the *DFA*, asking for information about the characteristics of connection and/or problems (e.g., bandwidth capabilities, transmission speed). The *MDProfile Agent* (of the *Connection MAS*) also communicates with the *DFA*, asking for the constraints and capabilities of a given type of *MD*.

The *ContentFilterAgent* (*CFA*) manages a *Knowledge Base* base which contains the preferences, intentions and characteristics of the users. The *CFA* communicates user's preferences to the *Receptor/Provider Agent* (which belongs to the *Information MAS*). The *Receptor/Provider Agent* adds them to the user's queries and checks if the results are adapted according to this information.

The *XML* files managed by the agents of the *Adaptation MAS* have been defined using the extensions introduced by Indulska *et al.* [11] to *CC/PP* [2]. These extensions include some user's characteristics (e.g., her/his location, application requirements, session features, etc.), together with the features of the *MD*, providing this way a complete description of the user and her/his device.

The agents of the *Connection*, the *Communication* and the *Information MAS* communicate with the *Adaptation MAS* agents for adding specific information to the user's queries and then to check the results provided by the *Router Agent* which belongs to the *Information MAS*.

4   PUMAS Scenarios

In this section, we present some scenarios in order to show the interactions which occur between *PUMAS* agents when a connection to an *ABWIS* is established, when a query is submitted to the system and finally, when the system returns the result for this query. In our proposition, interactions between agents rely on the messages exchanges according to the *Communication Acts* presented by Odell *et al.* in [12] (e.g., confirm, inform, propose, request, subscribe, propagate, etc.).

4.1   Connection Scenario

When a user wants to connect to the system using her/his *MD*, the *Mobile Device Agent* (*MDA*), which executes in the user's *MD*, sends a *"propose"* message (connection proposition) to the *Connection Controller Agent* (*CCA*). If there is no *Proxy Agent* (*PA*) for representing this *MDA*, the *CCA* creates one and it sends a *"subscribe"* message to the *Coordinator Agent* (*CA*) for subscribing this *PA* to the system. The *CA* informs the *MDProfile Agent* of this subscription. The *CCA* also sends to the *MDA* a *"confirms"* message when the subscription process is finished (see Fig. 2). When the *MDA* receives the confirmation message, a *UserAgent* (*UA*) is created in the central platform of *PUMAS* in order to manage the user's profile. This profile is defined in the *Current Session XML* file and is sent to the *UserAgent* by the *Mobile Device Agents*.

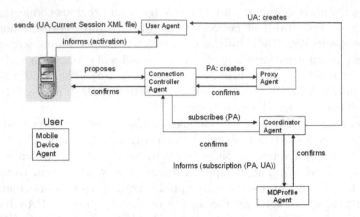

Fig. 2. Connection Scenario of *PUMAS*

4.2 Sending an Information Query

When a user sends an information query Q (see Fig. 3), the *Mobile Device Agent* (*MDA*) sends it to the *Connection Controller Agent* (*CCA*). If the user has established in her/his preferences (defined in the *User Profile XML* file) that her/his query Q depends on both her/his location and time of connection, the *CCA* adds up to Q the information about the time of connection, the user's location and the characteristics of the user's *MD* connection (these latter characteristics are exchanged with the *DisplayFilterAgent*). This leads to the production of a new query Q' (in Fig. 3, $Q'=Q + user's\ Spatio\mbox{-}Temporal$ - ST - features). Otherwise, the *CCA* only adds up to Q the characteristics of the user's *MD* connection. The Q' is then sent to the *Proxy Agent*. The Q' passes by the *Coordinator Agent* and then by the *MDProfile Agent*. The latter adds up to Q' some features related to the *MD*; these features are provided by the *DisplayFilterAgent* which have previously learnt them from the previous queries or retrieved them from its *Knowledge Base*. The new Q'' query (in Fig. 3, $Q''= Q' + MD\ features$) is sent by the *MDProfile Agent* to the *Receptor/Provider Agent* (*R/PA*). The *R/PA* adds up to Q'' the specific user's characteristics in the system by requesting the *ContentFilterAgent* (In Fig. 3, $Q'''=Q'' + user's\ preferences$). The *R/PA* sends Q''' to the *Router Agent* which decides (according to the query, the system rules and the fact in its *Knowledge Base*) which are the *ISAgents* able to answer. It can send the query to a specific *ISAgent* or to several *ISAgents* (e.g., waiting for the first to answer or different answers) or, it can divide the query in sub-queries which are sent to one or several *ISAgents*. The scenario in Fig. 3, shows for instance that Q''' is divided into $Q'''^{-1.1}$, $Q'''^{-1.2}$, $Q'''^{-1.3}$ and $Q'''^{-1.4}$ which are sent to the *ISAgents* executed on a server and different *MDs*.

When a user *U1* has an information query for another user (*U2*), both equipped with *MDs*, the query is propagated from the *MDA* executed on the *U1*'s *MD* towards the *Router Agent* which redirects it to the *MDA* executed in the *U2*'s *MD*. This *U2*'s *MDA* changes of role to become an *ISAgent*, i.e. the agent in charge of

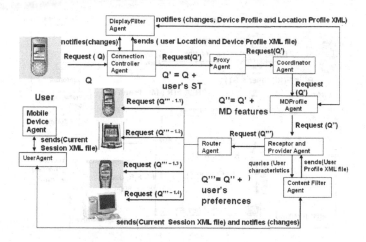

Fig. 3. Scenario of sending a query

answering the information query. This change of role is possible because a *MDA* has the knowledge for managing the information stored in the *MD* on which it executes and it has the capability of answering the information queries.

4.3   Receiving the Results of an Information Query

When the *Router Agent* receives all the results of the query from the *ISAgents* (in Fig. 4, the *Router Agent* receives partial results $R^{1.1}$, $R^{1.2}$, $R^{1.3}$ and $R^{1.4}$ sent by the *ISAgents* which are executed on a server and different *MDs*), it analyzes them before sending a message of *"confirms"* or *"disconfirms"* or *"not understand"* to the *Receptor/Provider Agent* (*R/PA*). This message includes the results of the query (*R*). The *R/PA* checks if the results can satisfy the specific characteristics of the user (in Fig. 4, *R'* is the result of applying the *Content Filter* to *R* according to the user's preferences, intentions, history) and redirects them to the *MDProfile Agent*. This agent checks if the results can be displayed according to the *MD* features and it performs the first step of the *Display Filter* (in Fig. 4, *R"* is produced by filtering *R'* according to the *MD* features). Then, *R"* is transmitted by the *Coordinator Agent* to the *Proxy Agent* and then to the *Connection Controller Agent*. The latter performs the last step of the *Display Filter* according to the technical features of the *MD* and to the user's *MD* connection characteristics (if the user is still connected, has changed of location, a timeout has occurred, etc.). Thanks to the *Content* and the *Display Filters*, the results of the query received by the *Mobile Device Agent* and displayed on the user's *MD* correspond to the more relevant information for the user.

It is worth noting that the scenario described above includes several results checking steps which might appear useless since the scenario of a query sending has already allowed to refine the query to take into account the user's and *MD* characteristics. However, this extra information added during the query

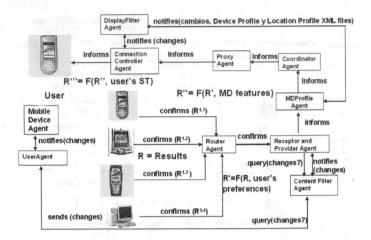

Fig. 4. Scenario of receiving the results of a query

sending scenario might not be still valid at result delivery time. Notably, the user's characteristics (location change, preferences changes) and the connection and communication means (bandwidth variation, different used *MDs*, network problems) might have evolved and therefore might impact the results expected by the user. The controls which are presented in the *"receiving the results of an information query"* scenario aim at eliminating some now possibly irrelevant retrieved information. In the next section, we illustrate the process performed by the agents of *PUMAS* using the example of a hospital *WIS*.

5   Example

Doctors equipped with *MDs* (e.g. *PDA*, cellular phone, etc.) access information which can be distributed between several *MDs* and/or one or several *WIS*. They can also receive information concerning their patients according to their location, preferences, technical characteristics of their *MDs* and considerations about their connection time (i.e., when visiting their patients, doctors with *MDs* can consult information about their clinic history, tests, medicaments, etc). For this, the application on her/his *MD* must consult the different *IS* of the hospital pharmacy, patients, etc. Doctors could also communicate with other doctors (peers) through their *MD* asking for a specific question (e.g. that can be answered only by the last specialist who has examined this patient).

The *Mobile Device Agent* which executes on the doctor's *MD* sends the doctor's queries (for instance, the query *Q* in Fig. 5). The queries are propagated through *PUMAS* core: they are first transmitted through the *Connection Controller Agent* (*CCA*). Let us suppose in our example that the system can identify a patient and get information about her/him from the location of this patient (e.g., room, floor, bed, etc.) and the current date. For this identification, the information about the patient's location can be directly entered by the doctor

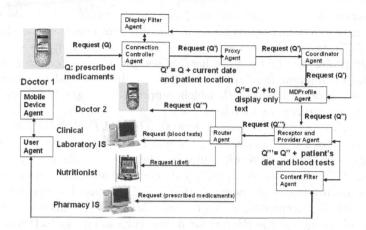

Fig. 5. Scenario of sending a query in the hospital example

or can be automatically got by means of a device located in her/his *MD* (e.g., *GPS*, bar-code reader, etc). The information about the current date can be got from the system. The *CCA* creates a new query *Q'* which contains *Q* and the information about the current date and the patient's location (In Fig. 5, *Q'= Q +* *current date and patient location*). Then, the query is sent to the *Communication MAS* agents (the *Proxy Agent*, the *Coordinator Agent* and the *MDProfile Agent*). The *MDProfile Agent* can add up into the queries some information related to the *MD* (e.g., *doctor's MD can not support images but only text files, then the doctor asks for the results test, she/he only could get them in a text format* which is illustrated in Fig. 5 as follows : *Q''= Q' + to display only text*). Then, the *MDProfile Agent* sends the queries to the *Receptor/Provider Agent* (*R/PA*). This agent can add up into the queries the preferences the doctor has previously expressed (e.g., *"when asking for a blood test, the system must also provide me with information about the patient's diet", "I do prefer graphical results"*, etc., in Fig. 5, *Q''= Q'' + patient's diet and blood tests*). Finally, the query comes to the *Router Agent*. This agent redirects the queries to the *ISAgent* located in the *IS(s)* which manage(s) the information about the patients in the hospital. All the queries follow the same path from the *Mobile Device Agents* towards the *Router Agent*. If the doctor wants to know the last medicaments prescribed to this patient, the *Router Agent* redirects the query to the *ISAgent* located in the *Pharmacy IS*. If the query concerns another doctor (peer), the *Router Agent* redirects the query to the *ISAgent* located in the peer's *MD*. A doctor can also ask for information about a specific patient to several of her/his peers. In this case, the *Router Agent* could send the query in a broadcast way or it could divide the query according to the receiver peer (e.g., queries relates to the heart for the cardiologist) or the defined criteria in the *User Profile XML* file (e.g., if the criterion is the location, the queries must only be redirected to peers at the same or closed location of the sender). The retrieved information is organized by the *Router Agent* (e.g., the latest prescribed medicaments, the peer's answers about this patient, etc.) and it is returned to the doctor who sent the query following the inverse path. The different agents checks the results because, for instance, the doctor may have disconnected from the system (due to network problems), and retaken her/his session in a new connection having characteristics different from the previous ones: she/he could now consult the system using another kind of *MD* which supports some graphical format (this new preference can now be satisfied).

Through this example, we can observe the *Hybrid P2P Architecture* of *PU-MAS*. The core of *PUMAS* centralizes the queries and it is in charge of applying the *Content* and *Display Filters* for adapting the answers. The main peer characteristics of *PUMAS* agents are: *i)* the agents have the autonomy of connecting to and disconnecting from the system, and *ii)* a *MD* can ask for a communication with a specific *IS* (executed on a server or on a *MD*) passing this information as a parameter of the query; the *Router Agent* transmits the query to this specific *IS* which exemplifies an agent to agent communication. This is for instance, the case when doctors directly exchange information about a patient using their *MDs*.

Another advantage offered by *PUMAS* is that it helps a user who does not know which specific *IS* to ask for information to find the more appropriate one(s). The *Router Agent* redirects the query to the "*right*" *IS* by means of an intelligent analysis of the query and the help of the *ISAgents* which achieve an intelligent search inside the different *IS* (pharmacy, clinical laboratory, patients, etc. in our example).

6   Related Works

We present here some agent-based architectures or frameworks for adapting information to users.

CONSORTS Architecture [13] is based on ubiquitous agents and designed for a massive support of *MDs*. It detects the user's location and defines the user's profile for adapting information to her/him. The *CONSORTS* architecture proposes a mechanism for defining the relations that hold between agents (e.g., communication, hierarchy, role definition), with the purpose of satisfying user's requests. However, it does not consider the distribution of information between *MDs* (which could improve response time) nor the user's preferences.

The work of Gandon *et al.* [14] proposes a Semantic Web architecture for context-awareness and privacy. This architecture supports the automated discovery and access of a user's personal resources subject to user-specified privacy preferences. Service invocation rules along with services ontologies and services profiles allow to identify the most relevant resources available to answer a query. However, it does not take into account the fact that information which can answer a query can be distributed between different sources.

PIA-System [15] is an agent-based personal information system for collecting, filtering and integrating information at a common point, offering access to the information by *WWW*, e-mail, *SMS*, *MMS* and *J2ME* clients. It combines *push* and *pull* techniques in order to allow the user on the one hand, to search explicitly for specific information and on the other hand, to be automatically informed about relevant information divided in slots according the activities performed during different parts of the day (pre, work and recreation). However, *PIA-System* only searches information in text format. It does not take into account the adaptation of different kinds of media to different *MDs*, nor the user's location.

7 Conclusion

In this paper, we have presented *PUMAS*, a framework based on agents and *P2P* approach. Peers characteristics of *PUMAS* appear in the cooperation developed by the agents in order to store and retrieve the information and in the possibility that two users equipped with *MDs* have to communicate in a direct way through the central platform offered by *PUMAS*. The architecture of *PUMAS* relies on three *Multi-Agents Systems* (*MAS*) for *Connection*, *Communication* and *Information* plus a transversal *MAS* dedicated to adaptation (the *Adaptation MAS*). *PUMAS* also benefits from the *P2P* characteristics of a hybrid *P2P* architecture: independence of the agents in connection, disconnection and reconnection to the system, direct communication between the peers (using both the agent identification and the central platform). *PUMAS* also provides a mechanism for identification, authentication and knowledge of the peers of an agent. In conclusion, *PUMAS* advantages are two-fold, the *intelligent* and *adaptive* information search done by means of agents, especially, the *Router Agent* which chooses the *WIS* or other *MDs* for routing the user's queries and then for compiling the answer(s). This search is *intelligent* because is based on the knowledge of the agent (proper, acquired and inferred knowledge) and its capability of reasoning. This search is also *adaptive* because it takes into account the nomadic user's profile, the characteristics of her/his *MDs* and the contextual features.

We are currently implementing and testing each *MAS* of *PUMAS*. Our future work aims at defining an extension for the *Agent Communication Language* (*ACL*) [16] which does not consider spatio-temporal features. To take into account these features in queries, we want to introduce primitives like *query-when*, *query-where*, etc. We also aim at defining the mechanisms and strategies of the *Router Agent* in order to achieve the *Query Routing* [17] process allowing to propagate the query towards the "*right*" *IS* and to compile the answers.

References

1. Shizuka, M., Ma, J., Lee, J., Miyoshi, Y., Takata, K.: A p2p ubiquitous system for testing network programs. In: Proc of Embedded and Ubiquitous Computing (EUC 2004)(Aizu-Wakamatsu, Japan, August 25-27, 2004). Volume 3207 of LNCS., Springer (2004) 1004–1013
2. W3C: OWL Web Ontology Language, Use Cases and Requirements (http://www.w3.org/TR/webont-req/). (2005)
3. Lin, F., Liu, H.: Maspf: Searching the shortest communication path with the guarantee of the message delivery between manager and mobile agent. In: Proc of Embedded and Ubiquitous Computing (EUC 2004)(Aizu-Wakamatsu, Japan, August 25-27, 2004). Volume 3207 of LNCS., Springer (2004) 755–764

4. Nieto-Carvajal, I., Botia, J., Ruiz, P., Gomez-Skarmeta, A.: Implementation and evaluation of a location-aware wireless multi-agent system. In: Proc of Embedded and Ubiquitous Computing (EUC 2004)(Aizu-Wakamatsu, Japan, August 25-27, 2004). Volume 3207 of LNCS., Springer (2004) 528–537
5. Rahwan, T., Rahwan, T., Rahwan, I., Ashri, R.: Agent-based support for mobile users using agentspeak(l). In: Proc of Agent-Oriented Information Systems, 5th Int. Bi-Conference Workshop (AOIS 2003)(Melbourne, Australia, July 14, 2003 - Chicago, USA, October 13, 2003). Volume 3030 of LNAI., Springer (2003) 45–60
6. Thilliez, M., Delot, T.: Evaluating location dependent queries using islands. In: Proc of Symposium on Advanced Distributed Systems (ISSADS 2004)(Guadalajara, Mexico, January 25-30, 2004). Volume 3061 of LNCS., Springer (2004) 126–136
7. Wooldridge, M., Jennings, N.: Intelligent agents: Theory and practice. The Knowledge Engineering Review **10 (2)** (1995) 115–152
8. Carrillo Ramos, A., Gensel, J., Villanova-Oliver, M., Martin, H.: Pumas: a framework based on ubiquitous agents for accessing web information systems through mobile devices. In: Proc. of the 20th Annual ACM Symposium on Applied Computing (SAC2005)(Santa Fe, USA, March 13-17, 2005), ACM Press, New York, NY (2005) 1003–1008
9. Lemlouma, T.: Architecture de Ngociation et dAdaptation de Services Multimdia dans des Environnements Htrognes. PhD thesis, Institut National Polytechnique de Grenoble, Grenoble (2004) (in French).
10. Panti, M., Penserini, L., Spalazzi, L.: A multi-agent system based on the p2p model to information integration. In: Proc of 1st Int .joint Conferences on Autonomous Agents and Multi-Agent Systems (AAMAS 2002)(Bologna, Italy,July 16, 2002), ACM Press, New York, NY (2002) 1288–1289
11. Indulska, J., Robinson, R., Rakotonirainy, A., Henricksen, K.: Experiences in using cc/pp in context-aware systems. In: Proc of 4th Int. Conf. on Mobile Data Management (MDM 2003)(Melbourne, Australia, January 21-24, 2003). Volume 2574 of LNCS., Springer (2003) 247–261
12. Odell, J., Van Dyke Parunak, H., Bauer, B.: Representing agent interaction protocols in uml. In: Proc of Agent Oriented Software Engineering (AOSE 2000)(Limerick, Ireland, June 10, 2000). Volume 1957 of LNCS., Springer (2000) 121–140
13. Kurumatani, K.: Mass user support by social coordination among citizen in a real environment. In: Proc. of Multi-Agent for Mass User Support. International Workshop (MAMUS 2003)(Acapulco, Mexico, August 10, 2003). Volume 3012 of LNAI., Springer (2003) 1–16
14. Gandon, F., Sadeh, N.: Semantic web technologies to reconcile privacy and context awareness. Journal of Web Semantics **1 (3)** (2004) http://www.websemanticsjournal.org/ps/pub/2004-17 (Last Access: March 2005).
15. Albayrak, S., Wollny, S., Varone, N., Lommatzsch, A., Milosevic, D.: Agent technology for personalized information filtering: The pia-system. In: Proc. of the 20th Annual ACM Symposium on Applied (SAC 2005)(Santa Fe, USA, March 13-17, 2005), ACM Press, New York, NY (2005) 54–59
16. FIPA: ACL Message Structure Specification (http://www.fipa.org/specs/fipa00061/SC00061G.html). (2005)
17. Xu, J., Lim, E., Ng, W.: Cluster-based database selection techniques for routing bibliographic queries. In: Proc of 10th Int. Conf. and Workshop on Database and Expert Systems Applications (DEXA 99)(Florence, Italy, August 30 - September 3, 1999). Volume 1677 of LNCS., Springer (1999) 100–109

Author Index

Lecture Notes in Artificial Intelligence (LNAI)

Vol. 4120: J. Calmet, T. Ida, D. Wang (Eds.), Artificial Intelligence and Symbolic Computation. XIII, 269 pages. 2006.

Vol. 4118: Z. Despotovic, S. Joseph, C. Sartori (Eds.), Agents and Peer-to-Peer Computing. XIV, 173 pages. 2006.

Vol. 4114: D.-S. Huang, K. Li, G.W. Irwin (Eds.), Computational Intelligence, Part II. XXVII, 1337 pages. 2006.

Vol. 4108: J.M. Borwein, W.M. Farmer (Eds.), Mathematical Knowledge Management. VIII, 295 pages. 2006.

Vol. 4106: T.R. Roth-Berghofer, M.H. Göker, H.A. Güvenir (Eds.), Advances in Case-Based Reasoning. XIV, 566 pages. 2006.

Vol. 4099: Q. Yang, G. Webb (Eds.), PRICAI 2006: Trends in Artificial Intelligence. XXVIII, 1263 pages. 2006.

Vol. 4095: S. Nolfi, G. Baldassarre, R. Calabretta, J.C.T. Hallam, D. Marocco, J.-A. Meyer, O. Miglino, D. Parisi (Eds.), From Animals to Animats 9. XV, 869 pages. 2006.

Vol. 4093: X. Li, O.R. Zaïane, Z. Li (Eds.), Advanced Data Mining and Applications. XXI, 1110 pages. 2006.

Vol. 4092: J. Lang, F. Lin, J. Wang (Eds.), Knowledge Science, Engineering and Management. XV, 664 pages. 2006.

Vol. 4088: Z.-Z. Shi, R. Sadananda (Eds.), Agent Computing and Multi-Agent Systems. XVII, 827 pages. 2006.

Vol. 4087: F. Schwenker, S. Marinai (Eds.), Artificial Neural Networks in Pattern Recognition. IX, 299 pages. 2006.

Vol. 4068: H. Schärfe, P. Hitzler, P. Øhrstrøm (Eds.), Conceptual Structures: Inspiration and Application. XI, 455 pages. 2006.

Vol. 4065: P. Perner (Ed.), Advances in Data Mining. XI, 592 pages. 2006.

Vol. 4062: G.-Y. Wang, J.F. Peters, A. Skowron, Y. Yao (Eds.), Rough Sets and Knowledge Technology. XX, 810 pages. 2006.

Vol. 4049: S. Parsons, N. Maudet, P. Moraitis, I. Rahwan (Eds.), Argumentation in Multi-Agent Systems. XIV, 313 pages. 2006.

Vol. 4048: L. Goble, J.-J.C.. Meyer (Eds.), Deontic Logic and Artificial Normative Systems. X, 273 pages. 2006.

Vol. 4045: D. Barker-Plummer, R. Cox, N. Swoboda (Eds.), Diagrammatic Representation and Inference. XII, 301 pages. 2006.

Vol. 4031: M. Ali, R. Dapoigny (Eds.), Advances in Applied Artificial Intelligence. XXIII, 1353 pages. 2006.

Vol. 4029: L. Rutkowski, R. Tadeusiewicz, L.A. Zadeh, J.M. Zurada (Eds.), Artificial Intelligence and Soft Computing – ICAISC 2006. XXI, 1235 pages. 2006.

Vol. 4027: H.L. Larsen, G. Pasi, D. Ortiz-Arroyo, T. Andreasen, H. Christiansen (Eds.), Flexible Query Answering Systems. XVIII, 714 pages. 2006.

Vol. 4021: E. André, L. Dybkjær, W. Minker, H. Neumann, M. Weber (Eds.), Perception and Interactive Technologies. XI, 217 pages. 2006.

Vol. 4020: A. Bredenfeld, A. Jacoff, I. Noda, Y. Takahashi (Eds.), RoboCup 2005: Robot Soccer World Cup IX. XVII, 727 pages. 2006.

Vol. 4013: L. Lamontagne, M. Marchand (Eds.), Advances in Artificial Intelligence. XIII, 564 pages. 2006.

Vol. 4012: T. Washio, A. Sakurai, K. Nakajima, H. Takeda, S. Tojo, M. Yokoo (Eds.), New Frontiers in Artificial Intelligence. XIII, 484 pages. 2006.

Vol. 4008: J.C. Augusto, C.D. Nugent (Eds.), Designing Smart Homes. XI, 183 pages. 2006.

Vol. 4005: G. Lugosi, H.U. Simon (Eds.), Learning Theory. XI, 656 pages. 2006.

Vol. 4002: A. Yli-Jyrä, L. Karttunen, J. Karhumäki (Eds.), Finite-State Methods and Natural Language Processing. XIV, 312 pages. 2006.

Vol. 3978: B. Hnich, M. Carlsson, F. Fages, F. Rossi (Eds.), Recent Advances in Constraints. VIII, 179 pages. 2006.

Vol. 3963: O. Dikenelli, M.-P. Gleizes, A. Ricci (Eds.), Engineering Societies in the Agents World VI. XII, 303 pages. 2006.

Vol. 3960: R. Vieira, P. Quaresma, M.d.G.V. Nunes, N.J. Mamede, C. Oliveira, M.C. Dias (Eds.), Computational Processing of the Portuguese Language. XII, 274 pages. 2006.

Vol. 3955: G. Antoniou, G. Potamias, C. Spyropoulos, D. Plexousakis (Eds.), Advances in Artificial Intelligence. XVII, 611 pages. 2006.

Vol. 3949: F.A. Savacı (Ed.), Artificial Intelligence and Neural Networks. IX, 227 pages. 2006.

Vol. 3946: T.R. Roth-Berghofer, S. Schulz, D.B. Leake (Eds.), Modeling and Retrieval of Context. XI, 149 pages. 2006.

Vol. 3944: J. Quiñonero-Candela, I. Dagan, B. Magnini, F. d'Alché-Buc (Eds.), Machine Learning Challenges. XIII, 462 pages. 2006.

Vol. 3937: H. La Poutré, N.M. Sadeh, S. Janson (Eds.), Agent-Mediated Electronic Commerce. X, 227 pages. 2006.

Vol. 3932: B. Mobasher, O. Nasraoui, B. Liu, B. Masand (Eds.), Advances in Web Mining and Web Usage Analysis. X, 189 pages. 2006.

Vol. 3930: D.S. Yeung, Z.-Q. Liu, X.-Z. Wang, H. Yan (Eds.), Advances in Machine Learning and Cybernetics. XXI, 1110 pages. 2006.

Vol. 3918: W.-K. Ng, M. Kitsuregawa, J. Li, K. Chang (Eds.), Advances in Knowledge Discovery and Data Mining. XXIV, 879 pages. 2006.

Vol. 3913: O. Boissier, J. Padget, V. Dignum, G. Lindemann, E. Matson, S. Ossowski, J.S. Sichman, J. Vázquez-Salceda (Eds.), Coordination, Organizations, Institutions, and Norms in Multi-Agent Systems. XII, 259 pages. 2006.

Vol. 3910: S.A. Brueckner, G.D.M. Serugendo, D. Hales, F. Zambonelli (Eds.), Engineering Self-Organising Systems. XII, 245 pages. 2006.

Vol. 3904: M. Baldoni, U. Endriss, A. Omicini, P. Torroni (Eds.), Declarative Agent Languages and Technologies III. XII, 245 pages. 2006.